MW00714021

William Borden

Comparative Approaches in Brief Dynamic Psychotherapy

Pre-publication
REVIEWS,
COMMENTARIES,
EVALUATIONS . . .

The Haworth Press, Inc.

The Haworth Press, Inc.

Comparative Approaches in Brief Dynamic Psychotherapy

Comparative Approaches in Brief Dynamic Psychotherapy has been co-published simultaneously as *Psychoanalytic Social Work*, Volume 6, Numbers 3/4 1999.

The *Psychoanalytic Social Work*™ Monographic "Separates"

Below is a list of "separates," which in serials librarianship means a special issue simultaneously published as a special journal issue or double-issue and as a "separate" hardbound monograph. (This is a format which we also call a "DocuSerial.")

"Separates" are published because specialized libraries or professionals may wish to purchase a specific thematic issue by itself in a format which can be separately cataloged and shelved, as opposed to purchasing the journal on an on-going basis. Faculty members may also more easily consider a "separate" for classroom adoption.

"Separates" are carefully classified separately with the major book jobbers so that the journal tie-in can be noted on new book order slips to avoid duplicate purchasing.

You may wish to visit Haworth's Website at . . .

http://www.haworthpressinc.com

. . . to search our online catalog for complete tables of contents of these separates and related publications.

You may also call 1-800-HAWORTH (outside US/Canada: 607-722-5857), or Fax 1-800-895-0582 (outside US/Canada: 607-771-0012), or e-mail at:

getinfo@haworthpressinc.com

Comparative Approaches in Brief Dynamic Psychotherapy, edited by William Borden, PhD (Vol. 6, No. 3/4, 1999). *Provides an introduction to contemporary models of brief dynamic psychotherapy and describes fundamental tasks and methods in time-limited intervention.*

Narration and Therapeutic Action: The Construction of Meaning in Psychoanalytic Social Work, edited by Jerrold R. Brandell PhD, BCD* (Vol. 3, No. 2/3 1996). *Nine contributors examine various aspects of narrative theory and its relationship to psychoanalysis and clinical social work.*

*Published under the title *Journal of Analytic Social Work*

Comparative Approaches in Brief Dynamic Psychotherapy

William Borden, PhD
Editor

Comparative Approaches in Brief Dynamic Psychotherapy has been co-published simultaneously as *Psychoanalytic Social Work*, Volume 6, Numbers 3/4 1999.

The Haworth Press, Inc.
New York • London • Oxford

Comparative Approaches in Brief Dynamic Psychotherapy has
also been published as *Psychoanalytic Social Work,* Volume 6,
Numbers 3/4 1999.

The development, preparation, and publication of this work has been undertaken with great care.
However, the publisher, employees, editors, and agents of The Haworth Press and all imprints of
The Haworth Press, Inc., including The Haworth Medical Press and Pharmaceutical Products Press,
are not responsible for any errors contained herein or for consequences that may ensue from use of
materials or information contained in this work. Opinions expressed by the author(s) are not necessarily those of The Haworth Press, Inc.

Cover design by Thomas J. Mayshock Jr.

The Haworth Press, Inc., 10 Alice Street, Binghamton, NY 13904-1580 USA

Library of Congress Cataloging-in-Publication Data

Comparative approaches in brief dynamic psychotherapy / William Borden, editor.
    p. cm.
    Includes bibliographical references and index.
    ISBN 0-7890-0833-5 (alk. paper) ISBN 0-7890-0844-0 (pbk. : alk. paper)
    1. Brief psychotherapy. 2. Psychodynamic psychotherapy.
    I. Borden, William.
RC480.55.C658 1999   99-43056
616.89'14-dc21   CIP

INDEXING & ABSTRACTING

Contributions to this publication are selectively indexed or abstracted in print, electronic, online, or CD-ROM version(s) of the reference tools and information services listed below. This list is current as of the copyright date of this publication. See the end of this section for additional notes.

- *Abstracts in Anthropology*
- *Applied Social Sciences Index & Abstracts (ASSIA) (Online: ASSI via Data-Star) (CDRom: ASSIA Plus)*
- *BUBL Information Service. An Internet-based Information Service for the UK higher education community*
- *caredata CD: the social and community care database*
- *CNPIEC Reference Guide: Chinese National Directory of Foreign Periodicals*
- *Criminal Justice Abstracts*
- *Digest of Neurology and Psychiatry*
- *Family Studies Database (online and CD/ROM)*
- *Family Violence & Sexual Assault Bulletin*
- *Human Resources Abstracts (HRA)*
- *IBZ International Bibliography of Periodical Literature*
- *International Bulletin of Bibliography on Education*
- *Mental Health Abstracts (online through DIALOG)*
- *NIAAA Alcohol and Alcohol Problems Science Database (ETOH)*
- *Periodica Islamica*
- *Psychiatric Rehabilitation Journal*
- *Psychological Abstracts (PsycINFO)*
- *Referativnyi Zhurnal (Abstracts Journal of the All-Russian Institute of Scientific and Technical Information)*

(continued)

- *Sage Family Studies Abstracts (SFSA)*
- *Social Planning/Policy & Development Abstracts (SOPODA)*
- *Social Work Abstracts*
- *Sociological Abstracts (SA)*
- *Studies on Women Abstracts*

Special Bibliographic Notes related to special journal issues (separates) and indexing/abstracting:

- indexing/abstracting services in this list will also cover material in any "separate" that is co-published simultaneously with Haworth's special thematic journal issue or DocuSerial. Indexing/abstracting usually covers material at the article/chapter level.
- monographic co-editions are intended for either non-subscribers or libraries which intend to purchase a second copy for their circulating collections.
- monographic co-editions are reported to all jobbers/wholesalers/approval plans. The source journal is listed as the "series" to assist the prevention of duplicate purchasing in the same manner utilized for books-in-series.
- to facilitate user/access services all indexing/abstracting services are encouraged to utilize the co-indexing entry note indicated at the bottom of the first page of each article/chapter/contribution.
- this is intended to assist a library user of any reference tool (whether print, electronic, online, or CD-ROM) to locate the monographic version if the library has purchased this version but not a subscription to the source journal.
- individual articles/chapters in any Haworth publication are also available through the Haworth Document Delivery Service (HDDS).

Comparative Approaches in Brief Dynamic Psychotherapy

CONTENTS

ABOUT THE EDITOR

William Borden, PhD, is Senior Lecturer in the School of Social Service Administration and the Department of Psychiatry at the University of Chicago, where he teaches courses on contemporary psychoanalytic thought, comparative personality theory, and clinical practice. He received his master's and doctoral degrees from the University of Chicago, and served as a fellow in the Harris Center for Developmental Studies at the University. He has published articles, essays, and book chapters on relational perspectives in contemporary psychoanlaysis, the contributions of D.W. Winnicott and the Independent Tradition in Great Britain, narrative perspectives in brief treatment, and empirical research on stress, coping, and development through the life course. He has worked as clinician, supervisor, and consultant in mental health settings since 1983. Prior to his current position, he was supervisory social worker in the University of Chicago student counseling service, where he provided advanced training in brief dynamic therapy. He has served on the faculties of the Institute for Clinical Social Work, Chicago; the Illinois State Psychiatric Institute, and the Jane Addams College of Social Work, University of Illinois at Chicago. His professional affiliations include the American Psychological Association, Division of Psychoanalysis; the National Association of Social Workers, and the Illinois Chapter of the Society for Clinical Social Work.

Introduction

William Borden

Although many writers relate the rise of short-term treatment to recent shifts in social and economic conditions, careful readings of the psychoanalytic literature remind us that clinicians have carried out various forms of brief intervention throughout the course of therapeutic practice. Our earliest conceptions of brief psychotherapy were set forth in the psychoanalytic tradition, following the pioneering efforts of Sandor Ferenczi, Otto Rank, Franz Alexander and Thomas French, and the major schools of psychoanalytic thought continue to shape emerging approaches to time-limited therapy.

As the articles in this volume show, the growing emphasis on theoretical pluralism and pragmatism in contemporary psychoanalysis has broadened the base of brief dynamic treatment. Although early approaches emphasized stringent selection criteria and limited the scope of intervention to a narrow range of problems, the realities of contemporary practice have forced clinicians to revise conservative models of short-term dynamic treatment. Practitioners have reconsidered classical notions of the therapeutic endeavor, enlarged their understandings of curative factors, and realized the need to develop more flexible treatment strategies in efforts to serve a greater range of clients with differing levels of functioning, relational capacities, coping strategies, social networks, and environmental conditions. Out of practical necessity, workers are carrying out what D. W. Winnicott would have called experiments in adapting to need (Winnicott, 1962/1965, p. 169).

While many clinicians continue to challenge the growing emphasis

[Haworth co-indexing entry note]: "Introduction." Borden, William. Co-published simultaneously in *Psychoanalytic Social Work* (The Haworth Press, Inc.) Vol. 6, No. 3/4, 1999, pp. 1-6; and: *Comparative Approaches in Brief Dynamic Psychotherapy* (ed: William Borden) The Haworth Press, Inc., 1999, pp. 1-6. Single or multiple copies of this article are available for a fee from The Haworth Document Delivery Service [1-800-342-9678, 9:00 a.m. - 5:00 p.m. (EST). E-mail address: getinfo@haworthpressinc.com].

1

on brief treatment and see short-term therapy as a limited alternative to more extended forms of intervention, we can anticipate even wider use of time-limited approaches in public and private domains of practice. Social, cultural, political, and economic forces continue to restrict the contexts and modes of service delivery, and the ascendancy of managed care has forced clinicians to revise patterns of practice and provide more focused and limited forms of treatment. Independent of the foregoing considerations, studies of clinical intervention in a variety of settings have repeatedly found that most persons stay in therapy for briefer periods than many practitioners would imagine, generally choosing to end treatment well within the range of sessions encompassed by current short-term models. Findings suggest that naturally occurring, consumer-defined brief therapies are the norm (Levenson, 1995; Stern, 1993). Finally, while critics argue that consumer advocate groups, employers, and managed care organizations have oversold the benefits of brief treatment, reviews of research show that time-limited interventions carry the potential to bring about substantial improvement in functioning and, by certain criteria, may be as helpful as more extended forms of intervention (see reviews in Messer & Warren, 1995). In view of the foregoing developments, it is hardly surprising that Michael Lambert, editor of the *Handbook of Psychotherapy and Behavior Change*, has decided to omit the customary chapter on short-term intervention in the forthcoming edition, scheduled for publication in 2001. He reasons: " . . . almost all therapy is brief therapy now" (Goode, *New York Times*, 11/24/1998).

The articles in this special issue show how comparative perspectives enlarge ways of seeing, understanding, and acting over the course of the therapeutic endeavor. In the opening article, "Pluralism, Pragmatism, and the Therapeutic Endeavor in Brief Dynamic Treatment," I place traditional models of brief therapy in historical perspective, review relational schools of thought that inform current approaches, and identify tasks in continued development of theory, research, and practice. I emphasize the need to consider a broader range of dysfunction and psychopathology in formulations of brief intervention and to develop realistic and flexible approaches for vulnerable and underserved populations.

In the following article, "Using Self Psychology in Brief Psychotherapy," Jill Gardner provides an overview of contemporary self psychology and shows how core concepts deepen our understanding of therapeutic tasks and curative factors in time-limited treatment. She presents an organizing framework that guides application of self psychological formulations in brief modes of intervention for a wider range of clients than workers have addressed in traditional models of brief dynamic treatment. From a self psychological perspective, she shows, use of relational elements in the therapeutic situation may strengthen the self, facilitate coping, and expand the capacity to derive psychological sustenance from other relationships. Even very brief courses of treatment, she emphasizes, carry the potential to reinstate processes of repair, structure building, and development.

In the next article, "Integrative Short-Term Treatment of the Borderline Patient," Eda Goldstein focuses on problems in functioning perpetuated by personality organizations that present particular difficulties in the clinical situation. She reviews conflict and deficit models of borderline functioning that inform current treatment approaches and presents an integrative, flexible framework for short-term dynamic intervention. She describes assessment procedures, establishment of the holding environment, selection of goals, maintenance of the treatment focus, management of countertransference experience, and use of educative, mirroring, and role modeling strategies as well as interpretive technique. While many workers continue to regard long-term, intensive therapy as the treatment of choice for more severe personality disorders, briefer modes of intervention can reduce symptoms, strengthen ego functions, promote coping capacities, limit self-defeating and destructive behaviors, and improve ability to negotiate interpersonal situations. Like Gardner, Goldstein believes that brief, supportive interventions carry the potential to facilitate reparative work and personality reorganization.

Although many workers view interpretation as the central curative factor in psychoanalytic psychotherapy, there has been surprisingly little study of interpretive process in dynamic intervention. In the following article, "Interpretation in Short-Term Therapy: The Role of Level of Patient Functioning," Carol Tosone, Paul Crits-Christoph, and Lester Luborsky report findings from a study of interpretative interventions in supportive-expressive, time-limited treatment. Theoretical formulations and clinical reports led them to expect that practitioners would modify the content and frequency of interpretations and vary verbal activity on the basis of differing levels of client functioning. The results of the study failed to support their hypotheses, however, and findings challenge widely held assumptions about the use and functions of interpretive strategies in analytic psychotherapy. The investigation promises to bring greater precision to further research on interpretive process and focus continued study of curative factors in brief dynamic treatment.

The next two articles examine ways in which developmental perspectives help workers formulate goals, understand curative elements, and evaluate outcomes in brief intervention at critical junctures through the life course. In "Development, Psychopathology, and Brief Psychotherapy," Erika Schmidt examines the interplay between psychopathology, developmental process, and therapeutic intervention. Drawing on contributions by such varied workers as R. N. Emde, Daniel Stern, Roy Schafer, and Winnicott, she shows how the inherent motivation, momentum, and self-righting tendencies of developmental processes can facilitate brief intervention during times of change and transition–what Winnicott had called "sacred moments," as she observes. A case report, describing the brief therapy of a late adolescent girl, shows how developmental concepts help us address difficulties in immediate contexts, formulate goals, and make use of curative elements in time-limited treatment.

In the following article, "Developmental Perspectives in Brief Treatment of Gay Youth," Nancy Stone examines ways in which the therapeutic process can help gay men negotiate the transition from late adolescence to young adulthood. Her case report, describing the short-term therapy of an 18-year-old in the early stage of the "coming out" process, illustrates how brief intervention can facilitate efforts to work toward greater authenticity in sense of self and identity, revise maladaptive relational patterns, and strengthen coping capacities. More generally, she suggests, time-limited intervention can provide a holding environment as youth renegotiate developmental discontinuities perpetuated by internalized homophobia and self-alienation.

Interpersonal perspectives in contemporary psychoanalysis have increasingly focused our attention on the role of the therapeutic relationship and the practitioner's contributions to the clinical situation, understood as a two-person process in an interactive field. Bertram Cohler examines representative tasks and difficulties in brief treatment of gay men from the perspective of the clinician in his report, "The Gay Therapist's Response to a Gay Client Practicing Unsafe Sex: A Dilemma in Brief Psychotherapy." Following careful review of the clinical literature, he describes the brief treatment of a young adult practicing unsafe sex in a venue that placed him at high risk for HIV infection. Drawing on self psychological perspectives and formulations of countertransference by Heinrich Racker, Cohler analyzes his own reactions in terms of concordant identifications based on vicarious introspection with the client's efforts to realize greater sense of personal coherence, integrity, and vitality, and complementary identifications emerging out of his own personal concerns and vulnerabilities. The therapist's reluctance to recognize and address personal feelings reciprocal to the client's problems in living may compromise the therapeutic process, he cautions, underscoring the importance of the clinician's continuing self-exploration in brief treatment of difficult and vulnerable populations.

The closing articles explore the essential ambiguity, uncertainty, and vulnerability of the clinical situation. Dennis McCaughan examines Harry Stack Sullivan's seminal contributions in his essay, "On Learning to Learn Again." He reviews his early encounters with Sullivan's ideas and offers a fresh reading of his classic work, *The Psychiatric Interview*. McCaughan argues that many clinicians moved beyond Sullivan before having fully engaged his views. His purposeful approach to treatment, so clearly centered on the interpersonal domain of experience, carries a relevance for contemporary practice that clinicians have scarcely as yet begun to appreciate.

James Clark explores the risk environment of brief dynamic treatment in "Clinical Risk and Brief Psychodynamic Therapy: A Forensic Mental Health Perspective." He argues that clinicians realize only limited benefits from profiles of high-risk clients and urges workers to focus on the contextual dynamics shaping clinical practice, including interpersonal processes in the therapeutic relationship, the therapist-client-party payer triangle, and the interface between the mental health and legal systems.

As a group, the articles in this volume provide an introduction to representative conceptions of short-term dynamic therapy and offer practical guidance for beginning and advanced practitioners in search of realistic, flexible approaches in the contemporary health care environment. The contributors promise to deepen our appreciation of the common elements and distinctive features of differing schools of thought and help us consider a greater range of options in our continuing efforts to carry out experiments in adapting to need.

REFERENCES

Goode, E. (1998). "How much therapy is enough? It depends." *New York Times*, Nov. 24., Section D1.

Messer, S. & Warren, S. (1995). *Models of brief psychodynamic therapy.* New York: Guilford.

Levenson, H. (1995). *Time-limited dynamic psychotherapy.* New York: Basic Books.

Stern, S. (1993). "Managed care, brief therapy, and therapeutic integrity." *Psychotherapy, 30,* 162-175.

Winnicott, D. W. (1962/1965). "The aims of psycho-analytical treatment." In *The maturational process and the facilitating environment* (pp. 166-170). New York: International Universities Press.

Chapter 1

Pluralism, Pragmatism, and the Therapeutic Endeavor in Brief Dynamic Treatment

William Borden

SUMMARY. This article places representative formulations of brief dynamic psychotherapy in the larger context of psychoanalytic thought, reviews relational perspectives that inform contemporary approaches to time-limited treatment, and identifies tasks in continued development of theory, research, and practice. In doing so, it emphasizes the need to consider a broader range of psychopathology, dysfunction, and need in formulations of brief intervention and to develop more flexible and realistic approaches in treatment of vulnerable and underserved populations. The growing emphasis on theoretical pluralism and pragmatism in therapeutic practice generally should facilitate efforts to broaden the base of brief dynamic treatment. *[Article copies available for a fee from The Haworth Document Delivery Service: 1-800-342-9678. E-mail address: getinfo@haworthpressinc.com <Website: http://www.haworthpressinc.com>]*

KEYWORDS. Brief dynamic psychotherapy, short-term therapy

William Borden, PhD, is Senior Lecturer, School of Social Service Administration and Department of Psychiatry, University of Chicago.

Address correspondence to: William Borden, School of Social Service Administration, University of Chicago, 969 East 60th Street, Chicago, IL 60637.

The author would like to thank Sharon Berlin, James Clark, Bertram Cohler, Irene Elkin, Miriam Elson, Allen Heinemann, and Linda Tartof for their critical comments and suggestions in the preparation of this article.

[Haworth co-indexing entry note]: "Chapter 1. Pluralism, Pragmatism, and the Therapeutic Endeavor in Brief Dynamic Treatment." Borden, William. Co-published simultaneously in *Psychoanalytic Social Work* (The Haworth Press, Inc.) Vol. 6, No. 3/4, 1999, pp. 7-42; and: *Comparative Approaches in Brief Dynamic Psychotherapy* (ed: William Borden) The Haworth Press, Inc., 1999, pp. 7-42. Single or multiple copies of this article are available for a fee from The Haworth Document Delivery Service [1-800-342-9678, 9:00 a.m. - 5:00 p.m. (EST). E-mail address: getinfo@haworthpressinc.com].

7

INTRODUCTION

"The fox knows many things," Archilochus wrote, "but the hedge-hog knows one big thing." This curious fragment of verse by the Greek satiric poet provides the point of departure for Isaiah Berlin in his classic essay on two types of intellectual temperament that lead to divergent ways of seeing, understanding, and acting (Berlin, 1953/1993). Berlin characterizes the hedgehog as the purist and describes one group of thinkers who seek order, unity, and coherence in their approach to experience, embracing a "single central vision," a "universal organizing principle" (p. 3). Plato, Dante, Dostoevsky, Nietzsche, and Proust are hedgehogs, in his view. The fox, on the other hand, favors a pragmatic pluralism and proceeds in light of the actual demands of the particular situation; here, Berlin focuses on a second group of workers who engage the concrete realities of life as we live it, refusing to privilege "any one unchanging, all-embracing," unitary vision (p. 3). Aristotle, Goethe, Moliere, Montaigne, Shakespeare, and Joyce are foxes, in his judgment. Although Berlin recognizes the limits of such broad classifications, he marks a basic distinction between the purist and the pluralist and captures the inevitable tension between the one and the many that divides thinkers and practitioners in diverse areas of human activity.

If the hedgehog has shaped our classical vision of the psychoanalytic endeavor, as a number of writers have argued in their interpretations of Freud, our earliest conceptions of brief psychotherapy are surely the work of the fox. The first attempts to revise therapeutic strategies and limit the length of treatment were carried out by workers who departed from Freud's vision of the "pure gold of analysis" (Freud, 1918, p. 168) and embraced more pragmatic approaches in their efforts to address a broader range of problems in living, restore prior levels of functioning, and facilitate adaptive ways of being and relating. The pioneering figures who emerge in historical accounts of brief psychotherapy, notably Sandor Ferenczi, Otto Rank, Franz Alexander, Harry Stack Sullivan, and D. W. Winnicott, were foxes by nature. They challenged orthodox notions of analytic practice, advocating experiments in adapting to need (Winnicott, 1962/1965, p. 169), and increasingly urged clinicians to employ a range of strategies in attempts to develop more active, focused, flexible, and efficient methods of intervention. The concerns, sensibilities, and values that informed their revisions of therapeutic practice prefigure the move toward theoretical pluralism and pragmatism in contemporary psychoanalysis and clinical social work.

Brief treatment has emerged as the prevailing form of intervention in public and private health care settings over the last decade, and it is likely that short-term therapy will become the primary mode of psychodynamic practice as workers respond to increased demands for service, shifts in health care delivery, and consumer preference for focused and efficient methods of help. While many writers relate the rise of short-term treatment exclusively to recent shifts in social, cultural, political, and economic conditions, close readings of the psychoanalytic literature remind us that clinicians have carried out various forms of brief intervention throughout the course of therapeutic practice. In this article I place representative conceptions of brief dynamic treatment in the larger context of psychodynamic thought, review relational lines of understanding that inform contemporary approaches to time-limited intervention, and identify tasks in continued development of theory, research, and practice. In doing so, I emphasize the need to (a) address a greater range of problems in living, dysfunction, and psychopathology in formulations of short-term intervention; (b) develop realistic and flexible strategies in treatment of vulnerable and underserved populations whose options for care are increasingly limited to brief contact; (c) strengthen research activities in efforts to document the efficacy and effectiveness of specific treatment approaches and determine whether certain methods are preferable under given conditions; and (d) expand opportunities for advanced training, supervision, and consultation in brief treatment for graduate students, educators, and experienced practitioners.

While many clinicians continue to see short-term treatment as a limited alternative to more intensive long-term therapy (see reviews by Bloom, 1992; Budman & Gurman, 1988; Goldstein & Noonan, 1999; Messer & Warren, 1995; Shechter, 1997; Strupp & Binder, 1984), we can expect greater interest in brief intervention and wider use of time-limited approaches in public and private sectors for several reasons.

First, social and economic forces continue to restrict contexts and modes of service delivery, and progressive changes in the reimbursement structure of mental health care have forced workers to revise patterns of practice and provide more focused and shorter forms of intervention. Social service agencies, health maintenance organizations, preferred provider groups, employee assistance programs, and private insurers continue to emphasize efficiency and accountability in evaluation of treatment outcomes, and financers of services limit sessions by number or dollar amounts in efforts to control costs. The move to managed care has created a series of ethical dilemmas and clinical challenges (see Bollas & Sundelson, 1995; Brandell, 1998; Myers, 1998; Reamer, 1997; Shechter, 1997), and many social workers have refused to participate in provider networks or panels. They identify a range of concerns, including shift of control for treatment from the practitioner to the payer, constraints on ability to provide services on basis of need, potential violation of client privacy and confidentiality, use of case reviewers with limited training in mental health care, and inefficient administrative procedures. In order to negotiate the demands of the marketplace and preserve their authority as service providers, however, many practitioners have decided that they must enlarge their understandings of brief treatment theory, master representative methods of short-term intervention, and revise traditional ways of working.

Second, there is considerable evidence that most persons use intervention over short periods of time and choose to end treatment well within the range of sessions encompassed by current definitions of brief therapy (see, e.g., Cummings, 1988; Levenson, 1995; Messer & Warren, 1995; Pekarik & Wierzbicki, 1986). Reviews of research conducted over the last two decades show that clients generally complete courses of treatment within 6 to 12 sessions in public and private settings (see Frank, 1990; Garfield, 1989; Koss & Shiang, 1994; Phillips, 1987); findings indicate that between 60 and 75 percent of all clients end treatment before the eighth session, even in open-ended dynamic therapy (Levenson, 1995; Pekarik & Wierzbicki, 1986). Further, even when clients do receive long-term treatment, findings suggest that marked improvements occur relatively early in the process, usually within the first six months of intervention (Howard, Kopta, Krause & Orlinsky, 1986; Kopta, Howard, Lowry & Beutler, 1994). Practitioners suggest that "naturally occurring brief therapies" (Stern, 1993) or "consumer-defined brief therapies" (Levenson, 1995) are the norm and urge workers to conduct short-term treatment *by design* rather than *by default* in view of the potential advantages of planned interventions (Bloom, 1992; Budman & Gurman, 1988).

Third, critical reviews of psychotherapy research findings show that time-limited interventions carry the potential to bring about substantial improvement in functioning (Koss & Shiang, 1994; Koss & Butcher, 1986; Luborsky, Singer & Luborsky, 1975; Orlinsky & Howard, 1986; Steenbarger, 1994). Messer and Warren (1995) provide a careful review of process and outcome studies over the last two decades and conclude that the effects of time-limited intervention appear to be as enduring as those of extended treatment; they emphasize, however, that beneficial outcomes appear to increase with length of treatment, and observe that breadth of change may be greater in long-term dynamic therapy. They note that acute and chronic symptoms generally improve earlier than problems in functioning associated with character structure. Workers acknowledge critical differences in the goals, processes, and outcomes of long-term psychotherapy and briefer forms of intervention; nonetheless, current findings provide strong support for use of shorter types of intervention.

Although clinicians emphasized stringent selection criteria and limited the therapeutic focus to a narrow range of problems in initial conceptions of brief dynamic treatment, the realities of contemporary practice have forced workers to revise conservative models of short-term treatment and reexamine approaches to time-limited intervention. Practitioners are enlarging their understandings of curative factors and developing more flexible treatment strategies in efforts to serve a greater range of clients with differing levels of functioning, relational capacities, coping strategies, social networks, and environmental conditions (see, e.g., Binder, Strupp & Henry, 1995; Borden, 1992a, 1992b, 1996; Elson, 1986; Goldstein & Noonan, 1999; Gustafson, 1995, 1997; Hoyt, 1995; Messer & Warren, 1995). Out of practical necessity, clinicians are carrying out what Winnicott would have called experiments in adapting to need. As Hans Strupp observes, the objective of treatment is no longer "the greatest amount of change, but rather the greatest amount of change that can be achieved relative to the available resources. All interested parties–consumers, therapists, third-party payers–have become thoroughly pragmatic" (Strupp, 1995, p. x).

By way of overview, the first part of the article traces the development of brief dynamic treatment, noting historical antecedents in the work of Freud, Adler, and Jung before focusing on the seminal contributions of Ferenczi, Rank, and Alexander and French. The second section shows how Freudian drive psychology influenced the first generation of brief treatment workers and describes representative models. The third section presents a series of relational models that have informed current approaches to time-limited intervention. The final section reviews current trends in the field of brief treatment and suggests possible directions in development of theory, research, and practice.

PSYCHODYNAMIC CONTEXTS OF BRIEF TREATMENT

In order to place contemporary models of brief treatment in historical perspective, I review overlapping lines of work in psychoanalysis and depth psychology that have shaped representative approaches to time-limited intervention. As a starting point I summarize antecedents in the work of Freud and two of his early followers, Alfred Adler and C. G. Jung, long-neglected in the contemporary psychoanalytic literature, who anticipate development of brief treatment approaches in their concerns with clinical technique and contexts of therapeutic practice. The remainder of the section reviews the contributions of Ferenczi, Rank, and Alexander and French, all of whom are recognized as seminal figures in the development of modern brief treatment.

FREUD

In his earliest efforts to develop the cathartic approach, Freud was forced to negotiate what we have come to recognize as fundamental dilemmas in the practice of short-term psychotherapy. In his pre-psychoanalytic period, Freud assumed that neurotic symptoms originated in repressed memories of traumatic events; the task of treatment, accordingly, was to help clients recover memories, process emotion associated with the experience (abreaction), and integrate awareness of past events. The therapeutic process allowed "strangulated affect . . . to find a way out through speech; and also subjects the idea to associative connection by introducing it into normal consciousness" (Breuer & Freud, 1893-95/1955). Breuer and Freud's discussion of selection criteria, curative elements, and therapeutic technique in *Studies on Hysteria* (1893-95/1955) foreshadows contemporary concerns in the development of brief treatment strategies, including assessment of motivation, establishment of the therapeutic alliance, maintenance of the focus, active provision of support and education, recognition and management of transference phenomena, and interpretation of defensive behaviors (resistance). Although Freud showed little interest in the question of time and therapeutic process as such, his emphasis on selection criteria, focal symptoms, activity, and support in his early formulations of therapeutic process anticipates what we have come to identify as the distinguishing features of brief dynamic treatment: selectivity, focus, activity, and brevity (see Bauer & Kobos, 1987; Flegenheimer, 1982, 1985; Groves, 1996; Gustafson, 1995; Messer & Warren, 1995; Strupp & Binder, 1984).

Freud's subsequent revisions of psychoanalytic theory and practice methods, following his abandonment of the cathartic method in favor of free association, changed the nature of the therapeutic endeavor; the task was not to work through repressed memories of traumatic experience and alleviate symptoms but to analyze and restructure the personality (Freud, 1905). In view of enlarged understandings of drive, motivation, development, psychopathology, and curative elements in the therapeutic situation, clinicians departed from the active, circumscribed approach of Freud's cathartic method and increasingly assumed a neutral, interpretive stance in efforts to trace childhood antecedents of neurotic conflict through analysis of transference phenomena. Interpretation and insight emerged as the chief agents of therapeutic change (for elaboration of these points see Messer & Warren, 1995; Mitchell, 1988; Strupp & Binder, 1984).

Although many writers have made connections between continued development of psychoanalytic theory and the increasing length of analytic treatments (see, e.g., Bauer & Kobos, 1987; Hoyt, 1995; Messer & Warren, 1995; Strupp & Binder, 1984), it is instructive to note that most of the treatments that Freud himself conducted were relatively brief by contemporary standards, often completed within weeks or months. By way of example, he provides reports of brief contacts with Katharina in 1885 and Lucy R. in 1892 (Breuer & Freud, 1893-95); his six-session treatment of the conductor Bruno Walter in 1906 (Sterba, 1951), and his four-hour consultation with Gustav Mahler in 1908 (Jones, 1955). His analysis of Sandor Ferenczi took place over two three-week periods in 1914 and 1916 (Jones, 1955).

Yet, while Freud was willing to carry out brief therapy, he tended to diminish the favorable outcomes of his short-term interventions, characterizing them as flights into health or transference cures, and he was increasingly critical of systematic attempts to limit the length of therapeutic work. In one of his final papers, *Analysis Terminable and Interminable* (1937), he explicitly addressed the issue of time and criticized attempts by Ferenczi and Rank to shorten the length of treatment; although he was initially receptive to their efforts, he dismissed Rank's revisions as failed attempts to "accelerate the tempo of analytic therapy to suit the rush of American life" (p. 234). In the end, Freud maintained that psychoanalytic psychotherapy–"the liberation of a human being from his neurotic symptoms, inhibitions, and abnormalities of character–is a lengthy business" (Freud, 1937/1963, p. 233).

ADLER AND JUNG

Adler and Jung established independent schools of thought, following their breaks with Freud, and writers in contemporary psychoanalysis are beginning to acknowledge the significance of their contributions in discussion of contemporary practice (see, e.g., Marcus & Rosenberg, 1998; Mitchell & Black, 1995, p. 21). While neither Adler nor Jung developed systematic methods of brief treatment, each of them experimented independently with clinical technique throughout the course of their work and varied strategies in efforts to focus the therapeutic process, shorten intervention, and improve outcomes. Like the early Freud of the pre-psychoanalytic period, Adler and Jung both stressed the importance of motivation, faith in the therapeutic method, active interpretation of relational experience, and use of cognitive and educational strategies in attempts to limit the length of therapy and promote adaptive functioning.

Adler emphasized the role of consciousness, personal meaning, and relational experience in his formulations of motivation, development, health, and the aims of the therapeutic endeavor. His school of thought, known as individual psychology, anticipates developments in modern ego psychology, interpersonal psychoanalysis, cognitive and humanistic perspectives, and narrative studies (see Stein & Edwards, 1998). Adler's view of the therapeutic process stressed the importance of empathy and active support, and he drew on cognitive, behavioral, and educational strategies in the development of particular techniques, including Socratic questioning, guided imagery, and role playing. Adler was troubled by the growing length of analytic therapy and attempted to minimize the frequency of visits and duration of treatment in his practice; he proposed that workers generally limit intervention to eight to ten sessions (Adler, 1932/1964, p. 201).

A growing number of writers have made connections between Jungian perspectives in analytical psychology and contemporary views of self, personality, and development (see, e.g., Mitchell & Black, 1995; Samuels, 1985; Young-Eisendrath & Dawson, 1997), but there has been surprisingly little consideration of Jung's particular contributions to clinical practice. By his own accounts, he was pragmatic in his therapeutic work. His primary focus was the individual's adaptive functioning; the fundamental goal of treatment, he believed, was to facilitate growth and adaptation to the world in view of actual circumstances and realistic prospects (Jung, 1931, 1935/1954). In a move that anticipates contemporary models of time-sensitive treatment, he distinguished four stages of psychotherapy (confession, elucidation, education, and transformation), any one of which provides potential stopping points in the treatment of a particular case (Jung, 1931/1954; see Stein, 1998). Jung increasingly advocated "individualization of therapeutic methods," in view of differing personality types, developmental stages, and particular problems-in-functioning, and emphasized the importance of "psychological knowledge" and "re-education" in efforts to complete treatment "as speedily as possible" (Jung, 1935/1954, p. 9, pp. 26-27). He believed that persons could make effective use of brief, focused consultations in efforts to negotiate developmental transitions, stressful life events, and loss.

FERENCZI AND RANK

Ferenczi and Rank are recognized as leading figures in the development of brief treatment, and they describe their revisions of psychoanalytic technique and therapeutic practice in a classic monograph, *The Development of Psychoanalysis* (Ferenczi & Rank, 1925/1986). Ferenczi experimented with more active ways of working in his efforts to shorten treatment and improve outcomes; he emphasized the importance of the therapeutic alliance, the focus on circumscribed difficulties and current life conditions, the confrontation of defensive operations, the role of emotion as a curative element, and the use of transference and countertransference experience in efforts to renegotiate the effects of earlier trauma (see papers in Ferenczi, 1926). Ferenczi and Rank proposed that analysis of "living out" tendencies in the immediacy of the therapeutic relationship–without extended exploration of childhood antecedents to current difficulties–was potentially sufficient to restore adaptive functioning (see Tosone, 1997). They reasoned that earlier experiences of childhood conflict are inevitably represented in current patterns of interaction; in their view, the relationship between client and therapist thereby serves as a facilitating medium in efforts to revise problematic patterns of interpersonal behavior and develop adaptive ways of being and relating. From this perspective, treatment is not an intellectual reconstruction, but an emotional reliving and renegotiation of earlier experience. Ferenczi enlarged ways of conceptualizing modes of therapeutic action (e.g., direct advice, suggestion, prohibition of behavior) and the functions of relational process in the clinical situation, anticipating formulations of the holding environment and the two-person interactive field in contemporary models of brief treatment. He was a major force in the development of object relations perspectives in the British School, following his treatments of Ernest Jones, Melanie Klein, John Rickman, and Michael Balint (see Borden, 1998); his views also influenced the development of the interpersonal tradition following his treatments of Clara Thompson and Sandor Rado (see Safran & Muran, 1998).

Rank increasingly focused on the role of separation and individuation in growth and development, and viewed problems in living as a function of unsuccessful efforts to negotiate coexisting needs for attachment and dependency, and separation and independence (Rank, 1936). He conceived of the will as an organizing, integrative force that facilitates efforts to negotiate basic existential dilemmas and promotes development and individuation of the self. The task of treatment, from this perspective, was to provide therapeutic conditions and relational experiences that would facilitate separation-individuation processes and empower the person to act and create. For Rank, the therapeutic situation was a present experience rather than a reliving of the past; he argued that knowledge of the origin of problematic behavior did not necessarily facilitate change, and he emphasized the curative functions of experiential learning in the course of therapeutic interaction. Following Ferenczi, he saw the therapeutic relationship as a medium in efforts to identify problematic patterns of interaction, learn more adaptive modes of relating, and anticipate application of new behaviors to representative situations following the end of treatment. The experience of ending provided a means of renegotiating issues of dependency, separation, and relatedness and he saw the termination date as a crucial feature of the therapeutic process. Recent evaluations of Rank's contributions emphasize his use of time limits and termination as a transformative element in the therapeutic process; he also stressed the role of client motivation and willingness to accept responsibility for behavior in favorable outcomes (Rank, 1936; see also Bauer & Kobos, 1987; Flegenheimer, 1982; Messer & Warren, 1995; O'Dowd, 1986).

ALEXANDER AND FRENCH

Although Franz Alexander and Thomas French presented their contributions as elaborations of earlier work by Ferenczi and Rank, they introduced important formulations in their own right and developed the first systematic approach to brief dynamic treatment. They believed that psychodynamic principles could inform briefer modes of intervention and they modified techniques in their efforts to provide services to a greater range of client populations (Alexander & French, 1946, p. 341). They clarified central tasks and concerns in time-limited intervention, including methods of assessment and collaborative treatment planning, formulation of goals, establishment of focus, recognition of the educational functions of treatment, use of transference experience, management of regressive states, and application of therapeutic learning to current life situations. Like Jung and Adler, they characterized the therapy process as "emotional re-education" (p. 95) and explicitly attempted to make therapy as brief as possible. They based treatment strategies on careful assessment of the client's psychodynamic organization and current life circumstances. They identified specific treatment goals and took an active role in efforts to maintain the focus, limit dependency and regressive experience, and promote adaptive modes of functioning. In attempts to foster independence and autonomy, Alexander and French varied the frequency of sessions, suspended treatment for brief periods, and set termination dates. Like Ferenczi and Rank, Alexander and French saw relational experience, rather than interpretation and insight, as the transformative element in therapeutic change. In the medium of the transference, Alexander believed, the client could recreate and re-experience problematic patterns of behavior and revise longstanding difficulties in interaction with the clinician. Alexander called this process the correc-tive emotional experience (p. 67).

THE DEVELOPMENT OF BRIEF TREATMENT MODELS

While the work of Ferenczi, Rank, Alexander, and French antici-pated the larger turn toward relational perspectives in contemporary psychoanalysis, their ideas remained marginal at the time and failed to influence prevailing methods of treatment. Instead, the tradition of drive psychology continued to shape clinical practice through the 1970s, and the first generation of brief treatment workers based their models on principles of classical psychoanalytic thought.

DRIVE MODELS

Michael Balint, David Malan, Peter Sifneos, and Habib Davanloo drew on Freud's theory of personality in their understandings of psy-chopathology and the therapeutic situation. Accordingly, they empha-sized notions of *impulse, anxiety, defense*, and *conflict* in their concep-tions of problems in functioning; they understood neurosis to operate in a closed system of drives and defenses (see Mitchell, 1988, pp. 282-283). Although they differed considerably in their formulations of selection criteria, their models favored clients with strong motivation, circumscribed problems in functioning, capacity for reflection and insight, and ability to negotiate the vicissitudes of therapeutic interac-tion. Conceptions of the therapeutic process emphasized the active role of the clinician in confrontation of defensive strategies, analysis of transference phenomena, and interpretation focused on a central conflict or limited aspects of psychopathology. Practitioners described systematic interpretive efforts focused on the experience of wishes, defenses, and conflict. Following classical lines of understanding, they conceptualized transference as the displacement of impulses, feelings, and attitudes from the past to the person of the therapist. The clinician made repetitive links between conflicts involving current persons, past persons, and the clinician, and interpreted defenses against painful emotion constellated in interpersonal experience. Presumably, inter-pretation provided missing information and insight, facilitating revision of distorted perceptions and adaptive modes of adjustment. In the context of short-term intervention, however, clinicians also emphasized the role of emotion in therapeutic change and saw abreaction as a curative element; a number of writers view this as a legacy of Freud's early cathartic approach.

Since each theorist has provided careful descriptions of supporting theory, selection criteria, assessment strategies, appropriate focal problems, technical procedures, and outcome research, this discussion summarizes the distinguishing characteristics of each approach and considers the relative strengths and limits of the models in the context of contemporary thought and clinical practice.

BALINT AND MALAN: INTENSIVE BRIEF PSYCHOTHERAPY

Under the leadership of Michael Balint, the Tavistock group in London initiated systematic studies of time-limited therapy in the mid-1950s and developed an approach they characterized as intensive brief psychotherapy (Balint, Ornstein & Balint, 1972; Malan, 1963, 1976a). Assessment procedures emphasized evaluation of current and prior levels of functioning, environmental support, and dynamic issues, but Malan placed particular importance on motivation for insight, initial patterns of interaction, and responses to trial interpretations in selection of clients. The approach required explicit formulation of a central conflict or focal problem that provided a means of organizing the therapeutic process. The clinician assumed an active role and limited interventions to the central issue, using "selective interpretation, selective attention, and selective neglect" to maintain focus and continuity over the course of intervention (see Malan, 1976a, p. 32). Malan employed two classical constructs in his formulations of the interpretive process: the *triangle of conflict* (representing core elements of conflictual experience, conceptualized as impulse, defense, and anxiety or symptom), and the *triangle of person* (representing three relational contexts of conflictual experience, described as history of childhood relationships with parents and other significant figures, current social relationships, and transference to the therapist). He recommended that interpretive efforts start with the triangle of conflict as it relates to the experience of others, and that they identify representative patterns of experience in past and present interaction, including transference reactions in the therapeutic situation. The therapeutic process sought to help clients identify psychic conflicts that have precipitated and perpetuated problems in living, revise maladaptive perceptions and reactions to situations, and establish more adaptive modes of negotiating interpersonal difficulties (see p. 259).

The number of sessions was flexible, ranging from 20 to 30, depending on levels of client functioning and therapist experience, but Malan emphasized the importance of establishing a termination date at the outset: ". . . a time limit gives therapy a definite beginning, middle, and end–like the opening, middle game, and end game in chess–and helps to concentrate both the patient's material and the therapist's work. . . . To adapt Dr. Johnson, being under sentence of termination doth most marvelously concentrate the material" (p. 257). His approach remained faithful to classical psychoanalytic principles but offered varying degrees of flexibility in selection of clients; Malan believed that persons with significant psychopathology could potentially benefit from this approach provided that they demonstrated sufficient motivation, capacity to engage in relational experience, and potential to make use of interpretation in initial interviews. Malan (1976a, 1976b) described research findings on two groups of clients that provided evidence for the effectiveness of his approach; the efficacy of the model in treatment of circumscribed problems in functioning has been supported in subsequent studies by Piper and colleagues (Piper, Debbane, Bienvenu & Garant, 1984; Piper, Azim, McCallum & Joyce, 1990).

SIFNEOS: SHORT-TERM ANXIETY-PROVOKING PSYCHOTHERAPY

Sifneos, working in Boston, developed an active, didactic approach that emphasized exploration of childhood conflict, transference phenomena, and interpersonal difficulties (Sifneos, 1972, 1979). The focal problem was defined in the context of the Oedipal situation (a *triangular relationship conflict*), and the therapeutic process stressed interpretation of anxiety, defensive strategies, and conflict as it appeared in the transference to the therapist. He believed that a fundamental technique of psychoanalysis, *genetic transference interpretations*, could also serve brief dynamic intervention, and attributed favorable outcomes to accurate interpretations of Oedipal concerns. The active style of interaction sought to intensify anxiety and resistance, presumably facilitating efforts to revise defensive strategies and develop adaptive modes of functioning. Like Malan, Sifneos limited interventions to the domain of the focal problem. The educational dimension of treatment examined problematic aspects of the client's psychodynamic organization and proposed strategies for management of interpersonal dilemmas. Sifneos did not recommend an explicit termination date but generally limited the length of intervention to 12 to 20 sessions. He attributed successful outcomes to stringent selection criteria, including strong motivation, specific chief complaint, focus on Oedipal concerns, history of meaningful relationship, receptivity to new ideas, and realistic goals. Sifneos conducted a series of controlled studies and reported beneficial outcomes in treatment of circumscribed difficulties in functioning (Sifneos, Apfel, Bassuk, Fishman, & Gill, 1980, Sifneos, 1987); subsequent investigations, carried out by Svartberg and Stiles (1992, 1994), emphasize the importance of fit between client and therapist in determining favorable outcomes.

DAVANLOO: INTENSIVE SHORT-TERM DYNAMIC PSYCHOTHERAPY

Davanloo, working in Montreal, developed an analytic form of short-term treatment that emphasized aggressive *confrontation of defensive strategies* and *systematic interpretation of transference phenomena* in efforts to reorganize core neurotic structures and restructure personality (Davanloo, 1978, 1980, 1988). He initiated fundamental aspects of the therapeutic process in the opening interview in order to evaluate the client's capacity to work with unconscious material, tolerate the vicissitudes of therapeutic interaction, and make use of interpretive interventions; he described eight phases of the trial therapy (Davanloo, 1988). He believed that defensive operations should be identified and challenged at the outset, and his approach is distinguished by the aggressive, methodical confrontation and interpretation of resistance in efforts to uncover unconscious experience and facilitate reorganization of personality structure. The length of intervention varied with the client's problems and rate of improvement, ranging from 1 to 40 sessions; treatments generally averaged about 20 sessions. The approach was used in a controlled study of brief treatment for clients with moderate personality disorders and appeared to be particularly effective in reducing depression (Winston, Pollack, McCullough, Flegenheimer, Kestenbaum & Trujillo, 1991).

DISCUSSION

The foregoing models shared fundamental characteristics that distinguished them from traditional modes of long-term treatment, including (a) specification of selection criteria; (b) formulation of focal problems and treatment goals; (c) rapid establishment of the therapeutic alliance; (d) active maintenance and monitoring of treatment focus; (e) active and systematic interpretation of transference phenomena, resistance, and other forms of defense; (f) use of emotion and abreaction; and (g) careful management of temporal limitations and termination process (for further discussion see Binder, Strupp & Henry, 1995, p. 51; also Bauer & Kobos, 1987, Koss & Butcher, 1986, and Messer & Warren, 1995). The first generation of workers demonstrated that psychoanalytic principles could be adapted to short-term therapy and they enlarged our understanding of basic tasks and representative dilemmas in briefer forms of intervention. Reviewers note their careful attention to technical procedures and early efforts to evaluate therapeutic outcomes (see, e.g., Crits-Christoph, 1992; Koss & Butcher, 1986; Malan, 1976a; Messer & Warren, 1995; Strupp & Binder, 1984).

In the context of contemporary practice, however, the drive models appear limited in scope and present a series of conceptual problems and practical difficulties. First, they are rooted in Freud's classical metapsychology and emphasize notions of drive, defense, and conflict in conceptualizing problems in living, treatment foci, curative elements, and the larger aims of intervention. As Binder, Strupp, and Henry (1995) observe: "The classical theory refers to highly abstract, impersonal forces and functions . . . far removed from subjective experience . . . (The) therapist who conceptualizes conflict in terms of this theory must engage in at least tacit translations into language understandable to the patient. The theory provides no guidelines for making these translations" (p. 52).

Second, formulations of curative factors privilege interpretation and insight over relational process and experiential learning in the context of therapeutic interaction. The theorists acknowledge the importance of the therapeutic alliance in discussion of relational factors but preserve classical formulations of transference and countertransference; accordingly, we find little consideration of the dyadic nature of the client-therapist relationship, particular patterns of interaction, or personal reactions to behavior in the therapeutic process. The models fail to reflect enlarged understandings of relational process and curative factors emphasized in contemporary views of treatment.

Third, the models are based on a single-cause approach to human difficulty and fail to consider alternate points of view. Pluralist and constructivist perspectives in contemporary psychoanalysis emphasize pragmatic use of varying perspectives in view of the particular requirements of the clinical situation. Further, the authoritarian character of the models challenges core social work values and practice perspectives that emphasize notions of agency, intention, personal meaning, and self-determination (Borden, 1992a; Messer & Warren, 1995; Witkin & Gottschalk, 1988). Clinicians have expressed concern that the models potentially encourage defensive compliance with the therapist's view of reality, perpetuate self-defeating ways of negotiating relational experience, and limit development of autonomy, initiative, and self-efficacy (Strupp & Binder, 1984, p. 107; Westen, 1986, p. 503; see review in Messer & Warren, 1995, pp. 109-110).

Finally, conservative selection criteria limit the range of applicability and favor clients with well-organized personality structures, circumscribed problems, capacity for reflection, and ability to negotiate relational experience; persons with low motivation, rigid defenses, difficulties in regulating emotion and controlling impulses, limited ability to make use of interpretation, and global, chronic, or severe dysfunction are excluded, thereby ruling out the majority of persons who need help most in mental health settings and social service agencies (Bloom, 1992; Goldstein & Noonan, 1999; Koss & Shiang, 1994).

RELATIONAL PERSPECTIVES

A second group of workers, departing from classical drive perspectives, pursued lines of study initiated by Ferenczi, Rank, Alexander and French and developed alternative ways of conceptualizing problems in living. Winnicott, the leading representative of the Independent Tradition in Great Britain, introduced developmental and clinical formulations that carried particular relevance for briefer modes of intervention. Although he eschewed formal treatment models, his clinical reports showed how brief contacts could help clients negotiate immediate problems in functioning in here-and-now contexts and restore "forward movement in the developmental process" (Winnicott,

1971, p. 5). Sullivan, a leading force in the interpersonal tradition, centered on the relational contexts of problems in living and set forth principles and procedures that were applied in briefer forms of treatment (Sullivan, 1954; see review by McCaughan, 1999). Finally, self psychological perspectives introduced by Heinz Kohut and his followers also informed practice methods in time-limited treatment; Kohut himself appreciated the potential benefits of brief intervention (see case reports in Kohut, 1987), and clinicians applied his ideas in short-term work with a range of populations (see Elson, 1986; Gardner, 1999).

Before we examine contemporary models of time-limited intervention, it will be helpful to review the fundamental assumptions of the relational perspective as set forth in contemporary schools of psychoanalytic thought. A number of writers have characterized the move from drive psychology to relational concepts as a paradigm shift. Stephen Mitchell (1988) argues: "Mind has been redefined from a set of predetermined structures emerging from inside an individual organism to transactional patterns and internal structures derived from an interactive, interpersonal field" (p. 17). According to this perspective, "the basic unit of study is not the individual as a separate entity whose desires clash with external reality, but an interactional field within which the individual arises and struggles to make contact . . . " (p. 3). From this point of view, the person elaborates self and constructs relationships on the basis of previous interpersonal experience; human difficulty emerges in the context of relational fields and encompasses representative dilemmas in negotiation of vulnerability, need, dependency, desire, safety and security, separation and individuation (for elaboration see Bollas, 1989; Messer & Warren, 1995; Mitchell, 1988, 1993, 1997; Sandler & Sandler, 1978). Conceptions of personality, psychopathology, and therapeutic interaction center on *internalized representations of self, other, and relational experience* as well as *actual modes of interaction in the interpersonal field*. The relational perspective encompasses a range of theoretical traditions that historically have emphasized either the intrapsychic domain or the interpersonal field, including object relations thought, self psychology, and interpersonal psychoanalysis. The "more profound significance of the term relational," Ghent (1992a) explains, is that "it stresses relation not only between and among external people and things, but also between and among internal personifications and representations" (p. xx).

Mitchell draws on self psychological, object relational, and interpersonal schools of thought in his efforts to explain representative problems in functioning: "The relational model rests on the premise that the repetitive patterns within human experience are not derived, as in the drive mode, from pursuing gratification of inherent pressures and pleasures. . . . but from a pervasive tendency to preserve the continuity, connections, familiarity of one's personal, interactional world" (Mitchell, 1988, p. 33). Psychopathology is self-perpetuating because it is embedded in more general ways of being and interacting that preserve continuity and coherence in sense of self, maintain connections with internalized representations of others, and provide safety and security in negotiation or interpersonal experience. As a group, the relational approaches emphasize the role of social experience in the emergence of object relations and interpersonal patterns that perpetuate problems in functioning, just as they underscore the adaptive functions of seemingly dysfunctional behavior in light of earlier developmental situations and conditions of care. We understand defensive behavior as efforts to regulate anxiety, promote safety and security, and preserve self (for elaboration see Mitchell, 1988, 1993, 1997; also Messer & Warren, 1995). The person actively constructs meaning and shapes interpersonal experience; from this perspective, transference phenomena reflect plausible readings of experience in view of prior patterns of interaction and anticipated outcomes. As Messer and Warren note, workers move away from exploration of past events and focus on current maintaining factors in maladaptive behavior: here, we understand psychopathology as a dynamic, self-fulfilling process "in which feared and anticipated relational events tend to be elicited and enacted by the individual" in interactions with others, who, in turn, respond in complementary ways (Messer & Warren, pp. 119-120). Formulations of curative factors emphasize the role of relational process and experiential learning rather than genetic reconstruction of past events, interpretation, and insight; the therapeutic relationship, including transference and countertransference states, provides crucial sources of experiencing and learning in facilitation of growth and development (see Borden, 1998; Casement, 1991). The clinician functions as a *participant-observer* and provides opportunities for revision of repetitive patterns of maladaptive behavior; we understand treatment as a two-person process in an interactive field.

The models developed by James Mann at Boston University (Mann, 1973; Mann & Goldman, 1982), Hans Strupp, Jeffrey Binder and colleagues at the Vanderbilt Center for Psychotherapy Research (Strupp & Binder, 1984), Lester Luborsky, Paul Crits-Christoph and colleagues at the University of Pennsylvania (Luborsky, 1984), and Mardi Horowitz and colleagues at the Center for the Study of Neuroses at the University of California at San Francisco (Horowitz, 1986, 1988, 1991) explicitly depart from drive concepts and emphasize relational formulations of motivation, development, psychopathology, and therapeutic intervention (for review of additional relational models see Bloom, 1992; Messer & Warren, 1995; Safran & Muran, 1998; Weiss, J., Sampson, H., and the Mount Zion Psychotherapy Research Group, 1986).

MANN: TIME-LIMITED PSYCHOTHERAPY

Mann drew on a range of psychoanalytic perspectives in the development of his model, but his approach most clearly reflects the concerns of object relations tradition. Building on Rank's developmental formulations, Mann reasoned that "life consists of a never-ending series of reunions, separations, and losses," that "separation and loss are never fully mastered," and that "better resolution of the separation-loss problem leads to a greater sense of self and greater independence . . . " (Mann & Goldman, 1982, p. 28). He placed presenting problems in the context of "universal conflict situations" precipitated by separation-individuation processes and used fixed time limits in attempts to help clients renegotiate earlier experiences of loss and develop more adaptive modes of functioning (Mann, 1973, p. 24; Mann & Goldman, 1982). In the context of the model, definitions of the therapeutic focus encompass the client's presenting problems but emphasize what Mann characterized as the person's "chronically endured pain" and negative self-image; he urged workers to elaborate the dysfunctional interpersonal consequences of the client's view of self in current life situations.

The initial phase of intervention focuses on immediate difficulties, but subsequent work explores the client's feelings about termination, which, in Mann's view, reflect universal reactions to separation and loss. Interpretive efforts relate earlier experiences of loss to feelings precipitated by the anticipated end of treatment. The larger aim of intervention is to provide opportunities to process earlier experiences of loss and to strengthen capacities to manage subsequent separation and individuation experiences through the life course. Presumably, the experience allows for more complete internalizations of relational experience. Mann explains: "This time the internalization will be more positive (never totally so), less anger-laden, and less guilty, thereby making separation a genuine maturational event" (Mann, 1973, p. 36).

The approach is carefully structured and requires strict adherence to time limits. The initial assessment phase is followed by 12 sessions, generally conducted on a weekly basis. Mann argued that careful client selection, the circumscribed frame of intervention, and a strong therapeutic alliance mediate fluctuations in emotion through the therapeutic process. He was willing to consider a wider range of functioning in his selection of clients than we find in the models of Malan, Sifneos, and Davanloo, reasoning that separation-individuation processes mediate behavior at all levels of organization. He believed that the approach is appropriate in treatment of more severe forms of psychopathology provided that persons demonstrate the capacity for rapid emotional engagement and ability to manage separation and loss in the context of the therapeutic situation. Messer and Warren (1995) review a series of process and outcome studies based on Mann's model and conclude that there is "good initial support" for the efficacy of the approach and the durability of its effects (see Messer & Warren, pp. 205-209).

LUBORSKY: CORE CONFLICTUAL RELATIONSHIP MODEL

Luborsky, Crits-Christoph, and colleagues developed a time-limited approach that focuses on circumscribed areas of maladaptive interpersonal functioning. The therapeutic process is organized around a *central relationship pattern* or *core conflictual relationship theme* that emerges from the client's accounts of representative dilemmas in negotiating interpersonal experience. Although development of the focal theme reflects the particular difficulties of the client, it addresses experience in three domains: (a) wishes, needs, or intentions, formulated in the context of relational experience; (b) responses from others, and (c) responses from the self. The theme "captures the central pattern, script, or schema that each person follows in conducting relationships" (Luborsky & Crits-Christoph, 1990, p. 1; see also Book, 1998; Luborsky, 1984). Accordingly, it reflects specific features of the client's particular problems in functioning rather than more universal conceptions of oedipal conflict or loss.

Luborsky and colleagues made important distinctions between "supportive" and "expressive" elements in formulations of therapeutic intervention. *Supportive techniques* encompass communication of respect, acceptance, realistic optimism, encouragement of self-expression, and establishment of collaborative conditions. *Expressive techniques* include identification of maladaptive relational patterns and interpretation of behaviors in the context of past, current, and transference relationships (the core conflictual relationship theme informs the content of interpretive interventions). The larger goal is to help the client revise negative expectations in negotiation of need with others and develop more adaptive modes of interpersonal functioning (Luborsky & Crits-Christoph, 1990). According to the guidelines of the model, the course of treatment is limited to 16 sessions, although some workers have extended the length of intervention up to a year. Luborsky and colleagues have developed treatment manuals that provide specific recommendations concerning establishment of the focus and use of techniques (see Book, 1998). Research carried out by Luborsky and associates over more than two decades suggests that supportive-expressive psychotherapy carries the potential to bring about substantial improvement in circumscribed areas of maladaptive functioning (see Luborsky, Crits-Christoph, Mintz & Auerbach, 1988; Messer & Warren, 1995; also Tosone, Crits-Christoph & Luborsky, 1999).

HOROWITZ:
BRIEF THERAPY OF STRESS RESPONSE SYNDROMES

Horowitz and colleagues developed a brief treatment model that focuses on problems in functioning following traumatic events (Horowitz, 1986, 1988, 1991a, 1991b). Horowitz' conceptions of personality and coping are based on psychoanalytic and cognitive perspectives, and his formulation of "person schemas" encompasses internalized representations of self, others, and relationships. He focuses on "enduring but slowly changing views of self and of other" and "scripts for transactions between self and other. Each individual may have a repertoire of multiple self schemas" (Horowitz, 1991a, p. 168). He assumes that unresolved dynamic conflicts and personality characteristics limit capacities to mediate adverse life events, leading to problems in functioning. The interpretive process centers on *internal structured role relationship configurations* and *interpersonal manifestations of dynamic patterns*. The task of intervention is to revise current internal working models of self, other, and the larger world in view of traumatic experience. Presumably, interpretive interventions modify and realign internalized representations of self and others. The process explores the particular meaning of events in the context of the client's life. Horowitz modifies the approach on the basis of representative fluctuations in self-organization and social functioning associated with traumatic experience. During the "intrusive-repetitive" phase of a stress response, for example, the clinician assumes a supportive stance that facilitates efforts to regulate, control, and reduce overwhelming emotional states; during the "denial-numbing" phase, the therapist takes an active role and encourages exploration of emotion, self-expression, and catharsis. Horowitz has adapted the model for treatment of problems associated with the personality disorders (Horowitz et al., 1984). The model is limited to 12 sessions. Outcome studies by Horowitz and associates suggest that the model carries the potential to bring about marked improvement in functioning following adverse events (Horowitz, 1991; Messer & Warren, 1995).

STRUPP AND BINDER:
TIME-LIMITED DYNAMIC PSYCHOTHERAPY

Strupp and Binder, working at Vanderbilt University, developed a relational model of time-limited dynamic psychotherapy that integrates core concepts in object relations thought, interpersonal psychoanalysis, cognitive psychology, and narrative theory. The model draws on a broader range of perspectives than any of the preceding approaches and anticipates current emphasis on theoretical pluralism and constructivist approaches. Following object relational and interpersonal lines of understanding, the model focuses on *internalized representations of relational experience* and *maladaptive patterns of interpersonal functioning* that perpetuate problems in living; psychopathology is understood as rigid, anachronistic internal working models or structured role relationships that predispose persons to maladaptive modes of being and relating. The *"cyclical maladaptive action pattern"* reflects the characteristic rigidity, chronic repetitiveness, and self-perpetuating nature of neurotic problems: "In these vicious cycles, self-confirming patterns of repetitive social interchange serve to verify patients' maladaptive views and to validate and reinforce their problematic actions . . . " (Strupp & Binder, 1984, p. 73). They conceptualize the focus as a *prototypic or schematic interpersonal narrative*. Although each client tells a particular kind of story, the focal narrative describes (a) human actions (b) embedded in context of interpersonal transactions (c) organized in a cyclical psychodynamic pattern that have been (d) a recurrent source of problems in living and are also a present source of difficulty (p. 70).

Selection criteria emphasize the client's potential to identify coherent interpersonal themes, ability to distinguish self from others, and capacity for concern and integrity in relational experience; Strupp and Binder observe that the foregoing characteristics appear throughout the range of diagnostic categories, so neither particular symptom configurations nor diagnosis of specific disorder categorically justify exclusion from treatment. They assume that efforts to improve maladaptive interpersonal patterns will, in principle, reduce difficulties associated with all forms of psychopathology (Binder, Strupp & Henry, 1995, p. 55).

They conceptualize the therapeutic process as a set of interpersonal transactions; the client casts the clinician in the role of a significant other and recreates maladaptive patterns of behavior that precipitate and perpetuate problems-in-living. Following views outlined earlier, psychopathology is understood as a self-perpetuating process; the person enacts modes of behavior and elicits feared reactions from others who assume complementary roles. The therapist provides new models for *identification*, in the role of *participant-observer*, and offers opportunities for *experiential learning* that facilitate revision of dysfunctional behaviors and development of new modes of interaction; exploration of transference and countertransference phenomena clarifies maladaptive interpersonal patterns. The clinician helps the client identify and revise these patterns in the course of therapeutic interaction. The larger goal of treatment is to facilitate change in *maladaptive internal relational configurations and their interpersonal correlates* (Strupp & Binder, 1984). The length of treatment varies with the nature of the presenting problem and the clinician's level of experience but is generally completed within 20 to 30 sessions (see Levenson, 1995; Strupp & Binder, 1984, p. 27). Research efforts carried out by Strupp and associates over the last quarter century have emphasized the quality of the therapeutic relationship in influencing treatment outcomes (Binder, Strupp & Henry, 1995).

DISCUSSION

The relational models are informed by a range of theoretical perspectives, empirical findings, and clinical experience and they show how comparative approaches may enlarge ways of seeing, understanding, and acting in the course of the therapeutic situation. On balance, they provide greater flexibility in selection of clients, establishment of the treatment focus, interpretive approaches, use of interpersonal experience, length of intervention, and termination procedures than we find in the first generation of drive approaches. Of the four models reviewed here, Mann's approach would appear to be the most restrictive. Although he encompassed a broad range of dysfunction in formulations of selection criteria, he followed a single-cause approach to problems in living and privileged separation-individuation issues in his understanding of human difficulty; in doing so, he limited formulations of treatment goals, interpretive possibilities, and concepts of therapeutic action (for critical discussion see Messer & Warren, 1995; Westen, 1986). The other approaches examined in this review depart from notions of universal conflict or prototypic dilemmas in their formulations of focal concerns and emphasize the specific content and particular contexts of problems in functioning. The time-limited dynamic model of Strupp and Binder provides the greatest flexibility in selection of clients, formulation of the focus, and concepts of therapeutic action. A number of workers have recognized the practical utility of the model and are adapting it in work with vulnerable and difficult clients who fail to meet selection criteria of traditional models (Borden, 1996; Levenson, 1995).

The approaches described by Luborsky and Crits-Christoph, Horowitz, and Strupp and Binder emerged in the course of ongoing research programs, and workers have carried out systematic studies of case formulations, characteristics of the therapist-client relationship, curative elements in the therapeutic process, and treatment outcomes (see reviews by Koss & Shiang, 1994; Messer & Warren, 1995; and Strupp & Binder, 1984). Such efforts have strengthened the empirical base of clinical practice and facilitated training efforts through development of standardized treatment manuals (for discussion of manual-guided training see Binder & Strupp, 1993).

EMERGENT ISSUES IN THEORY, RESEARCH, AND PRACTICE

Two fundamental perspectives in psychoanalytic thought have shaped contemporary formulations of short-term dynamic treatment, and, as we have seen, they provide divergent ways of understanding motivation, development, psychopathology, and modes of therapeutic action. The *drive position*, based on Freud's classical model of the mind, relates problems in living to maladaptive ways of negotiating conflict between instinct and defense. The task of treatment, broadly conceived, is to develop more functional ways of mediating conflictual experience. The *relational position*, encompassing object relational, interpersonal, and self psychological lines of understanding, emphasizes ways in which internalized representations of self, others, and interpersonal experience perpetuate maladaptive modes of functioning. The task of intervention, broadly understood, is to identify dysfunctional patterns, revise problematic behaviors, strengthen coping capacities, and develop more adaptive modes of functioning.

Although the modern schools of psychoanalytic thought have converged in their emphasis on relational concerns, contemporary writers provide differing views of the human condition, problems in living, and concepts of therapeutic action. The pluralist context of psychoanalytic studies has infused dynamic psychotherapy with renewed vitality, and workers are enlarging notions of psychodynamic thought to encompass emerging lines of work in such varied disciplines as the neurosciences, cognitive psychology, personality theory, social thought, narrative studies, and the humanities. In view of current circumstances and anticipated conditions, we can expect practitioners to expand conceptions of brief treatment and to draw on a wider range of theoretical formulations, empirical findings, and clinical experience in development of interventions. I briefly suggest possible directions in continued development of theory, research, and practice.

1. *Increasing focus on special needs of vulnerable populations.* Since the majority of clients in private and public settings presently receive short-term intervention–whether or not it would appear to be the treatment of choice–we must continue to address a broader range of need, dysfunction, and psychopathology in development of approaches. Practitioners have identified vulnerable groups who present particular challenges in briefer forms of treatment, encompassing a range of diagnostic categories and stressful life conditions (e.g., psy-

chotic, affective, and personality disorders, substance use, stress response syndromes and post-traumatic stress reactions, life threatening
illness, physical disability, and pervasive dysfunction perpetuated by
inadequate social environments and poverty). In spite of increased
pressure from managed care systems, professional organizations, and
the empirical practice movement to develop specific treatments for
particular disorders, practitioners continue to place less importance on
diagnostic categories per se and emphasize assessment and management of *personality characteristics* and *interpersonal processes* that
require special attention in the therapeutic situation (e.g., low motivation; inability to establish a central and circumscribed focus; poor
reality testing; limited ability to regulate emotion; impoverished, disorganized, or rigid modes of cognitive functioning; unstable object
relations and associated difficulties in negotiating interpersonal experience; underdeveloped or restricted coping capacities; stressful life
conditions, and lack of environmental resources).

   In view of the foregoing considerations, a number of clinicians have
described attempts to *adapt technique,* vary use of *curative elements,*
and *enlarge the focus of intervention* in time-limited treatment of
vulnerable client groups; in general, such modifications emphasize
increased flexibility in selection of focal problems and greater use of
relational processes, supportive strategies, supplemental treatment
modalities, and environmental resources (e.g., case management, support
groups, activity programs). By way of example, workers have applied
self psychological formulations in short-term treatment of problems in
functioning associated with character structure (see, e.g., Baker, 1991;
Basch, 1995; Elson, 1986; Gardner, 1991, 1999). Other practitioners
have emphasized object relational and interpersonal perspectives in
time-limited treatment of personality disorders (see, e.g., Alpert, 1992;
Borden, 1996; Budman & Gurman, 1988; Foote, 1992; Fosha, 1992;
Goldstein, 1999; Perry, 1989; Winston et al., 1991). Seruya (1997) has
developed a brief treatment approach that integrates self psychological
and cognitive perspectives. Leibovich (1983) describes a structured,
problem-focused approach in short-term treatment of pervasive problems associated with the borderline disorders. Rosengrant (1984)
draws on Winnicott's formulation of the holding environment in his
attempt to develop a general model of brief treatment for community
mental health settings. Dynamically-based narrative perspectives have
informed time-limited intervention following trauma and loss (Bor-

den, 1989, 1992a, 1992b). Continued experimentation and elaboration of approaches promise to deepen our understanding of curative factors in the context of specific needs, circumstances, capacities, and resources.

2. *Increasing emphasis on developmental contexts of problems in functioning.* We can expect increased application of developmental formulations and empirical findings in creation of specialized approaches for children, adolescents, and adults at vulnerable points in the life course. The goal of treatment, from a developmental perspective, is to help persons negotiate immediate tasks and demands, strengthen coping capacities, and revise life structures (see Budman & Gurman, 1988; Hoyt, 1995; Messer & Warren, 1995; Schmidt, 1999). Narrative approaches, informed by life-course perspectives, have proven particularly helpful in time-limited intervention following developmental transitions and traumatic events (see Borden, 1989, 1992a, 1992b). Emerging lines of research on brain function and its influence on development, self-organization, and behavior processes have generated considerable interest in the mental health disciplines, and we can expect findings to influence assessment procedures and methods of intervention.

3. *Increased flexibility in use of intervention methods and varied treatment approaches.* In their efforts to broaden the scope of brief treatment, workers are moving away from *purist notions of grand theory* as well as *conservative, restrictive models of therapy.* Contemporary views of time-sensitive treatment encompass varying modes and lengths of intervention, ranging from therapeutic consultations (Winnicott, 1971) and single session treatments (Bloom, 1992; Talmon, 1990) to more extended and intensive therapies lasting from 25 to 40 sessions. There is growing consensus that no single approach is appropriate for all clients, and writers increasingly urge practitioners to vary the type, frequency, and length of contact in view of varying needs, capacities, and resources (see, e.g., Bloom, 1992; Gustafson, 1995, 1997; Messer & Warren, 1995). We can expect practitioners to develop more integrative and flexible approaches informed by emerging understandings of problems in functioning, curative factors, and clinical experiments in adapting to need.

4. *Continued research on therapeutic process and outcome.* Researchers have made considerable progress in efforts to determine the global effectiveness of representative treatment approaches and fo-

cused our attention on the influence of common elements in therapeutic change (Butler & Strupp, 1986; Frank & Frank, 1991). Meta-analyses of research findings have suggested that the efficacy of varying therapeutic approaches would appear to lie more in shared features than in differing characteristics (see Lambert & Bergin, 1994; Luborsky, Singer & Luborsky, 1975; Shapiro & Shaprio, 1982; Stiles, Shapiro & Elliott, 1986), and workers have identified common elements believed to operate in all forms of intervention (e.g., use of relational processes; interpretive efforts to facilitate insight, understanding, and meaning; emotional expression and catharsis; problem-solving, modeling, and reinforcement; see Frank & Frank, 1991; Garfield, 1989; Messer & Warren, 1995). Although many clinicians have accepted the "dodo bird verdict" or "tie score effect," believing all therapeutic approaches to be roughly equivalent in effectiveness, researchers continue to call for greater precision and specificity of theory and method in empirical work and emphasize the need to consider potential differential effects of varying interventions in the context of client characteristics, specific disorders, focal problems, forms of intervention, and technical procedures (see Binder, Strupp & Henry, 1995; Reid, 1997).

5. *Increased interest in potential functions and outcomes of single session consultations.* In efforts to enlarge research activities we can expect increased study of the ways in which persons make use of briefer forms of intervention. Sullivan (1954) and Winnicott (1971) emphasized the potential benefits of the *therapeutic consultation* from dynamic perspectives, and a number of clinical researchers, notably Bloom (1992), Gustafson (1997), and Talmon (1990), observe that persons commonly report considerable improvement following single therapeutic contacts. Such findings challenge traditional understandings of curative factors and behavior change. Thus far, however, rapid improvers have received little attention in empirical study. Frank (1990) speculates that many practitioners underestimate spontaneous recuperative powers and problem-solving capacities of persons, and he urges workers to explore the varying functions and outcomes of single-session contacts.

6. *Increased opportunities for training, supervision, and consultation in brief treatment.* Although patterns of service use show that most clients use treatment over surprisingly brief periods, many clinicians report little or no training in methods of time-limited intervention (Hoyt, 1995; Levenson, 1995; Messer & Warren, 1995). Shorter

forms of intervention make considerable demands on the worker and require specialized training, as Strupp (1992) emphasizes. In view of consumer preference for efficient forms of treatment, fiscal concerns of the managed care movement, and current gaps in graduate programs and professional education, we can expect increased efforts to extend training, supervision, and consultation opportunities for students as well as experienced clinicians in public and private settings.

The field of brief psychotherapy encompasses a growing range of theoretical perspectives, treatment approaches, and practice models. The differing points of view allow workers to approach problems from varying positions and to shift ways of working in light of particular needs, capacities, resources, and constraints. From a comparative perspective, we view our theories and models as tools for thinking; each practice has its own purposes, domains, rules, strengths, and limits. Emerging needs, new demands, and changing circumstances inevitably force revision and elaboration of methods. Following the ways of the fox, workers are increasingly realistic about the potential benefits and limits of the therapeutic endeavor and would appear to embrace the pragmatism and pluralism that the pioneering figures in the field so clearly demonstrated.

REFERENCES

Adler, A. (1932/1964). Technique of treatment. In H. L. Ansbacher & R. R. Ansbacher (Eds.), *Superiority and social interest* (pp. 191-201). Evanston, IL: Northwestern University Press.

Alexander, F. & French, T. M. (1946). *Psychoanalytic therapy: Principles and application*. New York: Ronald Press.

Alpert, M. (1992). Accelerated empathic therapy: A new short term dynamic psychotherapy. *International Journal of Short-term Psychotherapy, 7*, 133-156.

Baker, H. S. (1991). Shorter term psychotherapy: A self psychological approach. In P. Crits-Christoph & J. P. Barber (Eds.), *Handbook of short-term dynamic psychotherapy* (pp. 287-322). New York: Basic Books.

Balint, M., Ornstein, P. & Balint, E. (1972). *Focal psychotherapy*. London: Tavistock.

Basch, M. F. (1995). *Doing brief psychotherapy*. New York: Basic Books.

Bauer, G. P. & Kobos, J. C. (1987). *Brief therapy: Short-term psychodynamic intervention*. Northvale, NJ: Jason Aronson.

Berlin, I. (1953/1993). *The hedgehog and the fox*. Chicago: Ivan R. Dee.

Binder, J. & Strupp, H. (1993). Recommendations for improving psychotherapy training based on experiences with manual guided training and research. *Psychotherapy, 30*, 571-773.

Binder, J., Strupp, H. & Henry, W. P. (1995). Psychodynamic therapies in practice: Time-limited dynamic psychotherapy. In B. Bongar & L. E. Beutler (Eds.), *Comprehensive textbook of psychotherapy* (pp. 48-63). New York: Oxford University Press.

Bloom, B. (1992). *Planned short-term psychotherapy.* Boston: Allyn and Bacon.

Bollas, C. (1989). *Forces of destiny.* London: Free Association Books.

Bollas, C. & Sundelson, D. (1995). *The new informants.* Northvale, NJ: Jason Aronson.

Book, H. (1998). *Brief psychodynamic psychotherapy: The core conflictual relationship method.* Washington, DC: American Psychological Association.

Borden, W. (1989). Life review as therapeutic frame in treatment of young adults with AIDS: A developmental approach. *Health and Social Work, 14,* 253-259.

Borden, W. (1992a). Brief psychotherapy of AIDS patients with cognitive impairment. *Neuro-Rehabilitation, 2,* 74-80.

Borden, W. (1992b). Narrative perspectives in psychosocial intervention following adverse life events. *Social Work, 37,* 135-141.

Borden, W. (1996). Relational perspectives in brief treatment of the borderline disorders. Lexington, KY: Paper presented to the Kentucky Society for Clinical Social Work.

Borden, W. (1998). The place and play of theory in practice: A Winnicottian perspective. *Journal of Analytic Social Work, 5,* 25-40.

Brandell, J. (1998). Editor's Introduction. *Journal of Analytic Social Work, 5,* 1-4.

Breuer, J. & Freud, S. (1893-95). *Studies on hysteria. Standard edition* (Vol. 2). London: Hogarth Press.

Budman, S. H. & Gurman, A. S. (1988). *Theory and practice of brief psychotherapy.* New York: Guilford Press.

Butler, S. F. & Strupp, H. (1986). Specific and nonspecific factors in psychotherapy: A problematic paradigm for psychotherapy research. *Psychotherapy, 23,* 30-40.

Casement, P. (1991). *Learning from the patient.* New York: Guilford.

Crits-Christoph, P. (1992). The efficacy of brief psychotherapy: A meta-analysis. *American Journal of Psychiatry, 149,* 151-158.

Cummings, N. A. (1988). Emergence of the mental health complex: Adaptive and maladaptive responses. *Professional Psychology: Research and Practice, 19,* 308-315.

Davanloo, H. (Ed.) (1978). *Basic principles and techniques in short-term dynamic psychotherapy.* New York: Spectrum.

Davanloo, H. (1980). *Basic principles and techniques in short-term dynamic psychotherapy.* New York: Jason Aronson.

Davanloo, H. (1988). The technique of unlocking the unconscious. *International Journal of Short-Term Psychotherapy, 3,* 99-121.

Elliott, R., Stiles, W. B. & Shapiro, D. A. (1993). Are some psychotherapies more equivalent than others? In T. R. Giles (Ed.), *Handbook of effective psychotherapy* (pp. 455-477). New York: Plenum.

Elson, M. (1986). *Self psychology in clinical social work.* New York: Norton.

Ferenczi, S. & Rank, O. (1925/1986). *The development of psychoanalysis.* Madison, CT: International Universities Press.

Ferenczi, S. (1926). *Further contributions to the theory and technique of psycho-analysis*. London: Hogarth Press.

Flegenheimer, W. V. (1982). *Techniques of brief psychotherapy*. Northvale, NJ: Jason Aronson.

Flegenheimer, W. V. (1985). History of brief psychotherapy. In A. J. Horner (Ed.), *Treating the oedipal patient in brief psychotherapy*. Northvale, NJ: Jason Aronson.

Foote, B. (1992). Accelerated empathic psychotherapy: The first self-psychological brief therapy? *International Journal of Short-term Psychotherapy, 7*, 177-191.

Fosha, D. (1992). The interrelatedness of theory, technique and therapeutic stance: A comparative look at intensive short-term dynamic psychotherapy anbd accelerated empathic therapy. *International Journal of Short-term Psychotherapy, 7*, 157-176.

Frank, J. (1990). Introductory essay. Talmon, M. *Single session therapy*. San Francisco: Jossey-Bass.

Frank, J. & Frank, J. (1991). *Persuasion and healing* (3rd edition). Baltimore: Johns Hopkins University Press.

Freud, S. (1893-95). Studies on hysteria. *Standard edition* (Vol. 2). London: Hogarth Press.

Freud, S. (1905). On psychotherapy. *Standard edition* (Vol. 7). London: Hogarth Press.

Freud, S. (1918). Lines of advance in psycho-analytic therapy. *Standard edition* (Vol. 17). London: Hogarth Press.

Freud, S. (1937). Analysis terminable and interminable. *Standard edition* (Vol. 23). London: Hogarth Press.

Gardner, J. (1991). The application of self psychology to brief therapy. *Psychoanalytic Psychology, 8*, 477-500.

Gardner, J. (1999). Using self psychology in brief psychotherapy. In W. Borden (Ed.) *The therapeutic endeavor in brief dynamic treatment: Theory, research, and practice*. Binghamton, NY: The Haworth Press, Inc.

Garfield, S. L. (1989). *The practice of brief psychotherapy*. Elmsford, NY: Pergamon.

Ghent, E. (1992a). Forward. In Skolnick, N. J. & Warshaw, S. C. (Eds.), *Relational perspectives in psychoanalysis* (pp. xiii-xxii). Hillsdale, NJ: Analytic Press.

Goldstein, E. (1999). Integrative short-term treatment of the borderline patient. In W. Borden (Ed.), *The therapeutic endeavor in brief dynamic treatment: Theory, research, practice and commentary*. Binghamton, NY: The Haworth Press, Inc.

Goldstein, E. G. & Noonan, M. (1999). *Social work treatment: An integrative perspective*. New York: Free Press.

Groves, J. E. (1996) (Ed.) *Essential papers on short-term dynamic psychotherapy*. New York: New York University Press.

Gustafson, J. (1986/1997). *The complex secret of brief psychotherapy* (second edition). Northvale, NJ: Jason Aronson.

Gustafson, J. (1995). *The dilemmas of brief psychotherapy*. New York: Plenum.

Horowitz, M. J., Marmar, C., Krupnick, J., Kaltreider, N., Wallerstein, R. & Wilner, N. (1984). *Personality styles and brief psychotherapy*. New York: Basic Books.

Horowitz, M. (1986). *Stress response syndromes*. Northvale, NJ: Jason Aronson.

Horowitz, M. J. (1988). *Introduction to psychodynamics*. New York: Basic Books.
Horowitz, M. J. (1991a). Short-term dynamic therapy of stress response syndromes. In Crits-Christoph, P. & Barber, J. P., *Handbook of short-term dynamic psychotherapy* (pp. 166-198). New York: Basic Books.
Horowitz, M. J. (1991b). *Person schemas and maladaptive interpersonal patterns*. Chicago: University of Chicago Press.
Howard, K., Kopta, S. M., Krause M. S., & Orlinsky, D. E. (1986). The dose-effect relationship in psychotherapy. *American Psychologist, 41*, 159-164.
Hoyt, M. (1995). *Brief therapy and managed care*. San Francisco: Jossey-Bass.
Jones, E. (1955). *The life and works of Sigmund Freud*. New York: Basic Books.
Jung, C. G. (1931/1954). The aims of psychotherapy. In *Collected Works of C. G. Jung* (Vol. 16) (pp. 36-52). Princeton, NJ: Princeton University Press.
Jung, C. G. (1935/1954). What is psychotherapy? In *The practice of psychotherapy, Collected works of C. G. Jung* (Vol. 16) (pp. 21-29). Princeton, NJ: Princeton University Press.
Kohut, H. (M. Elson, Ed.). (1987). *The Kohut seminars on self psychology and psychotherapy with adolescents and young adults*. New York: Norton.
Kopta, S. M., Howard, K. I., Lowry, J. L, & Beutler, L. E. (1994). Patterns of symptomatic recovery in psychotherapy. *Journal of Clinical and Consulting Psychology, 62*, 1006-1009.
Koss, M. P. (1979). Length of psychotherapy for clients seen in private practice. *Journal of Consulting and Clinical Psychology, 47*, 210-212.
Koss, M. P. & Butcher, J. N. (1986). Research on brief psychotherapy. In S. Garfield & A. Bergin (Eds.), *Handbook of psychotherapy and behavior change* (third edition) (pp. 627-70). New York: Wiley.
Koss, M. P. & Shiang, J. (1994). Research on brief psychotherapy. In A. Bergin & S. Garfield (Eds.), *Handbook of psychotherapy and behavior change* (fourth edition) (pp. 664-700). New York: Wiley.
Lambert, M. J. & Bergin, A. E. (1994). Effectiveness of psychotherapy. In A. E. Bergin & S. L. Garfield (Eds.), *Handbook of psychotherapy and behavior change*. New York: Wiley.
Leibovich, M. (1983). Why short-term psychotherapy for borderlines? *Psychother. Psychosom., 39*, 1-9.
Levenson, H. (1995). *A guide to time-limited dynamic psychotherapy*. New York: Basic Books.
Luborsky, L., Singer, B., & Luborsky L. (1975). Comparative sutdies of psychotherapies: Is it true that "everyone has won and all must have prizes?" *Archives of General Psychiatry, 32*, 995-1008.
Luborsky, L. (1984). *Principles of psychoanalytic psychotherapy: A manual for supportive-expressive treatment*. New York: Basic Books.
Luborsky, L., Crits-Christoph, P., Mintz, J. & Auerbach, A. (1988). *Who will benefit from psychotherapy: Predicting therapeutic outcomes*. New York: Basic Books.
Luborsky, L. & Crits-Christoph, P. (1990). *Understanding transference: The CCRT method*. New York: Basic Books.
Malan, D. (1963). *A study of brief psychotherapy*. New York: Plenum Press.

Malan, D. (1976a). *The frontier of brief psychotherapy: An example of the convergence of research and clinical practice.* New York: Plenum Press.

Malan, D. (1976b). *Toward the validation of dynamic psychotherapy: A replication.* New York: Plenum Press.

Malan, D. (1979). *Individual psychotherapy and the science of psychodynamics.* London: Butterworth.

Mann, J. (1973). *Time-limited psychotherapy.* Cambridge, MA: Harvard University Press.

Mann, J. & Goldman, R. (1982). *A casebook of time-limited psychotherapy.* New York: McGraw-Hill.

Marcus, P. & Rosenberg, A. (Eds.) (1998). Introduction. *Psychoanalytic versions of the human condition* (pp. 1-11). New York: New York University Press.

McCaughan, D. (1999). On learning to learn again. In W. Borden (Ed.), *The therapeutic endeavor in brief dynamic treatment: Theory, research and practice.* New York: The Haworth Press, Inc.

Messer, S. B. & Warren, S. (1995). *Models of brief psychodynamic psychotherapy: A comparative approach.* New York: Guilford.

Mitchell, S. A. (1988). *Relational concepts in psychoanalysis.* Cambridge, MA: Harvard University Press.

Mitchell, S. A. (1993). *Hope and dread in psychoanalysis.* New York: Basic Books.

Mitchell, S. A. (1997). *Influence and autonomy in psychoanalysis.* Hillsdale NJ: Analytic Press.

Mitchell, S. A. & Black, M. (1995). *Freud and beyond: A history of modern psychoanalytic thought.* New York: Basic Books.

Myers, R. (1998). Managed care as a transference object: A clinical study. *Journal of Analytic Social Work, 5,* 5-24.

O'Dowd, W. T. (1986). Otto Rank and time-limited psychotherapy. *Psychotherapy, 23,* 140-149.

Orlinsky, D. E. & Howard, K. I. (1986). Process and outcome in psychotherapy. In S. L. Garfield & A. E. Bergin (Eds.), *Handbook of psychotherapy and behavior change* (3rd ed., pp. 311-381). New York: Wiley.

Pekarik, G. & Wierzbicki, M. (1986). The relationship between clients' expected and actual treatment duration. *Psychotherapy, 23,* 532-534.

Perry, S. (1989). Treatment time and the borderline patient: An underappreciated strategy. *Journal of Personality Disorders, 3,* 230-239.

Phillips, E. L. (1987). The ubiquitous decay curve: Delivery similarities in psychotherapy, medicine, and addiction. *Professional Psychology: Research and Practice, 18,* 650-652.

Piper, W. E., Debbane, E. G., Bienvenu, J. P., & Garant, J. (1984). A comparative study of four forms of psychotherapy. *Journal of Consulting and Clinical Psychology, 52,* 268-279.

Piper, W. E., Azim, H. F., McCallum, M., & Joyce, A. S. (1990). Patient suitability and outcome in short-term individual psychotherapy. *Journal of Consulting and Clinical Psychology, 58,* 475-481.

Rank, O. (1936). *Will therapy.* New York: Knopf.

Reamer, F. (1997). Managing ethics under managed care. *Families in Society*, 96-101.

Reid, W. J. (1997). Long-term trends in clinical social work. *Social Service Review*, June, 200-213.

Rosengrant, J. (1984). Brief dynamic psychotherapy in community mental health settings: Providing a holding environment on a short term basis. *Psychoanalytic Psychology*, *2*, 157-164.

Safran, J. & Muran, C. (Eds.) (1998). *The therapeutic alliance in brief psychotherapy*. Washington, DC: American Psychological Association.

Samuels, A. (1985). *Jung and the post-Jungians*. London: Routledge.

Sandler, J. & Sandler, A. M. (1978). On the development of object relationships and affects. *International Journal of Psychoanalysis*, *59*, 285-296.

Schmidt, E. (1999). Development, psychopathology, and brief treatment. In W. Borden (Ed.), *The therapeutic endeavor in brief dynamic treatment: Theory, research and practice*. Binghamton, NY: The Haworth Press, Inc.

Seruya, B. (1997). *Empathic brief psychotherapy*. Northvale, NJ: Jason Aronson.

Shapiro, D. A. & Shapiro, D. (1982). Metaanalysis of comparative therapy outcome studies. *Psychological Bulletin*, *92*, 581-604.

Shechter, R. (1997). Time-sensitive clinical social work practice. In J. R. Brandell (Ed.), *Theory and practice in clinical social work* (pp. 529-550). New York: Free Press.

Sifneos, P. (1972). *Short-term psychotherapy and emotional crisis*. Cambridge, MA: Harvard University Press.

Sifneos, P. (1979/1987). *Short-term dynamic psychotherapy: Evaluation and technique*. New York: Plenum Press.

Sifneos, P., Apfel, R. J., Bassuk, E., Fishman, G. & Gill, A. (1980). Ongoing outcome research on short-term dynamic psychotherapy. *Psychotherapy and Psychosomatics*, *33*, 233-241.

Steenbarger, B. N. (1994). Duration and outcome in psychotherapy: An integrative review. *Professional Psychology: Research and Practice*, *25*, 111-119.

Stein, H. & Edwards, M. (1998). Alfred Adler: Classical theory and practice. In Marcus, P. & Rosenberg, A. (Eds.), *Psychoanalytic versions of the human condition* (pp. 64-93). New York: New York University Press.

Stein, M. (1998). Jung's vision of the human psyche and analytic practice. In Marcus, P. & Rosenberg, A. (Eds.), *Psychoanalytic versions of the human condition* (pp. 37-63). New York: New York University Press.

Sterba, R. (1951). A case of brief psychotherapy by Sigmund Freud. *Psychoanalytic Review*, *38*, 75-80.

Stern, S. (1993). Managed care, brief therapy, and therapeutic integrity. *Psychotherapy*, *30*, 162-175.

Stiles, W. B., Shapiro, D. A. & Elliot, R. (1986). Are all psychotherapies equivalent? *American Psychologist*, *41*, 165-180.

Strupp, H. & Binder, J. (1984). *Psychotherapy in a new key*. New York: Basic Books.

Strupp, H. (1995). Forward. In H. Levenson (1995), *A guide to time-limited dynamic psychotherapy*. New York: Basic Books.

Sullivan, H. S. (1954). *The psychiatric interview*. New York: Norton.

Svartberg, M. & Stiles, T. C. (1992). Predicting patient change from therapist competence and patient-therapist complementarity in short-term anxiety provoking psychotherapy: A pilot study. *Journal of Consulting and Clinical Psychology, 60*,
304-307.

Svartberg, M. & Stiles, R. L. (1994). Therapeutic alliance, therapist competence, and
client change in short-term anxiety provoking psychotherapy. *Psychotherapy Research, 4*, 20-33.

Talmon, M. (1990). *Single session therapy.* San Francisco: Jossey-Bass.

Tosone, C. (1997). Sandor Ferenczi: Forerunner of modern short-term psychotherapy. *Journal of Analytic Social Work, 4*, 23-41.

Tosone, C., Crits-Cristoph, P. & Luborsky, L. (1999). Interpretation in short-term
therapy: The role of level of patient functioning. In W. Borden (Ed.), *The therapeutic endeavor in brief dynamic treatment: Theory, research, and practice.* Binghamton, NY: The Haworth Press, Inc.

Weiss, J., Sampson, H., and the Mount Zion Psychotherapy Research Group (1986).
The psychoanalytic process: Theory, clinical observation, and empirical research.
New York: Guilford Press.

Westen, D. (1986). What changes in short-term psychodynamic psychotherapy?
Psychotherapy, 23, 501-512.

Winnicott, D. W. (1962/1965). The aims of psycho-analytical treatment. In *The
maturational process and the facilitating environment* (pp. 166-170). New York:
International Universities Press.

Winnicott, D. W. (1971). *Therapeutic consultations in child psychiatry.* New York:
Basic Books.

Winston, A., Laikin, M., Pollak, J. Samstag, L., McCullough, L. & Muran, J. (1994).
Short-term dynamic psychotherapy of personality disorders. *American Journal of
Psychiatry, 15*, 527-539.

Witkin, S. & Gottschalk, S. (1988). Alternative criteria for theory evaluation. *Social
Service Review, 62*, 211-224.

Young-Eisendrath, P. & Dawson, T. (Eds.) (1997). *Cambridge companion to Jung.*
Cambridge: Cambridge University Press.

Chapter 2

Using Self Psychology
in Brief Psychotherapy

Jill R. Gardner

SUMMARY. This article seeks to help clinicians make the translation from theory to practice when using self psychology to do brief psychotherapy. After a theoretical overview and review of the literature, a series of organizing questions and frameworks is provided to facilitate the clinician's capacity to apply a self psychological point of view to the understanding and conduct of brief treatment. *[Article copies available for a fee from The Haworth Document Delivery Service: 1-800-342-9678. E-mail address: getinfo@haworthpressinc.com <Website: http://www.haworthpressinc.com>]*

KEYWORDS. Self psychology, brief psychotherapy, short-term treatment

Jill R. Gardner, PhD, is Clinical Psychologist in private practice. She also teaches Self Psychology at the University of Chicago, School of Social Service Administration, and at the Chicago Institute for Psychoanalysis, Postgraduate Education Program.

Address correspondence to: Jill R. Gardner, 180 North Michigan Avenue, Suite 1915, Chicago, IL 60601 (e-mail: <jgardner@enteract.com>).

The author would like to express her appreciation to patients, students, and supervisees, who were sources of clinical examples incorporated in this article, and to Ernest Wolf and Carla Leone, who offered valuable suggestions on earlier drafts. The author is also very grateful for the wisdom, support, and editorial comments of Miriam Elson and for the legacy left to us all through the work of Michael Franz Basch.

[Haworth co-indexing entry note]: "Chapter 2. Using Self Psychology in Brief Psychotherapy." Gardner, Jill R. Co-published simultaneously in *Psychoanalytic Social Work* (The Haworth Press, Inc.) Vol. 6, No. 3/4, 1999, pp. 43-85; and: *Comparative Approaches in Brief Dynamic Psychotherapy* (ed: William Borden) The Haworth Press, Inc., 1999, pp. 43-85. Single or multiple copies of this article are available for a fee from The Haworth Document Delivery Service [1-800-342-9678, 9:00 a.m. - 5:00 p.m. (EST). E-mail address: getinfo@haworthpressinc.com].

43

Brief or time-limited psychotherapy is not usually seen as the province of self psychology, a theory which emerged in the context of psychoanalysis. Yet, as described previously (Gardner, 1991), I believe that brief psychotherapy is an eminently appropriate and fertile domain for the application of self psychology and that self psychology, in turn, can greatly enhance the effectiveness of brief treatment.

In this form of treatment, the therapist attends centrally to the state of the patient's self and the establishment of a selfobject bond with the therapist as a matrix for change. The core mutative process occurs through empathic interpretations which articulate and legitimize the patient's subjective experience, particularly his or her frustrated selfobject needs and longings. This process strengthens the self, leading to a reorganization of experience and reinstating a process of development, repair, and structure building. All of these events can and do occur even in the context of very time-limited therapeutic encounters.

The goal of the present article is to elaborate some of the practical steps involved in the application of this theoretical perspective. I address this goal primarily by providing a set of questions and organizing frameworks, intended to help clinicians conceptualize brief treatment from a self psychological point of view. Before turning to this material, I offer a revised and updated review of the summary of self psychology theory and literature on brief treatment presented in my earlier article (Gardner, 1991).[1]

THE PSYCHOLOGY OF THE SELF: A SUMMARY

Basic Concepts

The theory of self psychology, as developed originally by Kohut (1966, 1971, 1977, 1984; Kohut & Wolf, 1978) and his followers, provides an integrated view of normal development, psychopathology, and the treatment process.

Kohut defined the core of development as the maturation of a cohesive nuclear self, imbued with basic strivings for power and success, basic idealized goals, and basic talents and skills (Kohut & Wolf, 1978). This self is developed and sustained by the empathic response of others, who meet lifelong needs for validation, borrowed strength, and a sense of belonging.

The developing child has a need for admiring and confirming responses to his or her innate sense of vigor and greatness. With appropriate validation or mirroring, this early expansiveness matures into self-esteem, assertiveness, ambition, a healthy enjoyment of successes, and pleasure in the pursuit of interests and activities.

The child also has a need for closeness and support from an omnipotent source of calmness and strength. When the child is permitted to merge with the idealized calmness and strength of parental figures, these needs are transformed into ideals and values, idealized goals, and respect and admiration for others. Transformation of early idealizing needs also leads to the capacity for self-soothing, self-comfort, and self-regulation, particularly in regard to affect and tension states.

Finally, Kohut defined a basic need for twinship as the reassuring experience of essential alikeness, belonging, and kinship with others. He saw appropriate human closeness and twinship or alter-ego experiences as leading to a capacity to utilize optimally one's talents and skills.

The emergence of the self requires the presence of others who provide experiences that will evoke and maintain the self's cohesion (Wolf, 1988). These are called selfobject experiences. Selfobject refers to the internal, subjective experience of functions provided by others who are experienced as a needed part of the self (ibid.). The functions Kohut described were mirroring, idealizing, and alter-ego experiences. More recently, Lichtenberg (1991) emphasized that the term selfobject refers less to a function than to "a vitalizing affective experience," crucial for maintaining a cohesive and vital sense of self.

Although these ideas were initially developed in the context of Kohut's work with narcissistically disordered patients, they were expanded by Kohut and others into a general theory of human motivation and development. Self psychology holds that the guiding force in human development is the need for connections to sources of selfobject experiences throughout life. The forms that these experiences take change as selfobject relations mature (Wolf, 1980), but the needs do not go away. Kohut considered this to be a fundamental theoretical shift from the centrality of instinctual, biological drives to the motivational primacy of self experience, that is, the psychological need for a milieu of empathic selfobjects from birth to death (Kohut, 1984).

The adequacy of the early selfobject milieu in meeting the child's developmental needs determines the fate of the emerging self. The self crystallizes in the matrix of a particular selfobject environment, through a process of psychological structure formation Kohut called transmuting internalization. In this process, selfobject functions initially provided by others are internalized to become self functions, or inner psychic structure. Structure means having formerly external functions permanently in one's possession (Kohut, 1987). These functions or capacities include self-righting, self-soothing, self-regulation, and the maintenance of self-cohesion (M. Tolpin, 1971, 1983). With the acquisition of psychic structure, the self grows cohesive and firm.

Structure can also be described in terms of how experience becomes increasingly organized, through the empathic response of parents to the child's affect. As Stolorow (1998) put it, the concept of selfobject function emphasizes that "the organization of self-experience is codetermined by the felt responsiveness of others" (p. 7). Through early interactions of mutual influence between parent and child, the child develops expectancies regarding interactional patterns (Beebe & Lachmann, 1988). These patterns of interaction are then internalized to become part of the inner structure and regulatory capacities of the child (Elson, 1989). Thus, structure also refers to these "invariant organizing principles" (Stolorow & Atwood, 1992) which shape the child's inner world.

When the process of structuralization is incomplete, one's self experience is vulnerable to a loss of cohesion or vitality in the face of selfobject failure. A variety of narcissistic injuries, separations, or disruptions in relationships can precipitate the loss of requisite selfobject experience. This leads to fragmentation, enfeeblement, rage, and various measures to maintain or restore the integration of self experience and a subjective sense of well being.

The origin of psychopathology lies in disturbances in the self-selfobject relations of childhood. When the child's need for empathic responsiveness is not adequately met by caregivers, development becomes derailed, leading to structural deficits and pathological defenses. The latter are erected to safeguard or restore the fragile self and to prevent further fragmentation or traumatization. The resulting self disorder reflects an inability to regulate affect and self-esteem, pursue meaningful goals, or express and meet needs in mature and age appropriate forms. The problem is not one of conflict, as in classical libido theory, but of deficit: normal development has been derailed and needs to be resumed.

Thus treatment involves strengthening or rehabilitating the self. Kohut (1984) described the outcome of successful treatment in terms of both an increase in internal structure, reflected in greater firmness, cohesion, and vigor of the patient's self, and an expansion of the patient's selfobject milieu, reflected in an increasing ability to identify, seek out, and be sustained by appropriate selfobject experiences (both mirroring and idealizing), as currently available.

Placing more emphasis on the reorganization of experience, Fosshage (1998) described therapy as leading to new ways of organizing the sense of self, others, and relationships. Treatment outcomes also include expansion of awareness and improved capacities for self-righting (Lichtenberg et al., 1992, 1996).

Therapeutic Processes

Kohut consistently emphasized the importance of looking at the patient's experience from the patient's own perspective. The therapist gains access to this experience by the process of empathy, defined as "vicarious introspection" (Kohut, 1959, 1984). Empathy is a mode of observation which enables the therapist to grasp the affective state of the patient "while simultaneously retaining the stance of an objective observer" (Kohut, 1984, p. 175).

The therapist speaks to the patient's subjective experience and internal reality, communicating what he or she understands the patient to be saying. In this process, the therapist helps the patient to organize and clarify the meaning of his or her experience, while underscoring the salient feelings in the patient's statements. In particular, the therapist aims to articulate an empathic understanding and acceptance of the underlying needs, wishes, and longings which the patient's behavior reflects.

This way of responding enhances the patient's sense of the validity of his or her own experience. Kohut believed that faulty empathy in the past leads to a repudiation of needs which interferes with getting them met in the present. What is unacceptable to caregivers must be defensively warded off in order to protect the selfobject bond and, ultimately, the self, whose well being is contingent on that bond. In contrast, when the therapist shares his or her sense of the legitimacy of the patient's needs, it facilitates the patient's ability to integrate and transform them into their mature counterparts (Kohut, 1984).

The empathic mode of listening and responding makes contact with the patient's inner experience, enlivening his or her communications and engaging the patient in a "therapeutic dialogue" (Ornstein & Ornstein, 1986). The therapist's empathic responsiveness also creates an ambience and sense of safety that facilitate the patient's sharing and exploring previously repressed or disavowed aspects of experience, which formerly were too threatening to permit awareness. Once these become part of the dialogue, the therapist is in a position to offer the patient empathic interpretations of them. Such interpretations bring relief by virtue of their "giving meaning to otherwise frightening and bewildering affects and thoughts" (Ornstein & Ornstein, 1977, p. 349).

Wolf (1988) described how the ambience created in this process can lead to the resumption of development:

> . . . the accepting ambience of being in the presence of a respected person who is seriously, nonjudgmentally, and empathically interested in the patient's inner world may be the first such experience in their life. Treatment becomes the first occasion to be in a milieu that facilitates the healing of the self by allowing those aspects of the self which had been arrested in their development to resume developing. (p. 109)

This process occurs through the therapy relationship. Kohut (1984) described the reactivation of thwarted developmental needs as the essential driving force of the treatment process. As Elson (1986) elaborated, the therapist, functioning as a new source of selfobject experience and responding to the patient's emerging transference needs, reactivates development at the point at which earlier attempts to secure appropriate response from selfobjects failed. The patient's selfobject demands are viewed as legitimate expressions of his or her wish for the therapist to perform missing intrapsychic functions. In response to the patient's search for responses to these legitimate needs for structure building, the therapist becomes a source of selfobject functions that can be transmuted into the patient's own functional capacities, or inner psychic structure.

When the problem that brings the patient to treatment reflects a loss of previously established cohesion or vigor due to narcissistic injury or other disruptions in the selfobject milieu, the therapist similarly responds to the patient's selfobject needs in ways which allow the patient to restore his or her self to the previous level of functioning. For many people, a loss of requisite selfobject experiences is the precipitating and destabilizing event which weakens the self and leads to a search for therapy. Self psychology offers a particularly useful framework for understanding how cohesion and vitality can be restored in such cases, by use of the therapist as a selfobject for repair.

It is not that the therapist actively tries to put himself or herself in the role of selfobject; rather it is the spontaneous transference of the patient's needs onto the therapist which puts the therapist in this role (M. Tolpin, 1983). When the therapist is then optimally responsive to these needs, which have arisen out of deficits in prior selfobject relationships, a corrective or therapeutic selfobject experience occurs (Bacal, 1990).

Kohut (1959, 1984) defined empathy primarily as a mode of observation, a way of gathering the data needed to make interpretations. It was the understanding and explanation of disruptions in the selfobject transference bond with the therapist that he saw as transforming a potential trauma into an experience of "optimal frustration" and leading to the accretion of psychic structure.

Contemporary self psychologists place more emphasis on optimal responsiveness (Bacal, 1985, 1990, 1998) than optimal frustration and on the mutative value of the relationship itself. Terman (1988, 1989) described how the empathic bond with the therapist and the patient's experience of being understood are intrinsic parts of structure formation and the curative process. Terman argued that being understood is growth producing in its own right. The experience of the relationship with the therapist as different in significant ways from the relationships of childhood facilitates both the growth of new structure and the change of existing structure. In this process, previously thwarted developmental tendencies are able to resume in the context of an appropriate, facilitating response. Stolorow (1986) similarly described the therapeutic relationship as a "facilitating medium," which reinstates developmental processes of self-articulation and self-demarcation that had been previously aborted or arrested.

For Bacal (1990, 1998), therapy "cures" through a corrective selfobject experience, mediated via optimal responsiveness. Optimal responsiveness includes the therapist's communications which "that particular patient experiences as usable for the cohesion, strengthening, and growth of his self. That is, the analyst's communications that are therapeutic are experienced by the patient as the provision of selfobject functions" (1990, p. 361).

More recently, the concept of a "positive new experience" (Shane, Shane, & Gales, 1997), going beyond empathy and interpretation, has been introduced to define a range of interventions which certain patients require in order to experience a selfobject connection with the therapist.

Integrating these different threads, Fosshage (1998) defined the goals of treatment as being achieved through a combination of ongoing selfobject experience, analysis of ruptures in the therapy relationship, illumination of problematic organizing patterns, and new relational experiences with the therapist. It is the latter which enables the patient to develop new representational schemata.

In these more recent conceptualizations, change is described more in terms of the reorganization and integration of affect than the acquisition of structure. Socarides and Stolorow (1984, 1985) saw the integration and transformation of affect, leading to increases in both affect tolerance and articulation, as a central task of treatment. Even more pointedly, Basch (1988,1995) defined affect management as the essence of psychotherapy.

BRIEF TREATMENT AND SELF PSYCHOLOGY

The rather extensive literature on short-term, dynamic psychotherapy contains relatively few articles written explicitly from a self psychological perspective. Books by Basch (1980, 1988, 1992), Kohut (1987), and Elson (1986) and an article by Ornstein and Ornstein (1996b), though not about short term psychotherapy per se, do include a number of brief treatment cases which were informed by the authors' self psychological perspective. They provide, for this reason, useful illustrative material.

Although he did not explicitly write about short-term therapy, Kohut (1987) saw his ideas as very relevant for brief treatment. He felt that a little bit of help, emanating from the borrowed strength of the therapist's support, could accomplish a great deal.

Goldberg (1973) offered perhaps the earliest explicit attempt to apply the evolving insights of self psychology to short-term psychotherapy. Discussing the psychotherapeutic treatment of narcissistic injuries, he described a need for the patient to be able to use the therapist as a source of selfobject functions in order to restore self-esteem. It was specifically in the understanding and interpretation of the patient's frustrated selfobject longings that repair of the injured self was seen to occur.

Like Goldberg, Lazarus (1980) conceptualized the goal of brief therapy with narcissistic disturbances as one of reestablishing the patient's feelings of self-esteem and self-cohesion by allowing the patient to use the therapist as a source of selfobject experience. He saw the reinstatement of the patient's pre-morbid level of functioning as the primary outcome in most cases. However, he also believed that in some cases the patient might begin to internalize the therapist's functions, leading to an accretion of psychic structure and further working through of narcissistic problems after termination.

In a later paper, Lazarus (1988) described the use of self psychological principles to conduct brief psychotherapy with elderly patients whose entry into treatment was precipitated by a narcissistic injury or other selfobject loss. Lazarus again described how the relationship with the empathic therapist may serve as a bridge to restore self-esteem and enable the patient to reestablish a supportive selfobject milieu outside of the treatment context.

Chernus (1983) described the use of focal psychotherapy (a close precursor of this model) to treat a structural deficit in the self, thus expanding the terrain previously described by others. In the case she reported, the *primary* therapeutic goals were structure building and internalization of the therapist's selfobject functions, rather than the repair of the self and return to pre-morbid levels of functioning which had been emphasized by previous authors. (For an extended description of this case, see the report later published by the therapist, P. Ornstein, 1988.)

Chernus also suggested that the briefer the treatment, the more likely it was that the weight of the working-through process would occur in the context of the patient's external relationships and experiences, rather than in the transference to the therapist. Ornstein and Ornstein (1972) similarly found that working through occurred in meaningful ways outside of the therapeutic relationship.

In a detailed case report, Gardner (1991) also described a process of structural change occurring through brief, self psychological treatment. Baker (1991) published a paper around the same time which similarly summarized how self psychological principles could guide brief psychotherapy.

Taking a different approach, Ringstrom (1995) used a combination of intersubjectivity theory (Stolorow et al., 1987) and motivational systems theory (Lichtenberg, 1989) to suggest a new model of brief treatment. His focus was on the uncovering and modification of unconscious organizing principles, emerging in the intersubjective context of the transference relationship and illuminated through the analysis of paradigmatic model scenes (Lichtenberg et al., 1992). He also emphasized the importance of self-state assessment, a concept which is elaborated on at length later in the present article.

A major addition to the literature appeared with the publication of Basch's (1995) book on brief psychotherapy. One of Kohut's closest original collaborators, Basch integrated, applied, and extended the major developments in self psychology, creating a developmental model which emphasized affect while integrating cognition and information processing. Major emphasis was placed on the mobilization of the patient's strengths to facilitate brief treatment.

Finally, Seruya (1997) offered a model of "empathic brief psychotherapy" which integrated self psychology with cognitive-behavioral theory. While not exclusively self psychological in approach, her model draws on self psychology extensively, provides an excellent summary of the theory, and extends the model to brief work with couples.

Although the literature on self psychology and brief psychotherapy is not extensive, it is encouraging that it is increasing. As stated earlier, I believe that brief psychotherapy is fertile ground for the application of self psychology, which, in turn, can make brief psychotherapy more effective.

The concepts described above provide a conceptual roadmap for self psychologically informed brief treatment. However, the exact way these concepts are applied is not always clear to those who seek to practice this model. In the sections below, I address this issue by describing some pragmatic steps to assist clinicians in making the translation from theory to practice.

It is also important to note that there is not one approach to brief treatment within self psychology, but many. The literature just reviewed provides a variety of viewpoints regarding what we do, how we do it, and why it works. My own approach draws most heavily on the contributions of Basch and the Ornsteins, along with my experience doing and supervising brief treatment in the settings of a hospital-based, community mental health center and private practice. The model I describe is not a particular technique, but rather a series of components which, when put together, make treatment more efficient and briefer.

PATIENT SELECTION

Most approaches to brief therapy prescribe selection criteria. It is certainly logical to begin by trying to determine whether a given patient is a suitable candidate for self psychologically informed brief treatment. Yet this begs the question that most clinicians face. In some settings patients can indeed be directed to brief or open-ended treatment tracks at an intake level. In most cases, however, it is not the therapist but rather clinic policies, third party reimbursers, or the patient's own financial, time, and emotional limitations that dictate how long the patient and therapist will have to work together. When the length of the treatment is set arbitrarily by these extrinsic factors, the question becomes less one of who is appropriate and more one of how to use whatever time one has. Bellak (Bellak & Small, 1978) reflected this reality when he suggested that what we select, essentially, is problems and goals, not patients.

Another stumbling block to using well-established selection criteria is the lack of empirical data upon which to base them. Early models of brief dynamic treatment did have good outcome studies (see Messer & Warren, 1995, for a comprehensive review), but were criticized for using selection criteria which were so narrow as to exclude a majority of the patients who applied. A more recent approach (Basch, 1995), taking the opposite stance, suggests that we consider *all* patients as potentially suitable candidates for brief dynamic treatment until proven otherwise. How do we prove otherwise? Are there prognostic clues we can rely on? Fortunately, the lack of systematic outcome studies has not kept theorists from offering some suggestions.

Ornstein and Ornstein (1997) saw their capacity to formulate a focus early on as a key determinant for successful brief treatment. For the Ornsteins, a focus is not the presenting problem but a formulation that *explains* the presenting problem. Whether or not the therapist can arrive quickly at such an organizing formulation and focus the treatment around it is seen as a crucial prognostic indicator.

Ringstrom (1995) believed that the rapidity with which someone has a positive response to the therapist's empathy may be a good predictor of the efficacy of brief treatment. Drawing on Lichtenberg et al.'s (1992) observation that the state of the self depends on a person's responsiveness to empathy and vulnerability to lack of empathy, he urged therapists to consider questions such as: How restorative or fragmenting are the first sessions? How responsive is the patient to the therapist's attunement?

Most clinicians have had the experience of offering an empathic connection which is like water to a wilted plant for one patient and water off a duck's back to another. The former seems to grow firmer before our eyes, while the latter stares at us blankly, seeming to ignore whatever we say. Others respond aversively, with antagonism, withdrawal, or anxiety.

Basch (1995) emphasized the presence of an idealizing transference, stating that the success of brief treatment may depend on whether a positive (idealizing) transference is in place or can quickly be mobilized.

> . . . the question of whether or not short term therapy can be effective or whether lengthier treatment is needed depends often not so much on the nature of the problem *per se*, but on how soon patients can permit themselves to feel safe, supported, and enhanced in the therapeutic relationship. (p. 94)

When Basch used the term idealization, he was referring to the patient's capacity to rely on the therapist's guidance and support.[2] This is a necessary prerequisite for both trust and credibility: if the patient can't idealize or rely on the therapist, validation or mirroring from that therapist won't have any impact. Validation which is useful to us has to come from credible sources whom we can look up to in some fashion.

Basch also underscored how patients who are highly defended or resistant often require longer treatment to work through their shame over needing to rely on the therapist before any progress can be made. Because shame interferes with letting needs arise in therapy, it must be sufficiently resolved before the patient can tolerate both the therapeutic relationship and the underlying painful affects which have been protectively warded off (Basch, 1988, 1995; Kohut, 1984). It is through the vicissitudes and analysis of the transference that such patients' problems eventually become manifest and are resolved.

There were two other groups of people whom Basch defined as

usually *not* good candidates for brief treatment: people who need to make up for substantial developmental deficits and those needing prolonged support in order to function. He didn't believe that brief therapy could be a substitute for dealing with these problems in more open-ended treatment. At the same time, he saw people needing long-term psychoanalysis or long-term support as being at the ends of the bell curve, leaving a lot of people in the middle. He was fond of saying, "when all you have is a hammer, everything looks like a nail" (Basch, 1995, p. xii). By this he meant that it was our attachment to psychoanalysis and lack of alternative methodologies that led to our reluctance to realize that brief treatment might be the treatment of choice for many of our patients.

My own experience is that many people can work in circumscribed problem areas, leave major domains of character pathology untouched, and derive considerable benefit from relatively brief treatment. Others can reinstate a process of structural growth and change, impacting long standing patterns. (For case illustrations of the latter, see Chernus (1983) and Gardner (1991), in addition to Basch, 1995.)

The more conventional clinical indicators we usually consider in evaluating patients for brief treatment remain important: how pervasive the problems are, how limited, how long they have been going on, the presence of clear precipitants, the extent of substance abuse, and the degree of other internal resources and external supports, to name a few. But having been both surprised and wrong often enough, I have come to believe that it is more useful to begin with the assumption that the patient in front of us could potentially benefit from brief treatment and then look for what, if anything, would lead us to disconfirm that assumption. It might be severe, uncontrolled substance abuse; it might be massive defenses against enough idealization to make at least some use of what the therapist has to offer. It might become obvious in the first ten minutes; or it might take several sessions to determine.

Self psychologists, warning against the dangers of selectively perceiving or molding data to fit our preconceived conceptual schemata, have begun to suggest that we should "hold our theories lightly" (Orange, 1995). When we approach the task of determining which patients might benefit from brief treatment, we would do well to hold our assumptions lightly as well.

TREATMENT PLANNING AS A CLINICAL PROCESS AND COLLABORATIVE ACTIVITY

If what we select has more to do with *what* we work on than *whom* we work with, we need to turn our attention to how the relevant issues get selected. For many clinicians, the words treatment planning have come to signify onerous forms and administrative intrusion into the treatment process. Psychodynamic practitioners, in particular, often experience the idea of treatment planning as inimical to their way of working. Yet treatment planning is crucial to the success of brief treatment. What we need is another way to think about it.

I see treatment planning as evolving out of the clinical exploration of problems and goals, that is, as a clinical process not an administrative one. Treatment planning is a way of establishing an explicit understanding with the patient of the nature of why he or she is there and what's to be done. Most importantly, it involves engaging the patient as an active collaborator in defining the purpose of therapy.

Collaborative treatment planning reinforces the patient as a center of initiative in the therapy process. It promotes ownership and patient responsibility, helps to prioritize problems, and facilitates the establishment of a focus. Basch (1995) noted that "the process of establishing what the patient is there to accomplish is in itself therapeutic" (p. 52). If we just listen to problems without also hearing what the patient expects to see as an outcome, we may hamper a short term focus. Problems are not equivalent to goals. We also need to ask how the patients see therapy as helping or relevant to their presenting concerns. Questions regarding their view of what they need from us can be very helpful in clarifying the particular strengths they bring to the process, along with their difficulties.

The material which follows addresses, from several different perspectives, the issue of focusing the treatment, starting on a broadly conceptual level and then moving through some very specific ways of determining the issues to be worked on.

CENTRAL FOCUS ON SELF EXPERIENCE AND SELFOBJECT RELATIONSHIP WITH THERAPIST

In any kind of brief or time-limited treatment, the therapist must decide where to put his or her therapeutic energy, given limited resources. All forms of brief therapy address the issue of focus in one way or another. From a self psychological perspective, the therapist's central focus must be on the self experience of the patient and on the relationship between the patient and therapist as a new self-selfobject unit. This selfobject bond is the matrix in which change takes place. In brief treatment, as in longer term treatment, the emphasis is on strengthening the self.[3] When there has been a weakening or disorganization of self experience (manifested in decreased cohesion or vitality) due to changes and losses in the selfobject surround, then the selfobject relationship with the therapist functions as a bridge to restore the self to its previous healthier state.

Thus, whatever the specific precipitants, symptoms, or treatment goals may be, the therapist must (a) attend specifically to ways in which the self is vulnerable, injured, or arrested, (b) understand symptoms as manifestations of these deficits, and (c) enable the patient to establish the selfobject matrix required to facilitate repair and growth.

A. Ornstein (1986) suggested that concern with the state of the self should be the primary focus in the treatment of *all* patients, regardless of the nature of the pathology or form of the treatment. In any duration of treatment, feeling understood can lead to an increase in self-cohesion which allows an exploration of previously repressed or disavowed affects, wishes, fears, and fantasies. The emergence of these previously unavailable aspects of the patient's experience into awareness provides an opportunity to understand their meaning, and in so doing, to use the therapy relationship to strengthen the self.

Elson (1986) stated it eloquently:

> Self psychology clarifies the universal striving to secure a response to one's potential for individuality and significance. In even the most seriously deprived individual, underneath abrasive and cynical behavior, a vestige of the need to be confirmed remains alive to be rekindled. The very presence of the [therapist] may quicken this need. Many methods and approaches have been devised for responding to and controlling the relationship which ensues, but, regardless of method, how one orders what one sees and experiences, how one uses oneself on behalf of the individual, becomes more vivid through an explanatory system of human behavior that places the self of the individual at the center of one's observations and views the new self/selfobject unit as the medium for treatment. (p. 136)

STATE OF THE SELF

With the state of the self as a point of departure, assessment can be facilitated by a series of organizing questions which help both to conceptualize the clinical material and to establish a focus for treatment. These are described below under four broad headings: symptoms and deficits, adaptations, strengths, and transference.

Symptoms and Deficits

There are two lenses through which a self psychologist might look at symptoms. The first asks: How do the patient's presenting symptoms express a deficit in, or loss of, the self's cohesion or vitality?

Patients who exhibit agitation, anxiety, disorganized behavior, or a deterioration in appearance often signal through these symptoms a problem in the cohesiveness of their self experience. Incipient states of fragmentation are often characterized by debilitating disintegration anxiety (Tolpin & Kohut, 1980). One patient, usually meticulously groomed, arrived for her appointment in an agitated and disheveled state, saying that she felt "like humpty-dumpty." There is no more apt metaphor for fragmentation and the loss of cohesion than this nursery rhyme character who falls off a wall, splintering so irrevocably that "all the king's horses and all the king's men/cannot put humpty together again."

The patient suffering from a lack or loss of vitality, in contrast, sags rather than splinters. When we see symptoms that cluster around a lack of energy, motivation, and ambition, and the affect is melancholy, we think in terms of a devitalized or depleted sense of self.

Through the second lens on symptoms, we ask the question: In what ways do the patient's symptoms reflect attempts to restore or reorganize the weakened self? Substance abuse, eating disorders, and sexual acting out may be used to stimulate and enliven someone with a sense of deadness or depletion. Any of these symptoms might also be employed to calm or reverse an anxious state of fragmentation. Some people get high to feel alive; others drink to calm their nerves. Some people overeat when they're anxious, others when they're bored and lonely. When we see an increase in any of these symptomatic behaviors, we can begin to think in terms of how the behavior reflects an attempt to alter the underlying self state the patient is experiencing. Attending specifically to the patient's subjective experience of the symptomatic behavior and its sequelae will usually clarify what that underlying self state is.

For example, a man who often felt slighted by his boss and coworkers would go cruising in bars for sex on days he suffered these narcissistic injuries. Although his dangerous promiscuity created other problems for him, the affirmation he found in being sexually desired helped restore his self-esteem and sense of vitality.

Another patient was driving her family and coworkers to distraction with her angry, irritable, and controlling behavior. Her unreasonable attempts to force everyone to fulfill her minutest wishes could be understood as an effort to maintain eroding self-esteem and control over her selfobject world, as serious medical problems and job changes combined to make her feel totally out of control. This particular pattern of symptomatic behavior quite often is secondary to the sense of helplessness caused by illness, parenting problems, or job related stress.

Self psychologists generally view symptoms as the patient's best available means of protecting a fragile, vulnerable self against retraumatization or of revitalizing and reorganizing a depleted or fragmented self. Keeping these purposes in mind, we can ask the question: To what problem is this symptomatic behavior a solution? The answers help us make the translation from symptom to self state, an important step in determining the focus of treatment. It is a shift in understanding from the level of behavior, e.g., this person abuses cocaine, to the level of dynamics, e.g., this person has a crushing sense of deadness and he is devoid of other (internal) resources to counteract it. Symptoms reflect efforts to achieve both a reintegration on the level of self organization and a shift in the subjective experience of self.

When we evaluate problematic affect, cognition, and behavior, we also need to determine whether we are dealing with transient symptoms or ongoing deficits. Again, a series of questions is helpful: What deficits are apparent in the patient's self experience? Are they acute? Chronic? In other words, has this individual ever acquired the self-soothing and regulating functions needed to maintain self-esteem and regulate affect? To judge this, it would be helpful to know how prone the patient is to fragmentation or depletion experiences. Light could be shed on this by asking: Is the current upset less than, as bad as, or worse than what the person has felt before? Is this a pretty typical way of feeling or is it unusual? As always, subjective experience is crucial.

What one person considers an alarming sign of impending breakdown may for another be an everyday experience of self, albeit a painful or distressing one. To evaluate symptoms of anxiety or absent-mindedness, for example, it matters whether one is a person who is generally unflappable or one who is always worried, one who never misplaces things, or one who can lose keys while holding them in hand.

In a sense, I am discussing the pervasiveness and chronicity of presenting problems. Generally speaking, the more that symptoms reflect a *loss* of cohesion or vitality rather than a *lack* of them, the more likely it is that brief intervention may help the individual get back on course. Both Kohut (1987) and Elson (1986) offer several examples of this among student populations.

Adaptations

In conjunction with deficits, we also need to know: How, typically, has the person tried to compensate for these deficits? Here I am referring to the range of defensive adaptations, compensatory structures, and characterological solutions which people devise, over the course of development, to deal with whatever trauma and selfobject failures they have experienced.

Most people have characteristic ways of coping, i.e, maintaining cohesion, competence, or adaptive functioning and avoiding anxiety. These ways of dealing with trouble and maintaining a viable sense of self include both internal mechanisms (functional capacities) and external supports (sources of needed selfobject experience).

The search for treatment is often precipitated by something which triggers an inability to cope. Usually the trigger is a loss or a new challenge. The situation then exposes what we might think of as "fault lines." These are structural deficits which are exposed when the usual defenses are overwhelmed. Precipitating stresses disrupt the previous adaptations and strain them to the point where they cannot hold. Although this development is often preceded by an initial redoubling of usual defensive efforts, these emergency measures eventually fail as well. It is at this point that the underlying problems may come more into view and can therefore become a focus of treatment.

For example, some people protect themselves against unbearable feelings of dependency by developing a pattern of defensive self-sufficiency. When external events, such as an accident, illness, or job loss, necessitate requesting or accepting help from others, they become acutely anxious. The anxiety is associated with the memory of pre-vious traumatic failures in the face of needs. It is the inability to employ the usual solution which reveals the underlying vulnerability. A more obvious example is phobic avoidance. As long as the object of one's phobia can be avoided, the patient appears asymptomatic. If the defense of avoidance is precluded or fails, however, the underlying anxiety immediately becomes apparent.

A similar problem can be observed in patients who rely on defen-sive isolation or distance to regulate their anxiety about intimacy. They often become symptomatic when external events necessitate more closeness than they are used to or comfortable with. Obvious examples are signs of increased commitment to a relationship, such as moving in with a partner, getting engaged, or getting married. These are common times for us to see symptoms emerge. This problem can also be precipitated, however, by a change as innocuous seeming as needing to share an office at work. The loss of the physical wall or partition may subjectively constitute the loss of a psychological wall which enabled the person to function within a range of acceptable emotional distance.

One patient became increasingly anxious as her pregnancy pro-gressed. Exploration revealed her ever-expanding abdomen as the focus of her distress. As we explored the meaning of this concern, she described her father's bitter disappointment in not having a son and his disdain for his two daughters. Desperately needing an antidote to her depressed mother, she managed to evoke some affirmation from her father by becoming a star athlete, winning a place on the national team in her sport. What her advancing pregnancy made clear was how her flat stomach had always been not only a source of pride, but a crucial symbol of the one thing that she felt made her valuable in the eyes of her father, securing the selfobject bond with him she urgently needed to maintain her self-esteem.

Sports and physical activity are often used to regulate tension, as well as self-esteem. It is not uncommon to see patients who rely on this outlet become both depressed and anxious when an injury pre-vents them from their usual routine. While others may simply become irritable or feel less energetic when they can't run or work out, for this kind of person more extensive underlying deficits in self-regulation become apparent.

The pressures in many workplaces brought about by downsizing and other cost-cutting measures create particular difficulty for people whose compulsivity and perfectionism are defensively tied to their psychological security. When one now has three jobs to cover, it is impossible to cover all the bases as thoroughly. A related pattern is the person who manages to stave off vulnerability and anxiety by being extremely competent, always on top of things. When external demands create more than anyone could humanly manage, no matter how skilled he or she is, the underlying vulnerability in self-esteem is revealed. It is usually the concurrence of several stressful events which triggers the problem in this type of individual.

Finally, and perhaps most prevalently, there is the person who must ward off affect to maintain his or her psychological equilibrium. It seems to matter less which particular defenses are used than it does that unmanageable (usually dysphoric) affect is kept at bay. When precipitating events mobilize too much affect to suppress, the person experiences emotional flooding, anxiety, and symptoms. The characterological defenses against affect simply cannot handle the emotions which have been stimulated.

Some of these people say things like, "I'm a coper," "I'm a minimizer," or "I'm a control freak." When something then happens which the person can't cope with, minimize, or control, symptoms develop. It is often then not the presenting symptoms, or even the defenses, but rather the meaning of the need to minimize or control in the first place that becomes the focus of treatment. As the patient's usual means of sequestering underlying anxieties and affects fail, these experiences can be brought to light, understood, and explained.

The conception of treatment I am elaborating here is very close to the model of focal psychotherapy developed by Balint and the Ornsteins (Balint, Ornstein, & Balint, 1972; Ornstein & Ornstein, 1972; P. Ornstein, 1988). As defined by Chernus (1983), focal psychotherapy involves the exploration and working through of a focal conflict precipitated by a recent event which has overwhelmed the patient's characterological defense mechanisms. That characterological weakness becomes the focus of treatment. In contrast to the goal of crisis intervention, which is a return to the previous homeostasis, the goal of focal psychotherapy is a modification of the maladaptive defensive structures.

More recently, the Ornsteins (1997) have updated their description of brief focal psychotherapy in ways that clarify how the examination of symptoms, deficits, and adaptations can create a focus in brief treatment. They suggest that rather than trying to examine the whole personality, we should look at a slice or sector of the personality in depth. This look would cut across the levels of surface or presenting problems, attempts to cope with the problems, and core or nuclear problems. They emphasize that the current problem should make sense in terms of who the person has been for an entire life. In other words, the therapist must establish the dynamic connection between the current problem, precipitated by some kind of stress, and what has gone on in the person's life before. When such a formulation can be expressed in terms of an interpretive comment to the patient, it creates a focus for the treatment. As stated earlier, for the Ornsteins the focus is not the presenting problem, but rather a formulation which explains the presenting problem. Also, if the focus provides an explanation for the current problem, while at the same time touching on the patient's character pathology, then work on the immediate problem includes working on the chronic problems.

Wolf (personal communication) expressed a similar idea by emphasizing that precipitating events often resonate with earlier events which have similar affective themes. It is these similarities which amplify the impact of the precipitating events and create continuity between past and present.

My own experience has been that successful cases of brief treatment often conform to these models. A woman referred by her employer because of the irritability and stress she was exhibiting at work reported a history of several recent medical problems, all quite serious. While she was aware of sadness and anger in connection with these problems, she was not in touch with her considerable anxiety. She only knew she was snapping at everyone around her. As she described her situation, she revealed herself to be a high-functioning, very competent person, who characteristically downplayed both needs and dysphoric feelings. She said she was a "minimizer" who had "no tolerance for self-pity." However, as her sense of choice and control was being rapidly eroded by her health problems, she was confronted with feelings she could not successfully minimize and her previous defenses no longer served to protect her from the anxiety such feelings created in her. Successful treatment focused on increasing her affect awareness and tolerance. When she could experience and express her feelings more directly, feeling entitled to them as legitimate, she regained her equilibrium and was able to terminate the treatment. I saw her a total of six times.

In another case, the patient came requesting help to better manage the tension associated with several external stresses in both his family and work life. His presenting complaint was depression. What quickly became apparent was his great difficulty in asserting himself effectively with a disabled relative who was making enormous demands on him. Although massively frustrated, he was trying very hard to be compassionate, understanding, tolerant, and helpful. His history revealed that he had responded to a very critical and guilt-inducing parental environment with a combination of compliance, resentment, and withdrawal. This was a man who had learned to sit on feelings until they reached a boiling point, at which point they felt too dangerous to express, leading him to retreat and to become depressed. Treatment focused on his long-standing fears regarding self-assertion. As with the previous case, effective treatment involved enabling him to identify and express his own needs and feelings more directly, even in the face of significant others in his life whose needs seemed to him much greater. It was this change in relation to his internal life that enabled him to achieve his original goal of managing the external stresses more effectively.

In both cases, it was a focus on the underlying problem in the self which was exposed by the failure of characteristic defenses that led to successful brief treatment. These cases also underscore Socarides and Stolorow's (1984-1985) emphasis on the central role of the selfobject transference bond in the "articulation, integration and developmental transformation of the patient's affectivity" (p. 112).

Strengths

When working with people in brief treatment, attention to their strengths becomes pivotal. We need to ask: What strengths are apparent in the patient's self experience and functioning? What has the patient used in the past to maintain or restore vitality and cohesion? Which self-restorative efforts have been helpful? In what areas does the patient continue to exhibit strength now?

Basch, in particular, emphasized the need to elicit and foster strengths and to focus on how the strengths no longer serve the patient, rather than focusing on the origins of problems in childhood. In his view, the patient is seen as possessing the resources to cope with his or her problem; the therapist's job is to mobilize them. He described the patient as an agent for change in the present rather than simply a victim of the past and saw patients' strengths as the leverage to help them do something about their problems (Basch, 1995).

> When we work successfully, we are not solving patients' problems *per se*; rather we are helping them to use or enhance what they have on the plus side to minimize, offset, and occasionally eradicate what is on the minus side. We are helping them to right themselves so that *they* will be in a position to solve the problems that brought them to us in the first place. (pp. 6-7)

Basch felt that people come to therapy because their strengths are no longer working. The fostering of self-righting, which he is describing above as a goal of treatment, has been emphasized by other self psychologists as well (M. Tolpin, 1983; Lichtenberg et al., 1992). Kohut actually talked twenty years earlier about mobilizing the patient's strengths. In a 1975 lecture he stated:

> In those cases in which the essential task is the analysis of a disturbed core self, the crucial work deal[s] predominantly with opening up the possibility of new choices . . . with the freeing of sources of strength that were not present before . . . the primary analytic task is understood to be an effort that will enable the patient to use something that is in him by freeing it or putting it in working order . . . it is not that one is finally able to see that he has an unacceptable drive that has to be discarded, but that he has a central source of strength that was not available before. (Tolpin & Tolpin, 1996, pp. 370-371)

Consistent with Kohut's, and later Basch's, emphasis on potentials for strength and growth, we need to emphasize what the person is doing right and support it. The orientation in our training towards pathology often interferes with this focus on strengths. A simple inquiry regarding what patients feel they need from us can be useful in supporting their capacities to define their own resources and limitations, reinforcing our view of them as active collaborators in the therapeutic endeavor.

On a practical level, Basch (1995) suggested that we note the content associated with shifts from negative to positive affect as the patient tells his or her story. He felt that such shifts towards brighter affect signal the hidden strengths and adaptive coping mechanisms one hopes to mobilize.

When the clinician then encourages an elaboration of the material following the shift, dramatic results can occur. One man had appeared in the first few sessions to be an inhibited and passive person, lacking drive or ambition, experiencing little pleasure in life, and seeming drained rather than energized by his various activities. His presenting complaint was his inability to make commitments. In our conversations, he was formal, polite, and subdued, often running out of things to say. However, when he began talking about a college friend he was reminded of by a dream, his face lit up with admiration and enthusiasm.

His obvious, vicarious enjoyment of his friend's wild antics and joie de vivre, in contrast to his own inhibited approach to life, led me to inquire whether there had ever been anything he felt he could put himself into fully. As he recalled an early artistic talent, his face again lit up. Guided by this shift in affect, I actively encouraged him to elaborate on things he had enjoyed. This revealed talents, creativity, imagination, and humor which I could not have imagined he possessed and with which he, too, had long lost contact. The pleasure he experienced in remembering and sharing these more vibrant parts of himself marked a turning point in the treatment, seeming to infuse him with a newfound energy as he began to make decisions and actively take hold of his life.

Another man came to treatment with a crisis of confidence as he stood on the threshold of his professional career. He believed that only regaining a previously felt (and defensively held) sense of invincibility would cure his anxiety, inhibition, and fear of competing in the marketplace. Hearing that he had been a soccer player, I asked him what he did when he was playing a game and fell down. With great emphasis, he replied, "I got up and got back in the game! If I gave up a goal, I was embarrassed, but then I tried even harder." This allowed me to suggest that perhaps what he had lost confidence in was not his invincibility, but his resiliency. Drawing on his history, I pointed out how over and over he had been able to turn an initial disappointment to advantage and move his life forward. Looking at this pattern helped him realize that even when he hadn't been invincible, he had nevertheless been successful. Armed with a new sense of confidence in his own resiliency, he became able to accept the much more attainable goal of "getting back in the game" following whatever setbacks might occur. With this shift, it took only a few sessions for him to come out of the malaise which had overtaken him and feel more secure about launching his career.

Sometimes the mobilization of strengths involves less reconnecting with previous experiences than reframing them. Basch (1995) was particularly effective at doing this. With one man who took his children's rather minor misconduct as disrespectful insults and challenges to his authority, complaining that *he* never behaved that way as a child, Basch replied that the man never had a chance to *be* a child, never behaved in all the ways that are typical of children and frustrating to adults. The fact that his kids could afford to do this was a compliment to what he had achieved psychologically for them. In contrast to his own, anxiety-filled childhood, his children had a basic confidence and trust that he would be there to take care of them, whether they responsibly performed every chore or not. Basch noted that this interpretation validates the patient's achievement, while protecting his fragile self-esteem. Reframing weakness to strength is a familiar process to self psychologists, who emphasize the adaptive and protective functions of behavior generally.

Transference Manifestations of Selfobject Needs

Manifestations of selfobject needs in the relationship with the therapist provide another way to understand the organization of self experience and state of the self. Insufficiently met selfobject needs lead to vulnerabilities in the self and defenses which are erected to protect the precariously organized self from retraumatization. When a patient enters therapy, the needs, vulnerabilities, and defenses all become manifest in the transference. The unmet developmental needs are reflected in the "selfobject dimension" of the transference, while the vulnerabilities and defenses are reflected in the "repetitive/conflictual dimension" (Stolorow et al., 1987). Therefore, it is helpful to ask ourselves: What needs of the self are being expressed in the patient's behavior towards the therapist? What selfobject experiences is the patient appealing to us to be a source of? How are these manifested (or defended against)?

The patient who provides detailed descriptions of his activities and accomplishments, for example, may be seeking mirroring and validation through which to bolster self-esteem. The one who wants to "chat" may be searching for some kind of enlivening engagement with the therapist, not resisting deeper issues. A clamor for advice and direction may reflect an appeal to the therapist to be a source of idealizing selfobject functions which would organize and make sense out of the patient's experience. On the other hand, the patient who engages in hostile, provocative behavior towards the therapist may be trying to protect a vulnerable self from being retraumatized, by rejection or misunderstanding. Through behaviors which create distance and mask underlying vulnerabilities, the patient prevents exposure of previously thwarted selfobject needs. Kohut (1984) described this protective function as the fundamental goal of all defenses. When the therapist recognizes and affirms the legitimacy of whatever selfobject needs are evident in the transference, the self is strengthened. When the therapist fails to do so, the self is threatened and symptoms may worsen.

Careful attention to the selfobject dimension of the transference may also clarify the specific nature of underlying deficits or recent injuries, since patients tend to reactivate in the transference those selfobject needs which have been thwarted. In an early paper, Goldberg (1973) described two brief treatment cases who presented in nearly opposite ways to the therapist. The first patient "entered the hour as a storm-tossed and agitated man who wanted smoothing of his ruffled feathers and agreement and reflection of his outrage" (p. 724). The therapist was implicitly beseeched to admire the patient (his "charm, wit, and presence") and to refrain from any kind of criticism. In the second case, the patient immediately assigned to the therapist the role of an expert, who would tell him what was wrong with him and what to do about it.

These obvious bids to meet mirroring and idealizing needs, respectively, paralleled the internal meaning of the narcissistic injuries which had brought these patients to treatment. In the first case, the man became symptomatic after a group of students whom he had hoped to impress called him pompous; in the second, the patient's symptoms were triggered by his boss' failure to be the omnipotent protector for whom he longed.

By recognizing a patient's appeal in the transference for the therapist to be a source of reparative selfobject experiences, the therapist is alerted to the nature of the underlying difficulty. The specific problems which emerge through this process clarify deficits in the self and point to a potential focus for treatment. An analogous process for exploring precipitating events is described below.

As a final note regarding transference, it is important to reiterate the need to evaluate the extent to which a positive transference is either in place or is able to be mobilized quickly (cf. Basch, 1995). Even if more archaic needs emerge and are addressed, the therapist must be used for mature selfobject functions in the present and this requires the idealization or reliance described earlier. When deeply entrenched defenses prevent such engagement, brief treatment may not be possible.

SUBJECTIVE (INTERNAL) MEANING OF PRECIPITATING EVENTS

All therapists seek to understand the role of precipitating events in the patient's presenting problems and search for treatment. This is the familiar question, "What brings you in now?" A self psychologically informed version of this question would ask: What is the meaning of the precipitating events in terms of their impact on the patient's self experience and selfobject surround? More specifically, how do the stresses which led the person to seek therapy involve the loss of important selfobject experiences? Which kinds of selfobject experiences were lost or became less available? And finally, what role did these experiences play in sustaining an inner sense of vitality and cohesion? All of these questions aim to clarify the nature of the *internal* problem that has to be addressed. As therapists, we respond not to external events, but to the subjective experience of those events. An empathic mode of inquiry is used to determine what the subjective experience is.

The internal loss might be precipitated by a loss or rupture in a relationship, leading to a temporary loss of cohesion, depletion, or fragmentation. Or it may be precipitated by the loss of a role that was affirming, like a job or parenting. Depending on the nature of the relationship or role, the selfobject experiences afforded might have met mirroring needs, such as the need for affirmation and appreciation, or idealizing ones, such as the availability of idealized strength and guidance.

When the normal process of psychic structure building is incomplete, an individual is more vulnerable to a loss of needed selfobject experiences. If a relationship is disrupted or ends, the selfobject loss is then more pronounced. For example, if the mirroring functions of a relationship were necessary to stabilize and maintain self-esteem, then with the other person could go the capacity to feel good about oneself. One patient, struggling with feelings about her physical appearance after breaking up with her boyfriend, expressed this very concretely:

> I miss the feedback I got from Perry. He always told me I looked good and made me feel attractive. Now I look in the mirror and I don't know what to think. I can't tell. I feel like I have to go to such effort to make myself look good and I don't always feel like it. But I would feel terrible if I went out and people saw me looking awful. With Perry, he just told me I looked good no matter what and I felt OK.

This description underscores the difficulty she is having regulating her self-esteem in the absence of her boyfriend's mirroring affirmation.

If, on the other hand, the calming and soothing functions of an idealized other are needed because of deficits in the person's own capacity for self-soothing, then with the loss of this selfobject dimension of the relationship may go the capacity for affect regulation and the ability to calm down. Increased anxiety and decreased cohesion usually follow. This is a very common pattern in patients with borderline personality disorders because of the extremely tenuous nature of their underlying self organization (P. Tolpin, 1984).

It becomes easier to understand how people stay in apparently destructive relationships when we consider these selfobject functions being served by them. A similar dynamic underlies the dissolution of relationships as well. As Wolf (1988) described:

> Much of the irritation of people with each other, the quarrels that tear up marriages, and the misunderstandings that lead to loss of spouse, friend, or job can be traced back to the ups and downs of self-esteem when individuals with fragile selfs try to use others to make themselves feel stronger and more whole. (p. 42)

It is also important to keep in mind, as Stolorow (1986) noted, that selfobject failure does not refer to objectively assessed shortcomings of the other person, but rather to a "subjectively experienced absence of requisite selfobject functions" (p. 389).

One of the reasons a focus on the selfobject dimension of precipitating events is so important is for the light it sheds on the state of the self, the quality of the patient's selfobject world, and the connection between the two. There is generally an inverse relationship between the strength of the internal psychic structure and the strength of the external selfobject surround. When less has been organized internally, more is needed externally. Thus the individual is more vulnerable to disruptions in those externally stimulated selfobject experiences. Conversely, the more cohesively organized one's internal experience is, the less vulnerable the individual is to the vicissitudes of the selfobject surround or to debilitating narcissistic injury in the face of selfobject failure.

Thus one person's wobble is another person's earthquake. One person can shrug off the boss' scowl as reflecting a bad mood, while a coworker is devastated by even a hint of criticism. This is why a knowledge of external events tells us nothing without a corresponding understanding of their meaning to the patient.

That meaning has to be understood with a great deal of specificity. For example, one patient reported that marine boot camp was one of the best periods of his life. Surprised by this statement, I encouraged him to elaborate. He described how competent he felt at doing what was required of him physically and how much he enjoyed the sameness of uniforms and haircuts. It became clear that he loved boot camp for its structure, discipline, and challenge. These qualities, which had been sorely lacking in his family growing up, helped him with self-regulation, self-esteem, and a sense of belonging. Conversely, when he was off the base and not in uniform, his military haircut made him feel painfully *out* of place and contributed to a discomfort which ultimately was so intolerable he decided to leave the service.

Basch (1992, 1995) constantly enjoined therapists to get examples when a patient described a problem, believing that it was the specific details which would clarify the meaning of the events and issues the patient reported.

When someone reports difficulty getting over a relationship, I've found it particularly helpful to ask, "What do you think about when you think about him (or her)?" Does the person describe missing the affirmation of an admirer, the company of a playmate, or the solace of being held in the dark of the night? These point to differing internal experiences and needs.

In describing her boyfriend, one patient said, "Don is amazing . . . when he holds me his strength just seems to flow into me, wrapping around me and keeping me safe." When she later broke up with Don, the lost selfobject experience for her was very different from the woman described earlier who struggled with her appearance after her boyfriend left.

This question of what the patient thinks about is relevant to any loss, whether of a relationship, a job, or health and faculties. It is equally relevant to new challenges. Moving away from home, starting a new school or job, getting married, having a baby, and retiring are all life changes that have highly subjective, personal meanings.

For one patient, struggling with feelings of depletion after leaving her large and chaotic family, the significance of the change was in the loss of stimulation provided by all the commotion and activity at home. Suddenly on her own, her underlying emptiness became apparent. The appropriate focus of treatment was not anxiety about either separation or the new challenges she faced, but rather the need for external stimulation in order to mobilize or sustain any sense of vitality.

For another woman, who spent years nursing a failing spouse, her husband's death triggered a loss of structure and meaning. Her sense of self had become organized around the caregiving role, a pattern not uncommon for people in her situation. Treating this only as a problem of grief and mourning would miss what in fact became a more relevant concern for the treatment: finding a new basis for a sense of purpose, in order to restore her self-esteem. Finding new ways to sustain self-esteem constitutes a very different focus for treatment than resolution of an object loss or grief reaction.

Sometimes what is lost is a hope or fantasy. Bergart (1997) studied the losses and challenges involved when a woman closes the door on unsuccessful fertility treatment. Both Moses (1987) and Fajardo (1987) described the loss of dreams when a parent gives birth to a disabled child. Benetar (1989) similarly outlined the narcissistic issues stimulated in parents when their children marry someone very different from the parents' wishes and expectations.

The question of what comes to mind when the patient thinks about the presenting problem is helpful when dealing with trauma as well as loss. The specifics of traumatic memories provide clues to the nature of the underlying problem, continuing difficulties, or both. This is true of a wide range of situations, including assaults, accidents, and abuse.

When a hospital chaplain told me she was stymied by a patient who seemed unable to resolve the death of his wife, I asked her what he talked about when he talked about his spouse. In fact, the man always returned to exactly the same point, the experience of discovering her in the bathroom, dead of cardiac arrest, shortly after bringing her home from the hospital. Rather than suffering from an unresolved grief reaction, he was suffering from an acute anxiety reaction, more specifically post-traumatic stress, triggered by the way in which he discovered his wife's death. What he needed was help in integrating the shock, the sense of helplessness, and the other affects connected with this traumatic memory. This is, again, a very different focus from his grief over his lost partner.

This example, as well as several of the ones above, bring to mind what I consider the quintessential story for brief treatment.[4] As the story goes, an army general, very frustrated when his men are unable to fix his broken jeep in a foreign land, calls for a local mechanic. After looking under the hood for a bit, the mechanic asks for a hammer and gives the engine a bang. To the general's amazement, the car starts right up. Impressed and grateful, the happy general asks how much he owes. The mechanic says, "That will be $100." Taken aback, the general responds, "$100? For one bang?" "No," said the mechanic. "$1 for the bang, and $99 for knowing *where* to bang."

For treatment to be brief, we need to avoid wasting time either trying to address the wrong problem or trying to solve a problem on the wrong level. Using an empathic mode of observation to investigate the patient's subjective experience of precipitating events and problems helps us know "where to bang," where the internal problem in the self is.

As described earlier, ultimately our inquiry always comes back to understanding the ways in which the self is vulnerable or disrupted and to establishing a selfobject relationship which will strengthen vitality and cohesion. The more rapidly we can translate the precipitants, symptoms, deficits, strengths, and transferences into statements about the organization of self experience, the more readily we will be able to do this.

It is through an empathic mode of observation, facilitated by the questions described above, that we are able to understand the selfobject dimension and subjective meaning of the patient's experience. It is through empathic interpretations that we communicate that understanding to the patient.

ADDRESSING SELFOBJECT EXPERIENCE THROUGH EMPATHIC INTERPRETATIONS

Empathic interpretations accept, understand, and explain the meaning of the patient's experiences (Ornstein, 1986), including their frustrated selfobject needs or longings. Understanding phenomena from the point of view of the patient's subjective experience allows the therapist to offer the selfobject responsiveness needed to restore cohesion and enable symptoms to abate.

To illustrate, using an empathic interpretation to capture his patient's experience of losing his girlfriend, one therapist declared, "When she left it was like all your good feelings about yourself walked out with her." Another therapist, responding to a young man who was upset by the cold water his father had thrown on his ideas, replied, "You wanted support for your plan and an expression of confidence in you, not twenty questions about how you'd get it to work." When the patient's older brother offered a similarly disappointing response to an accomplishment, the therapist said, "You wanted him to take pride and pleasure in your achievement, not be competitive and resentful about it."

Such interpretations belatedly legitimize underlying needs or wishes. We are accustomed to reflecting the feelings which are reactive to needs not getting met, usually feelings of hurt, anger, sadness, or disappointment. But when we go beyond these reactive affects to the underlying longings and fantasies, our interpretations can have a powerful mutative effect. As Goldberg (1973) observed:

Behind the sadness of the adolescent who is rejected for a date is the image of a dashing and irresistible hero whom no one can resist. His anger at the girl who turns him down is secondary to feeling injured. Relief comes when someone can understand the hidden image of himself without ridicule or condemnation. Behind the disabling depression of the chronically ill is the fantasy of the perfect body that is intact and beautiful and cannot be damaged. (p. 726)

A cancer patient, successfully treated in brief psychotherapy for problems stimulated by her illness, described feeling enraged when people told her that the way she felt was "normal" when it was anything but normal for her. What she wanted was understanding, not reassurance that couldn't really be offered. When the doors closed behind the people leaving the room where she received radiation, she wanted someone to simply appreciate the fear she felt at that moment, to understand her sense of aloneness and helplessness. She needed this experience accepted and confirmed.

An elderly man home alone recovering from major surgery complained that the physical therapist wasn't showing up and his home-delivered meals weren't coming on time. Looking at the internal meaning of his situation, it becomes clearer that he was upset at being failed by those who were supposed to take care of him, adding salt to the injury that he couldn't take care of himself. He missed his strong, capable body and was disappointed and furious with the idealized caregivers who were not coming through for him.

He railed at the therapist, "I'm still waiting for my meals, can you believe it? I am so upset, I don't know what to do! I can't get well. I want to get strong, so I can go out. Do you understand?!" She replied, "I do. I understand that you are trying to get better, stronger, how you used to be. You want to recover from the surgery, so that you can get back to doing all these things like cooking meals for yourself, so you won't have to wait for a delivery. And the fact that you have to wait, sometimes not getting meals, is standing right in the way of your getting better, getting back to where you want to be. It's frustrating you in reaching your goal." With a huge sigh and great sense of relief, he replied, "Yes, exactly, that's it." He wanted her to appreciate his destination, not just his frustration.

The use of empathic interpretations to clarify and legitimize needs, affect, and experience is a crucial mutative tool in any self psychologically informed treatment. In brief treatment, it occupies center stage. We constantly articulate our understanding of what events and experiences mean to the patient; and we do so in a very active, explicit, and ongoing way.

In addition to its general mutative power, using an empathic mode of observation and response to focus on internal experience and specific meanings also saves time because of its power to mitigate defensiveness and resistance. Consider, for example, this excerpt from the second session of a brief treatment case:

PT: I don't understand why I am here with you, you're just going to send me home after we talk. Maybe I should leave now.

TH: You're worried that what we do here won't be enough. You're wondering if it's even worth it.

PT: Sometimes I think I'd be better off in the hospital for a while. Then I could try to deal with everything that has happened to me. I wouldn't have to worry about being strong and responsible or taking care of everyone else.

TH: Although you're feeling a lot of your own pain, you don't feel you have time to deal with that because you're too busy taking care of everyone else. Perhaps you see the hospital as a place where you'd have permission to stop worrying about everyone else and just take care of *you* for a while.

PT: Yes. Even when I'm here with you, I'm thinking about everything else I have to do. I can't let myself focus on all my problems, or let you push me to talk about them, because when I go home I have to be strong and pretend like everything is okay. No one would know what to do if *I* fell apart. Who would take care of me?

TH: You want to know that someone cares about you and would take care of you if *you* fell apart.

PT: You don't care about me. You're only here because it's your job, picking people apart! You're supposed to open me up so you can see what's wrong with me, explain it to me, and then leave me to deal with it. You know, just when the going gets tough, you get going!

TH: So you expect that I'll open you up and then just leave you all alone to deal with what's wrong, right when you most need my help. From what you said earlier, this is something you have experienced before. You've gotten used to people getting inside you and then rejecting what they see. You're afraid that I will do the same thing, and you don't want to be hurt like that again.

At this point the patient began to cry. The therapist's empathic attunement and understanding, of both her wishes and her fears (i.e., the protective functions of her anger and defensiveness) enabled her to feel understood. Her affect changed markedly as she began to talk about her earlier experiences of rejection, expressing painful feelings in a way she had previously been unable to do.

In describing the profound effect on the state of the self which this kind of empathic understanding has, Ornstein and Ornstein (1996a) explained: "Feeling understood is the adult equivalent of being held, which on the level of self-experience results in firming up or consolidating the self" (p. 94). The underlying feelings and needs made available by the ensuing suspension of defense are then integrated and transformed through the therapist's empathic interpretations.

In the example above, the therapist sought to convey her understanding without further investigation of her own contribution, in the present, to the patient's experience of the therapist as someone who didn't care about her, wanted to push her to talk, would pick her apart, and would leave her to deal with her problems alone. This would be an appropriate and expected focus in a self psychologically informed treatment and certainly could have been meaningfully pursued here. At the same time, it is important for the brief therapist to realize that an empathic interpretation of the patient's subjective experience, without such exploration of the joint contributions of both parties to that experience, may be sufficient to mitigate defensiveness and gain access to underlying affects.

To summarize, empathic interpretations constitute the therapist's most powerful tool for communicating understanding, clarifying experience, legitimizing affect and needs, mitigating defensiveness, facilitating the reorganization of affective experience, and strengthening the self. In addition, for most patients the experience of being responded to in this way constitutes a new relational experience, which is in itself a potent aspect of the mutative process.

ADDRESSING SOMETHING
WITHOUT ADDRESSING EVERYTHING

Correction in Course

With brief treatment our goal is less to get something finished than to get something started. We're aiming for a correction in course. Whether what gets started is a process of understanding, of stabilization, or of change, we're trying to strengthen the self, to help the patient develop more internal and external resources for dealing with life. This process does not need to be completed at the time of termination for continued working through and growth to occur afterwards.[5]

In other words, in brief treatment, we can address *something* without addressing *everything*. Yet a little bit can go a long way. Sometimes what the patient emerges with is a new experience of what is possible, both in relation to themselves and to others. One patient, faced with the need to end treatment because her therapist was moving away, said, "All my life I was waiting for someone who could understand me. You came along and now you're leaving and I won't have that anymore." After reflecting the patient's feelings of loss, the therapist added, "So you'll never again have the experience of feeling that there's no one who could ever understand you." "Right," the patient responded, "it makes me feel like less of a freak."

The therapist's response to this isolated and disconnected woman underscored that there was some experience of the relationship that would remain with her, whatever else might be lost in their termination. Once she has felt understood in this way, she can no longer go back to seeing herself as incomprehensible or the world as a place where such an empathic connection would never be possible. She might believe that it will never happen again. However, much as the task of clearing a path in the woods which has become overgrown is much less difficult than the task of carving it out the first time, finding one's way back to an experience is usually easier than getting there initially. This patient's experience with her therapist opens the door to her being able to seek out and find similar experiences with others.

Mutative Moments

Experiences like those of the woman just described are powerful events, which can permanently change the internal landscape. Elson (1995), encouraging therapists doing brief treatment to appreciate the enormous potential of even brief encounters, drew on an experience of Dostoevsky's to illustrate:

> We not infrequently despair over the brevity of our work with the individuals who come to us or are mandated for treatment. I would like to share an illustration of the manner in which a weakened and endangered self can be sustained by the brief experience of a selfobject function which becomes transformed

into psychic structure capable of restoring cohesion and strength to that self.

When Dostoevsky was but twenty four, he spent more than a year revising and editing a work of fiction called *Poor Folk*. Finally he read it to a friend, who in turn showed it to other friends, who woke him in the middle of the night to give him hugs and congratulations. One friend took it to a much feared and revered Russian critic, urging him to read the manuscript and likening its author to a new Gogol. Skeptical at first, he roared, 'Bring him to me!' His enthusiasm and praise were unstinting. And Dostoevsky left him in a daze, wondering, 'Am I really such a great man?'

Many years later he wrote, 'This was the most blissful moment of my life. Every time I remembered this moment when I was in Siberia (where his wrists and ankles were shackled for four years, leaving permanent scars) I found new courage and strength. Still today I remember it with joy.' (Geir Kjetsa, *Fyodor Dostoevsky: A Writer's Life*, 1987, p. 45).

Our clients and patients perhaps do not have the genius of a Dostoevsky, yet the experience of being the center and focus of our empathic attention, the experience of being understood, does not go away. It remains as a beacon and may assist an individual in his lifelong quest for meaningful goals and relationships.

As therapists, we can reflect on moments both in our own lives and in our own treatment when this kind of powerful experience left a lasting impression. We might think of our appreciation of small gestures of understanding when grief stricken, our swelling with pride when affirmed by someone we particularly admire, or our deep sense of connection and well being when someone responds to us by sharing their own experience in a way which makes us feel known and understood in the depth of our being. It is not the duration, but the affective intensity of such experiences which gives them their tremendous mutative power.

Termination: Object Loss and Selfobject Loss

When termination occurs before the therapist or patient feels the work is fully done, which is often the case in brief treatment, there can be concern about what will be lost by stopping. It is helpful here to distinguish between object loss, which concerns the therapist as a separate, valued person, who might be missed or mourned, and selfobject loss, which has to do with sustaining functions or experiences of which the therapist has been the source. When selfobject loss is a concern, there is a fear that with the loss of the therapist will come a loss, for example, of the capacity to be self-regulating, the ability to calm or motivate oneself, or (like the patient above) the opportunity to be understood and appreciated. One patient preparing to end his brief psychotherapy asked the therapist for a tangible possession, something of hers that would be a reminder (or transitional object) to aid in his struggle to internalize their bond and the functions it provided (Gardner, 1991).

When we evaluate how people might do after termination, this selfobject dimension of the relationship is important to examine. It is helpful to ask ourselves what the patient will be able to sustain internally without us, either because there has been an increase in self-esteem or self regulating capacities and the self is more firmly structured, or because there has been an expansion of the selfobject milieu and the person is better able to find others who can be a source of sustaining selfobject experiences. These are connected: one has to believe a feeling or need is legitimate before one dares to express or seek to meet it. Being validated in therapy leads to more ability to assert one's needs outside of therapy.

It is useful to talk to people directly about these issues. One patient, announcing she no longer felt the need for me, stated, "I can validate myself now." Some people have described how they imagined writing in a journal or turning more to other people to sort out their feelings, once they stopped coming to therapy. Others described recalling specific words I'd said or concepts we'd discussed, to help them stay calm or hopeful when anxiety or despair threatened to overwhelm them.

Keeping in mind that brief treatment often ends at a time when the structure-building process and reorganization of self experience have been set in motion but not completed, it is appropriate to help patients think through the consequences of leaving the selfobject matrix of the therapy relationship. This can best be accomplished by exploring together the current state of the patient's internal and external resources for sustaining a cohesive and vital sense of self.

COMPONENTS OF A MODEL
TO FACILITATE BRIEFER TREATMENT

Earlier I stated that the model I describe is less a particular technique than a series of components, whose combined use can make treatment more efficient. These components include:

1. Eliciting patient expectations and active collaboration in defining the goals of treatment, reinforcing the patient as a center of initiative in the process;
2. Emphasizing and using the patient's strengths;
3. Illuminating and addressing underlying vulnerabilities which are exposed when usual defenses and solutions are overwhelmed;
4. Using an empathic mode of observation to focus on the selfobject dimension (internal meaning) of precipitating events; and
5. Using empathic interpretations to clarify and validate subjective experience, needs, and frustrated longings.

There is nothing new in these activities per se or different from what one might do in long term treatment. But any one of them might be less emphasized in longer term therapy. That is not the case here. It is the combined and active use of *all* of these steps which makes the difference.

Focus is crucial, in both assessment and intervention. We are constantly looking for specific things, through particular lenses; we look, for example, not simply at precipitating events, but at the selfobject dimension of those events. By utilizing strengths and clarifying vulnerabilities, we can move rapidly to the interpretation of focal issues.

Careful assessment of changes in the state of the self and associated selfobject surround, using the frameworks described above to determine how self experience is vulnerable to disruption, enables the therapist to understand what must be addressed in order to enhance the self's vitality and cohesion. When we then communicate our understanding of the patient's subjective experience through empathic interpretations, we strengthen the self, mitigate defensiveness, facilitate the formation of a selfobject bond, and provide a new relational experience, all of which advance the therapeutic process.

Once this process has been mobilized, it may well continue on its own momentum after the treatment relationship ends. Thus a correction in course, rather than a completed journey, may be sufficient to produce benefit from brief treatment. Although developed in the context of long term, intensive psychotherapy and psychoanalysis, the conceptual framework provided by self psychology is ideally suited to facilitate treatment of any duration, no matter how brief. When translated from theory to practice, this framework provides a roadmap which can help us use whatever time we have to maximally help our patients.

NOTES

1. Those seeking a comprehensive overview of contemporary self psychology are also referred to the excellent summary statement provided by Fosshage (1998) in a previous issue of this journal.

2. In his final book (Basch, 1995), Basch actually dropped the term idealization and began using the word reliance to denote this aspect of the patient's needs and transference.

3. For sake of convenience, I use the term "the self" in the remainder of this article to refer to the subjective sense of self and to the organization of self experience. I do not mean to imply, by this term, an entity, agent, or fixed structure.

4. I don't know who originated this story, but credit Leo Bellak with bringing it into the domain of brief dynamic treatment.

5. For a detailed clinical report of changes that were achieved and those still in progress at the time of termination in brief treatment, see Gardner (1991).

REFERENCES

Bacal, H. (1985). Optimal responsiveness and the therapeutic process. In A. Goldberg (Ed.), *Progress in self psychology, Vol. I* (pp. 202-227). New York: Guilford.

Bacal, H. (1990). The elements of a corrective selfobject experience. *Psychoanalytic Inquiry, 10*, 347-372.

Bacal, H. (1998). *Optimal responsiveness: How therapists heal their patients.* Northvale, NJ: Jason Aronson.

Baker, H. (1991). Shorter-term psychotherapy: A self psychological approach. In P. Crits-Christoph & J. Barber (Eds.), *Handbook of short-term dynamic psychotherapy* (pp. 287-322). New York: Basic Books.

Balint, M., Ornstein, P., & Balint, E. (1972). *Focal psychotherapy: An example of applied psychoanalysis.* London: Tavistock.

Basch, M. F. (1980). *Doing psychotherapy.* New York: Basic Books.

Basch, M. F. (1988). *Understanding psychotherapy: The science behind the art.* New York: Basic Books.

Basch, M.F. (1992). *Practicing psychotherapy: A casebook.* New York: Basic Books.

Basch, M. F. (1995). *Doing brief psychotherapy.* New York: Basic Books.

Beebe, B., & Lachmann, F. (1988a). Mother-infant mutual influence and precursors of psychic structure. *Progress in Self Psychology, Volume 3*, 3-26. Hillsdale, NJ: Analytic Press.

Bellak, L. & Small, L. (1978). *Emergency psychotherapy and brief psychotherapy*, 2nd edition. New York: Grune & Stratton.

Benetar, M. (1989). "Marrying off" children as a developmental stage. *Clinical Social Work Journal, 17*, 223-231.

Bergart, A. (1997). Women's views of their lives after infertility treatment fails. Doctoral Dissertation. University of Chicago.

Chernus, L. (1983). Focal psychotherapy and self pathology: A clinical illustration. *Clinical Social Work Journal, 11*, 215-227.

Elson, M. (1986). *Self psychology in clinical social work*. New York: Norton.

Elson, M. (1989). Kohut and Stern: Two views of infancy and early childhood. *Smith College Studies in Social Work, 59*, 131-145.

Elson, M. (1995). Pathways to health in self psychology. Seventy Second Annual Meeting, American Orthopsychiatric Association, Chicago, Illinois, April 26, 1995.

Fajardo, B. (1987). Parenting a damaged child: Mourning, regression, and disappointment. *Psychoanalytic Review, 74*, 19-43.

Fosshage, J. (1998). Self psychology and its contributions to psychoanalysis: An overview. *Journal of Analytic Social Work, 5*, 1-17.

Gardner, J. (1991). The application of self psychology to brief psychotherapy. *Psychoanalytic Psychology, 8*, 477-500.

Goldberg, A. (1973). Psychotherapy of narcissistic injuries. *Archives of General Psychiatry, 28*, 722-726.

Kohut, H. (1959). Introspection, empathy and psychoanalysis. *Journal of the American Psychoanalytic Association, 7*, 459-483.

Kohut, H. (1966). Forms and transformations of narcissism. *Journal of the American Psychoanalytic Association, 14*, 243-272.

Kohut, H. (1971). *The analysis of the self*. New York: International Universities Press.

Kohut, H. (1977). *The restoration of the self*. New York: International Universities Press.

Kohut, H. (1984). *How does analysis cure?* Chicago: University of Chicago Press.

Kohut, H. (1987). *The Kohut seminars on self psychology and psychotherapy with adolescents and young adults* (M. Elson, Ed.). New York: Norton.

Kohut, H. (1996). *The Chicago Institute Lectures*, P. Tolpin & M. Tolpin (Eds.). Hillsdale, N.J.: The Analytic Press.

Kohut, H., & Wolf, E. S. (1978). Disorders of the self and their treatment. *International Journal of Psychoanalysis, 59*, 413-425.

Lazarus, L. (1980). Brief psychotherapy of narcissistic disturbances. *Psychotherapy: Theory, Research and Practice, 19*, 228-236.

Lazarus, L. (1988). Self psychology: Its application to brief psychotherapy with the elderly. *Journal of Geriatric Psychiatry, 21*, 109-125.

Lichtenberg, J. (1989). *Psychoanalysis and motivation*. Hillsdale, NJ: Analytic Press.

Lichtenberg, J. (1991). What is a selfobject? *Psychoanalytic Dialogues, 1*, 455-479.

Lichtenberg, J., Lachmann, F., & Fosshage, J. (1992). *Self and motivational systems: Toward a theory of technique*. Hillsdale, NJ: Analytic Press.

Lichtenberg, J., Lachmann, F., & Fosshage, J. (1996). *The clinical exchange: Technique derived from self and motivational systems*. Hillsdale, NJ: Analytic Press.

Messer, S. & Warren, C. (1995). *Models of brief psychodynamic therapy: A comparative approach*. New York: The Guilford Press.

Moses, K. (1987). The impact of childhood disability: The parent's struggle. *Ways*, 6-10.

Orange, D. (1995). *Emotional understanding: Studies in psychoanalytic epistemology*. New York: The Guilford Press.

Ornstein, A. (1986). "Supportive" psychotherapy: A contemporary view. *Clinical Social Work Journal, 14*, 14-30.

Ornstein, A. & Ornstein, P. (1986). Empathy and the therapeutic dialogue. In *The Lydia Rappaport lecture series* (pp. 3-16). Northampton, MA: Smith School of Social Work.

Ornstein, P. (1988). Multiple curative factors and processes in the psychoanalytic psychotherapies. In A. Rothstein (Ed.), *How does treatment help?* (Workshop Series of the American Psychoanalytic Association, Monograph 4, pp. 105-126). Madison, CT: International Universities Press.

Ornstein, P. & Ornstein, A. (1972). Focal psychotherapy: Its potential impact on psychotherapeutic practice in medicine. *Journal of Psychiatry in Medicine, 3*, 311-325.

Ornstein, P., & Ornstein, A. (1977). On the continuing evolution of psychoanalytic psychotherapy: Reflections and predictions. *The Annual of Psychoanalysis, 5*, 329-370.

Ornstein, P., & Ornstein, A. (1996a). I. Some general principles of psychoanalytic psychotherapy: A self-psychological perspective. In L. Lifson (Ed.), *Understanding therapeutic action: Psychodynamic concepts of cure* (pp. 87-101). Hillsdale, NJ: The Analytic Press.

Ornstein, A., & Ornstein, P. (1996b). II. Speaking in the interpretive mode and feeling understood: Crucial aspects of the therapeutic action in psychotherapy. In L. Lifson (Ed.), *Understanding therapeutic action: Psychodynamic concepts of cure* (pp. 103-125). Hillsdale, NJ: The Analytic Press.

Ornstein, A., & Ornstein, P. (1997). Brief but deep: Finding the focus in "focal psychotherapy." Twentieth Annual International Conference on the Psychology of the Self, Chicago, Illinois, November 13, 1997.

Ringstrom, P. (1995). Exploring the model scene: Finding the focus in an intersubjective approach to brief psychotherapy. *Psychoanalytic Inquiry, 15*, 493-513.

Seruya, B. (1997). *Empathic brief psychotherapy*. Northvale, NJ: Jason Aronson.

Shane, M., Shane, E., & Gales, M. (1997). *Intimate attachments: Towards a new self psychology*. New York: The Guilford Press.

Socarides, D., & Stolorow, R. (1984-1985). Affects and selfobjects. *The Annual of Psychoanalysis, 12/13*, 105-119.

Stolorow, R. (1986). Critical reflections on the theory of self psychology: An inside view. *Psychoanalytic Inquiry, 6*, 387-402.

Stolorow, R. (1998). Foreword. In I. Hardwood & M. Pines (Eds.), *Self experiences in group: Intersubjective and self psychological pathways to human understanding* (pp. 7-8). London: Jessica Kingsley Publishers.

Stolorow, R. & Atwood, G. (1992). *Contexts of being: The intersubjective foundations of psychological life.* Hillsdale, NJ: The Analytic Press.

Stolorow, R., Brandchaft, B., & Atwood, G. (1987). *Psychoanalytic treatment: An intersubjective approach.* Hillsdale, NJ: The Analytic Press.

Terman, D. (1988). Optimum frustration: Structuralization and the therapeutic process. In A. Goldberg (Ed.), *Learning from Kohut: Progress in self psychology, Vol. 4* (pp. 113-126). Hillsdale, NJ: Analytic Press.

Terman, D. (1989). Therapeutic change: Perspectives of self psychology. *Psychoanalytic Inquiry, 9*, 88-100.

Tolpin, M. (1971). On the beginnings of a cohesive self. *The Psychoanalytic Study of the Child, 26*, 316-352.

Tolpin, M. (1983). Corrective emotional experience: A self psychological reevaluation. In A. Goldberg (Ed.), *The future of psychoanalysis* (pp. 363-380). New York: International Universities Press.

Tolpin, P. (1984). Discussion of "A current perspective on difficult patients" by B. Brandchaft and R. D. Stolorow, and "Issues in the treatment of the borderline patient" by G. Adler. In A. Goldberg & P. Stepansky (Eds.), *Kohut's Legacy* (pp. 138-142). Hillsdale, NJ: Analytic Press.

Tolpin, M. & Kohut, H. (1980). The disorders of the self: The psychopathology of the first years of life. In S. I. Greenspan & G. H. Pollock (Eds.), *The Course of Life* (pp. 425-442). Bethesda: NIMH Tolpin, P. & Tolpin, M. (1996).

Wolf, E. S. (1980). On the developmental line of selfobject relations. In A. Goldberg (Ed.), *Advances in self psychology* (pp. 117-130). New York: International Universities Press.

Wolf, E. S. (1988). *Treating the self: Elements of clinical self psychology.* New York: Guilford.

Chapter 3

Integrative Short-Term Treatment of the Borderline Patient

Eda G. Goldstein

SUMMARY. The realities of current practice necessitate that clinicians engage in briefer forms of treatment with borderline patients despite the fact that long-term treatment has been considered the treatment of choice because of their entrenched and pervasive personality difficulties, severe developmental arrests, and history of trauma. Most short-term treatment models are ill-suited for work with the borderline population because they favor highly motivated and well-functioning patients who have circumscribed problems. Nevertheless, there is a considerable body of practice principles that can be adapted to brief treatment with borderlines. This paper reviews the clinical features of borderline disorders and current views on their origins and treatment and then describes the components of an integrative short-term treatment framework. *[Article copies available for a fee from The Haworth Document Delivery Service: 1-800-342-9678. E-mail address: getinfo@haworthpressinc.com <Website: http://www.haworthpressinc.com>]*

KEYWORDS. Borderline disorders, short-term treatment, brief treatment, difficult patients, developmental arrests

INTRODUCTION

Clinicians tend to view patients who are diagnosed with borderline personality disorder as difficult to engage and treat successfully.

Eda G. Goldstein, DSW, is Professor and Director, PhD Program in Clinical Social Work, New York University Shirley M. Ehrenkranz School of Social Work, 1 Washington Square North, New York, NY 10003.

[Haworth co-indexing entry note]: "Chapter 3. Integrative Short-Term Treatment of the Borderline Patient." Goldstein, Eda G. Co-published simultaneously in *Psychoanalytic Social Work* (The Haworth Press, Inc.) Vol. 6, No. 3/4, 1999, pp. 87-111; and: *Comparative Approaches in Brief Dynamic Psychotherapy* (ed: William Borden) The Haworth Press, Inc., 1999, pp. 87-111. Single or multiple copies of this article are available for a fee from The Haworth Document Delivery Service [1-800-342-9678, 9:00 a.m. - 5:00 p.m. (EST). E-mail address: getinfo@haworthpressinc.com].

Leading lives of not-so-quiet desperation, borderline individuals frequently exhibit a shifting and fluid sense of themselves and their
identities. They show contradictory feelings and behavior, fear separation from others, and have problems being alone, soothing themselves,
and containing their impulses. They do not tolerate stress well and
they become flooded with anxiety, anger, and other strong affects.
They often have histories of sexual and physical abuse. Because they
tend to yearn for and fear closeness, are sensitive to perceived slights
and rejections, fluctuate dramatically in their self-esteem, and alternate between attempts to merge with and distance from others, their
relationships are quite volatile. They also are prone to addictive, suicidal, and other types of self-destructive behavior. Their lives are
riddled with crises and they live in the immediacy of their experience.
Tending to blame others for their difficulties, they seek relief from
their troubling inner states or from the problems that result from their
usual ways of functioning in the world without seeing that it is their
own characteristic behavior that gets them into trouble.

Consequently, their motivation for treatment ceases after their most
pressing concerns recede. Those who are self-reflective have difficulty
using their insight to manage their thoughts, feelings, and behavior.
Even successful treatments are stormy. Borderline patients arouse
strong emotions in therapists and challenge their usual notions about
what is supposed to occur in treatment. They miss appointments,
threaten to leave, mutilate themselves, make suicide threats and attempts, and do not comply with agency or therapeutic requirements.
They request personal information, additional time, or extra-therapeu-
tic and sometimes physical contact.

The DSM IV (APA, 1994) refers to borderline as a specific type of
personality disorder defined by overt signs and symptoms. Others
point to a unique and pathological structural organization originating
in early development that underlies numerous personality disorders
(Kernberg, 1975, 1984); a group of disturbances that are manifested
by developmental deficits in ego functioning, attachment, separation-
individuation, internalized object relations, or self cohesion (Blanck &
Blanck, 1974, 1979; Mahler, Pine, & Bergman, 1975; Adler & Buie,
1979; Kohut, 1971, 1977; Brandchaft & Stolorow, 1984a & b); or a
complex variety of posttraumatic stress disorder related to the presence of childhood sexual trauma (Herman, 1992; Kroll, 1993). Re-

gardless of how borderline is defined, individuals who are so diagnosed are a challenge to even the most skilled practitioner. In keeping with the deeply rooted, pervasive, and chronic nature of their difficulties, the voluminous literature on the treatment of borderline patients advocates a variety of long-term approaches. The realities of today's practice arena, however, in which there is increasing pressure to provide short-term treatment to everyone who seeks mental health services, necessitate that practitioners engage in briefer forms of treatment on a planned basis. This need is heightened by the lack of studies on the efficacy of long-term treatment with borderline patients and the tendency of these patients to leave treatment suddenly and prematurely so that they actually receive short-term treatment by default both in private and agency practice (Kroll, 1993).

Numerous short-term psychotherapeutic models have been put forth. Most of these, however, are ill suited for work with the borderline population because of their clearly defined selection criteria that favor highly motivated and well-functioning patients who have circumscribed problems (Cornett, 1991; Messer & Warren, 1995). Goldstein and Noonan (1999, pp. 7-14), in reviewing the well-known approaches of Malan (1963, 1976), Sifneos (1972, 1979, 1987), Davenloo (1978, 1980, 1991), and Mann (1973, 1991), note that among these authors' selection criteria are high motivation for insight, good ego strength, favorable reactions to interpretation, psychological mindedness, motivation beyond symptom relief, willingness to make accommodations and sacrifices, receptivity to new ideas, realistic goals, the ability to deal with emotional reactions to termination, and the ability to tolerate loss. It is clear that the use of these criteria would exclude most borderline patients from brief treatment.

Nevertheless, some major contributions of these models, as well as those of Strupp and Binder (1984), Luborsky (1984), Stadter (1996), and Baker (1991), are their positive attitudes toward short-term treatment for the purposes of personality change and their emphasis on developmental issues, quick assessment, active goal setting, and focused interventions in the context of the therapeutic relationship (Goldstein & Noonan, 1999, p. 8).

The cognitive-behavioral approaches to the treatment of borderline individuals (Linehan, 1993, Dungee-Anderson, 1992; Heller & Northcut, 1996), which are related to but distinctive from the psychodynamic models, have their own strengths and limitations. On the positive side, they lead to the systematic identification of selected aspects of the borderline's difficulties that are most salient and that become targets of highly focused interventions. Although some of these frameworks acknowledge the importance of the therapeutic relationship and its reparative potential, others tend to be highly confrontative and require rather strict contracting. Like the psychodynamic models, the cognitive-behavioral approaches are more suitable to those who are highly motivated, possess high ego strength, and are able to tolerate certain procedures. Moreover, although these approaches stress individualization with respect to their specific focus, they run the risk of being applied in a rigid and mechanical way.

Despite the limitations of both the long- and short-term treatment of borderline individuals, there is a considerable body of theory and practice principles that can be adapted to briefer forms of intervention with this population. The first half of this paper reviews the clinical features of borderline disorders and current views on their origins and treatment. The second half describes the components of an integrative short-term treatment framework for their treatment.

THE CLINICAL PICTURE

The various psychodynamic developmental frameworks differ in their view of borderline disorders. Kernberg (1975, 1984), a conflict theorist, argues that they reflect ego weakness and a rigid and pathological defensive structure that arises to ward off anxiety and conflict centering around the expression of unneutralized constitutional aggression. Similarly, Masterson (1972, 1976) and Masterson and Rinsley (1975) see the borderline individual as revealing a split rewarding and punishing internal object relations unit and concomitant defenses and associated problems in ego functioning centering around problems related to separation-individuation. In contrast, deficit theorists view borderline disorders as reflecting gaps or missing elements in the personality as reflected in attachment and separation-individuation issues and other types of ego weakness (Blanck & Blanck, 1974, 1979), the absence of good internal objects (Adler, 1985; Adler & Buie, 1979) or undeveloped self-structure and the presence of severe narcissistic vulnerability (Kohut, 1971, 1977; Brandchaft & Stolorow, 1984a & b).

Drawing on both the conflict and deficit perspectives, the following discussion reflects 12 major characteristics that are important in diagnosing borderline disorders from a developmental perspective (Goldstein, 1990).

Identity Disturbances

Borderline individuals are confusing, contradictory, and unpredictable. They tend to portray themselves either as "all good" or "all bad" or they shift radically in their feelings, attitudes, behaviors, and goals so that it is difficult to get a clear or three-dimensional sense of who they are. Sometimes they use others to supply them with an identity; sometimes they develop a false self that covers a more real sense of self.

Splitting and Related Defenses

Conflict model theorists think of the main defense of borderline individuals as splitting, which keeps apart two conscious, contradictory, or opposite feeling states, such as love and hate, so that they are not integrated. Selected personality traits also become associated with goodness and badness and are split so that the person cannot acknowledge the coexistence of certain traits. Borderline individuals often tend to use other related defenses of *denial*, in which there is an inability to acknowledge selected aspects of the self or of others that conflict with their perceptions of self and others; *idealization*, in which there is a tendency to see themselves or others as totally good in order to ward off anxiety-provoking feelings about them; *devaluation*, in which there is a penchant to see themselves or others as all bad; *omnipotent control*, in which those with a highly inflated sense of self attempt to control others; and *projective identification*, in which they continue to have an impulse, generally an angry one, which, at the same time, is projected onto another person, who then is feared and controlled.

Problems in Impulse Control

Borderline individuals generally show chronic or episodic impulsiveness that sometimes is triggered by even minor disappointments, more major blows to self-esteem, experiences of loss and rejection, and threats of abandonment.

Problems in Anxiety Tolerance

Many borderline individuals are anxious most of the time or they have recurrent, disabling bouts of diffuse anxiety. They may experience dread when they awake in the morning or even in the middle of the night. Increases in stress are disorganizing or overwhelming. They also may experience panic reactions intermittently in response to life events, especially separations.

Problems in Affect Regulation

Borderline individuals often escalate rapidly in their feelings so that, for example, irritation becomes rage; sadness becomes despair; loneliness becomes aloneness; and disappointment becomes hopelessness. They become overwhelmed by intense positive or negative feelings. Seemingly happy at one moment, they plunge into a painful depression the next or they show inappropriate anger or temper tantrums.

Negative Affects

Often complaining of chronic depression, many borderlines show persistent feelings of anger, resentment, dissatisfaction, and envy. Sometimes they experience inner emptiness and feel bereft of positive or meaningful connections to others.

Problems in Self-Soothing

Borderline individuals lack the capacity for self-soothing and are at the mercy of any upsurge of uncomfortable feelings. They have "no money in the bank" to draw upon in moments of stress and become overwhelmed by feelings of panic, rage, and aloneness. Conflict model theorists see unmodulated and intense aggression at the root of this problem while deficit model theorists view it as related to the absence of good internal objects. Whatever the reason, even minor separations such as leaving a therapy session can generate panic that prompts them to engage in desperate efforts to make contact. Some immerse themselves in constant activities or engage in addictive or other types of self-destructive behavior in order to escape from their feelings.

Abandonment Fears

Borderline individuals commonly show fears of abandonment. Some attempt to merge with others in efforts to deny or ward off their aloneness and to reassure themselves that they will never be abandoned. Conflict model theorists believe that the borderline individual's anger at the object produces this fear, while deficit model theorists stress the borderline's lack of a stable good internal object and the failure to have achieved object constancy. Borderline individuals seek constant proximity to or contact with those upon whom they are dependent and want to know their exact whereabouts or minute details of their activities. At the same time, they often exhibit a need-fear dilemma that makes them ward off or withdraw from the positive experiences with others for which they long or show an oscillating cycle of clinging and distancing behavior. When they are not feeling intense loneliness, many borderline individuals manage their abandonment fears by regulating interpersonal closeness and engage in many superficial relationships, avoiding intimacy.

Problems in Self-Esteem Regulation

Borderline individuals lack a sound ability to regulate their self-esteem and may be driven to seek attention, affirmation, and praise from others. They are vulnerable to even minor criticisms and disappointments as well as extremely sensitive to rejection, disapproval, failures, or setbacks. Some show either grandiose or devalued conceptions of their abilities and talents and tend to feel either entitled to special treatment or unworthy of help or they fluctuate between these extremes.

Super-Ego Difficulties

While some borderline individuals show an absence of guilt and empathy in their dealings with others and are capable of ruthless and exploitative acts, many experience remorse, self-contempt, and self-recriminations after they mistreat others. Nevertheless they find themselves unable to stop the very behavior that they hate.

Intense and Unstable Interpersonal Relationships

Intimacy is a problem since the borderline tends to merge with others or regulates closeness so that it is not threatening. Moodiness, possessiveness, insecurity, and highly charged interactions are common. Fights, accusations, and sudden break-ups frequently occur and are usually related to feelings of being rejected or abandoned. Feelings of victimization are frequent. Separations are difficult, however, and cause anxiety and severe depression. They may lead to desperate and often seemingly manipulative and attention-getting behavior, such as suicide threats and attempts.

Problems in Self-Cohesion

Some borderline individuals are vulnerable to psychotic decompensation under stress. They have a profound lack of self-cohesion that leaves them susceptible to transient periods of fragmentation that can be quite disturbing. When in equilibrium, borderline individuals can maintain their self-cohesiveness by regulating the degree of intimacy in their relationships, avoiding the loss of ego boundaries involved in closeness.

TREATMENT PERSPECTIVES

The long-term intensive psychodynamic treatment models that have been applied to the treatment of borderlines aim at either modifying their pathological defenses, personality structure, and patterns of relating or at building their internal ego, object relations, or self structure and thereby improving their overall functioning. For example, Kernberg's conflict-based treatment approach argues for an insight-oriented, highly confrontative and interpretive approach, sometimes in conjunction with strict limit-setting and external structuring of the patient's life in order to modify the patient's pathological defenses, improve identity integration, and manage self-destructive and disruptive behavior. Recommending similar techniques, Masterson (1972, 1976) and Masterson and Rinsley (1975) emphasize helping patients to identify and modify their rewarding and punishing split object relations units and their associated pathological defenses and problems in ego functioning.

In contrast to conflict model writers, more deficit model theorists argue that most borderline patients cannot tolerate and will not benefit from a relentless attack on their defenses. Instead, they advocate a

treatment that facilitates the development of internal ego, object relations, and self structures. For example, the Blancks (1974, 1979) suggest an ego-building approach that is geared to the correcting and
repairing of ego deficits stemming from separation-individuation sub-
phases and the mastery of separation-individuation tasks. Likewise,
Adler (1985) and Adler and Buie (1979) underscore the necessity of
helping borderline patients to overcome their need-fear dilemma, to
acquire more stable internal good objects, and to develop their unique
strengths and capacities. Applying self psychology, Brandchaft and
Stolorow (1984a & b) focus on enabling patients to develop greater
self-cohesion and to overcome their severe narcissistic vulnerability.
This group of diverse theorists places importance on the establishment
of a therapeutic holding environment that has empathic and non-
threatening elements, the need for the therapist to supply more measured gratifications or more empathic self-object experiences, and the
importance of a reparative use of the therapeutic relationship. Interpretations are aimed at helping patients mobilize their highest level of
functioning, overcome their fears of the treatment relationship, repair
disruptions in the therapeutic relationship, and make sense of their
current needs and behavior in the light of the developmental experiences that have led them to respond in certain ways. A clinical issue
that arises in the course of this approach involves how to address the
more impulsive, self-defeating, self-destructive, and therapy-interfering aspects of the borderline's behavior without resorting to the heavy
use of confrontation and strict limits advocated in more conflict-based
treatment models (Goldstein, 1990).

Another important contribution to the treatment of borderline patients arises from the recognition that dissociated experiences of childhood trauma, usually related to sexual abuse, are at the root of an
unusually high percentage of those individuals who are diagnosed as
borderline. There are those who argue that they have been mis-
diagnosed and really are trauma survivors suffering from a complex
variety of post-traumatic stress disorder (Gunderson & Chu, 1993;
Herman, 1992; Herman, Perry, & van der Kolk, 1989; Corwin, 1996;
Kroll, 1993).

Some over-zealous practitioners have pressed patients to deal with
early trauma only to find that this approach has a disorganizing effect.
Most skilled clinicians are more cautious and recognize that trauma-
based treatment is no less complicated or time-consuming than other

long-term approaches. In addition to the more usual borderline symptomatology that patients with a trauma history present, they are highly distrustful of relationships, use defenses and engage in behaviors that protect their traumatic memories and that have helped them to survive, often cannot tolerate confrontative techniques, tend to become involved in situations in which they experience repeated revictimization, and are not readily able to do the work of the treatment because of their lack of a sense of safety and their variable ego functioning which may make it hard for them to tolerate the working through of their traumatic experiences. This necessitates considerable attention to the creation of a holding environment for these patients, validation of their survival skills, efforts to help them avoid situations in which they are revictimized, and sensitive timing of interventions that engage patients in the trauma recovery work.

In addition to the psychodynamic models used in the treatment of borderline patients, there are numerous cognitive-behavioral approaches (Linehan, 1993; Dungee-Anderson, 1992; Heller & Northcut, 1996) that rely heavily on educative and cognitive restructuring techniques, task assignment, modeling, exercises, and problem-solving. For example, Heller and Northcut (1996) give examples of their use of cognitive/behavioral techniques in working with the borderline's affective/cognitive splitting, affect dysregulation, and faulty attributions. Likewise, Dungee-Anderson (1992) recommends what she calls a self-nurturing approach that teaches the patient "to recognize and differentiate both the underdeveloped reality ego and developmentally arrested child components of the split-ego structure by their affective and behavioral characteristics" (p. 295). The mastery of separateness and independence/autonomy are central to the work although the tasks involved in this are unique to each patient based on their history and developmental issues. The therapist is a teacher and a modeler of more positive skills that the patient is helped to practice in exercises. Finally, Linehan (1993a & b), who has the most systematic and well-studied but also strict, confrontative, and unrelenting approach of this kind in order to increase and sustain the patient's level of motivation and commitment to treatment, advocates for relentless attention to modifying the patient's most disruptive target behaviors. Her first-stage target behaviors involve decreasing suicidal, therapy-interfering, and quality-of-life-interfering behaviors and increasing behavioral skills in the areas of core mindfulness skills, interpersonal effectiveness, emotional regulation, distress tolerance, and self-management. Her second-stage goals aim at reducing posttraumatic stress and her third-stage goals include increasing respect for self and achieving individual goals.

AN INTEGRATIVE SHORT-TERM TREATMENT FRAMEWORK

Drawing on the full repertoire of approaches to the treatment of borderline individuals, the following discussion suggests the major components of an integrative short-term treatment framework. The exact time frame of the treatment will vary but this approach can be used in 20-30 sessions of generally weekly contact. Sessions may be spaced, however, to meet the needs of the patient.

Belief in the Efficacy and Conscious Use of Short-Term Treatment

In order to employ a short-term treatment model effectively, it is important for practitioners either to hold the conviction or be open to the possibility that borderline patients can make improvements in their lives within a limited time-frame and that they be willing to engage in the planned use of brief treatment. This is not to suggest that short-term treatment is a panacea that is appropriate for everyone, or that clinicians should abandon their efforts to get managed care organizations to make exceptions to their usual guidelines, or that they not continue to work for changes within the health care system that allow for differential treatment arrangements. All too often, however, for understandable reasons, given the enormity of borderline patients' difficulties generally and their issues around loss and abandonment and apparent need for a stable good object in their lives specifically, clinicians are pessimistic if not completely negative about the use of short-term treatment with borderline individuals. They may communicate this directly or indirectly to their patients. This attitude may be accompanied by the hope that patients will find a way to prolong treatment when financial or insurance constraints exist. Consequently, they do not modify their treatment approach in keeping with potential time constraints and thus do not employ short-term intervention in a planful manner even though, as noted earlier, treatment ends earlier than planned. Opportunities are lost to provide patients with the hope, structure, and focus that they need to make progress in the time available for treatment and to motivate them to extend the treatment should this be possible. Even if short-term intervention is not optimal in a given case, there is good reason to believe that a period of brief treatment that provides patients with some sense of connection and accomplishment will be helpful in enhancing patients' motivation to return for additional treatment at a later time.

Drawing on Diverse Theoretical Formulations and Frameworks

Using the full repertoire of frameworks regarding the borderline, it is important for clinicians to draw on diverse theoretical formulations and models and to think of borderline pathology as reflecting a range of developmental difficulties that necessitate highly individualized and attuned therapeutic interventions. This eclecticism in the short-term treatment of borderline patients does not imply that the clinicians "fly by the seat of their pants" or use any model or assemblage of interventions that strike their fancy. Being able to conduct treatment from the vantage point of different perspectives allows practitioners to expand their ability to understand what is most salient for a particular patient in the assessment process, which must be rapid out of necessity as will be discussed further. This is important because it is likely that borderline patients have difficulties at multiple and different levels, that some aspects of their problems may be more prominent at one time than another, and that some of their problems may be more readily explained and worked with from one framework than another. Each of the various psychodynamic perspectives on viewing the origins and treatment of borderline patients has value when one considers the full range of patients although they are not always compatible in a particular individual. Areas of conflict and deficit can coexist in the same individual. Likewise, the accumulating evidence about the incidence and role of childhood sexual abuse and trauma in women who are diagnosed as borderline is compelling. It requires that practitioners be alert to the presence of childhood trauma in borderline patients and to use their understanding of the significance of this type of event, its sequelae, and its treatment implications in planning and implementing intervention and in managing the therapeutic relationship.

High Level of Therapist Activity

The active structuring and focusing of short-term treatment from the outset of the interventive process is important because of its time-limited nature, which creates pressure for the work to be done; the diffuse and sometimes chaotic nature of the borderline's inner life and external behavior, and the borderline's particular defenses and deficits. This involves the therapist's efforts to establish a holding environment, assess the patient, set realistic goals, select and maintain a focus, enhance the patient's motivation for treatment, anticipate and help the patient to address aspects of his or her behavior that might interfere with the treatment, and enable the patient to manage life outside of the treatment. This requirement for a high level of activity may clash with therapists' usual style or preferences about how to conduct treatment and may result in forced interventions. It is important to bear in mind that the need to be active should not be interpreted as license to impose a strict and mechanical treatment structure, to minimize the establishment of a positive therapeutic relationship, to impose one's agenda on the patient, to confront aspects of the patient's thoughts, feelings, and behavior that the therapist thinks are problematic, to ignore the patient's concerns, or to vigorously and quickly address issues that are too overwhelming or stressful for the patient to tolerate. It necessitates that the therapist strike a delicate balance between being empathically attuned to and responsive to patients, going at a pace they can handle, being alert to the features of the patients' problems that can have potentially destructive consequences in their lives and on the treatment itself, and assuming responsibility for fostering the conditions that are essential to the therapeutic work.

Establishment of a Therapeutic Holding Environment

In most psychodynamic treatment, it is customary to underscore the significance of the therapist's development of a therapeutic alliance in which the patient's reality ego perceives that the therapist is there to be helpful. This enables the patient to agree to the requirements of therapy. But this feature of the treatment is only one component of the task of creating a therapeutic holding environment that is essential in work with patients who show severe developmental arrests, generally and particularly with those individuals with histories of childhood sexual abuse and other types of early trauma.

Borderline individuals often come to treatment at a time of crisis when they are emotionally labile and unable to regulate or manage their intense feelings and impulses. They are lacking in certain ego functions that therapists take for granted in other patients; they yearn for closeness but are fearful and distance themselves from relationships; they are suspicious of but sometimes try to provoke revictimization. For these patients, the establishment of a therapeutic environment that helps to stabilize them, helps them feel safe, enables them to contain and verbalize their feelings, and helps them trust the therapist is essential.

It is not easy, however, for the most caring and empathic therapist "to hold" borderline individuals. The provision of consistency, clarity about expectations, empathy, genuineness, acceptance, interest, clear boundaries, and respect for diversity, that should be present in most forms of treatment, are necessary first steps. Beyond these general therapist characteristics, the optimal treatment framework likely will require other elements and should be individualized and flexible based on the therapist's understanding of what a particular patient requires.

Thus, the establishment of a holding environment is closely linked to the assessment, the nature of which will be discussed below. For example, some borderline patients who are angry, provocative, demanding, erratic in their session attendance, disorganized, or highly impulsive may benefit from the establishment of clear guidelines and limits to help them maintain control of their behavior. Likewise their difficulties in adhering to the treatment structure and therapists' expectations may need to be addressed in a forthright and firm manner. Or, some borderline individuals, as a result of their addictive or suicidal behavior, may require active and protective interventions such as day treatment, 12-step programs, family involvement, or other types of external structure. There are those borderline patients whose lack of object constancy makes them unable to maintain a sense of connection to the therapist outside of sessions and who tend to experience anxiety and panic states that they are unable to overcome easily. They require other measures. Some authors (Wells & Glickauf-Hughes, 1986) have suggested that therapists use transitional objects, journals, and visualization to help such patients while others (Adler, 1985) suggest that therapists be willing to talk to patients briefly by telephone at designated times or send post cards during vacation periods. In the author's discussions of this issue in the professional community, numerous therapists have concurred with her observation that telephone answering machines often appear to serve as transitional objects and patients themselves speak of wanting to hear the message on the device rather than necessarily speaking to the therapist directly. It is likely that some patients have discovered their therapists' E-mail addresses and are utilizing this means of contact as well.

The practices of remaining neutral and refraining from the selective gratification of patients' needs for additional time, advice, direct questions, or requests for personal information about the therapist are not always useful and often can be detrimental in the treatment of many borderline patients. This stance may reexpose many patients to what feels like the unrealness, neglect, and indifference in their early lives (Goldstein, 1994). While maintaining therapeutic and ethical boundaries so as not to threaten or overstimulate patients, therapists may need to be more real and willing to meet some of their patients' needs. If therapists are not prepared or willing do so, it is important not to interpret patients' requests as manipulative or inappropriate or to tell them that what they want is not good for their treatment. Instead, it is possible to convey understanding of why patients may make certain requests while taking responsibility for not feeling able to grant them. What is important is providing a type of "optimal responsiveness" (Bacal, 1985) based on what will help foster the therapeutic holding environment and work of the treatment.

In the creation and maintenance of a good-enough holding environment, therapists must consider not only the patients' developmental needs but also the interpersonal or environmental triggers to their current crises. For example, Cornett (1991), in using self psychological principles in short-term treatment of patients who are not likely to benefit from more traditional models that favor highly functioning and well-motivated patients, urges therapists to consider whether patients' current crises and desire to seek help have been precipitated by disruptions in their experience with previously helpful selfobjects in the mirroring, idealizing, or twinship/alterego spheres. Such awareness not only helps therapists to understand what is contributing to patients' more acute distress or seeking of help but also can inform how therapists use themselves in their relationships with patients. Thus, therapists' willingness to function as selfobjects may enable patients to regain their equilibrium, which itself may constitute the main goal of some brief treatment or it might help to foster patients' motivation to work on other aspects of their difficulties.

Empathy and selective gratification may not be sufficient to hold certain borderline patients. The setting of limits and the provision of external structure may be necessary. To the degree that this is so, it is important for therapists to engage patients collaboratively in a problem-solving effort about what will enable them to contain their impulses and self-destructive behavior. The unilateral establishment of strict rules should be avoided. Although it might be helpful in some cases to employ the practice recommended by some authors (Kernberg et al., 1989; Linehan, 1993) of utilizing written contracts with clear consequences if patients fail to live up to the rules, this is a rather extreme approach. Moreover, therapists need to recognize borderline patients' vulnerability to slips and difficulties in doing what is good for them. There should be sufficient flexibility in the treatment structure to help patients through these occurrences without their being viewed as "non-compliant" or terminated from treatment. For example, many borderline patients present with alcohol or drug abuse, a severe eating disorder, or self-mutilating behavior. The therapist's expectation that such patients become totally abstinent as a prerequisite for treatment assumes that they are healthier than is usually the case. It may be necessary to address this issue firmly when the destructive behavior is out of control and is having obvious and immediate destructive consequences for the patient or others. In most instances, however, therapists' timing in placing expectations for ceasing and desisting such actions is important. Waiting does not imply that the therapist ignores the problem. Rather the therapist continues to address the behavior by keeping it in focus, exploring its current triggers or underlying causes, identifying the gratification obtained from it and resistance to giving it up, and helping the patient find other ways of managing urgent feeling states. The therapist might eventually help the patient to take decisive action but it may take a period of work before this tactic can be effective.

Similarly, when it is necessary for therapists to address patients' behaviors that are interfering with the treatment such as missing sessions, coming late, drinking or smoking marijuana before sessions, or not paying fees in a timely fashion or behaviors that are likely to disrupt the treatment, such as a history of repeated sudden terminations, it is tempting to resort to confrontation as is sometimes recommended. This usually results in patients feeling attacked, particularly when therapists actually are irritated, if not angered, by patients' behavior. It generally is preferable to comment on the more immediately problematic aspects of patients' behavior in non-judgmental ways that show an understanding of their inner states, fears, and difficulties while also problem-solving with them about how to manage themselves better. In order to do this, it is necessary for therapists to see beyond their patients' often rageful, provocative, grandiose, and seemingly manipulative behavior to their underlying anxiety, fears of being victimized, injured self-esteem, anticipation of rejection and abandonment, and attempts to distance and preserve autonomy.

Rapid Assessment

It follows from the preceding discussion that therapists must engage in a rapid assessment of borderline patients that draws on their understanding of the major features of borderline disorders. Careful attention should be paid to understanding patients' here and now functioning before the exploration of historical background. The assessment has seven foci: (a) main current problems and symptomatology; (b) ego functioning, separation-individuation issues; self concept, selfobject needs, and self-esteem regulation, and internalized object relations; (c) the main developmental issues that are associated with patients' most pressing problems; (d) current triggers for patients' more acute distress or help-seeking; (e) environmental supports or conditions that are stimulating or perpetuating the patients' difficulties; (f) strengths, level of motivation, and ability to sustain treatment; (g) ability to manage their lives outside the treatment; and (h) therapy-interfering behaviors.

Because of the demands of time and the complex nature of the borderline patients' difficulties and the confusing, unfocused, and contradictory ways in which they communicate, the assessment process is challenging. Therapists need to balance the act of seeking crucial information with the need to be attuned to patients' pace and style of relating. Therapists should not adhere to a set pattern of questioning but should be clear about what they need to know and how to acquire the information that they need. Because borderline patients often do not discuss significant data or occurring events, therapists need to be quite active in surveying important areas of patients' lives. It may be necessary, however, to refrain from probing into what appear to be sensitive topics. Alternatively, if a patient indicates that he or she is having suicidal thoughts, the therapist's exploration of the nature and severity of this ideation should take precedence over asking about other issues.

Although borderline patients' problems are embedded in chronic and enduring aspects of their personality, these are not necessarily the focus of intervention. An important part of the assessment is the determination of what areas of a patient's overall personality functioning are causing or perpetuating the presenting difficulties and need to be addressed. For example, the fact that a patient is lacking in object constancy and has fears of abandonment may not be contributing to his or her problems with authority at work that result in repeated job loss. Instead, it appears to be faulty self-esteem regulation, poor judgment, and impulsiveness that render the patient sensitive to the absence of positive feedback or the presence of overt criticism and lead to self-defeating behavior. It is these features of the patient's functioning that should be the focus of treatment.

One of the significant areas about which therapists must be alert in the assessment phase relates to the presence of early trauma, particularly sexual abuse in patients' lives and current triggers for stimulating memories or feelings related to these events. Likewise, therapists should take special note of separations and losses, absence of selfobjects or severe disruptions in experiences with those that existed, and the presence of strong highly perfectionist or negative views of the self.

Goal Setting and Focusing

Many borderline patients enter treatment at a time of crisis in a life punctuated by frequent upheavals. Others are experiencing their characteristic chaos, turmoil, and unhappiness. With those who are experiencing more acute distress, a crucial focus of treatment is to foster the stabilization process. After this is accomplished, other goals might be undertaken. With those who are showing the effects of their usual and ongoing difficulties, the goals may involve helping them to identify what gets them into trouble, enabling them to diminish the more self-defeating and self-destructive aspects of their functioning, developing better ways of coping with their pressing needs and impulses, and building or modifying their inner structure.

Partialization makes the work more manageable and less overwhelming to both therapist and patient. Because patients often present with multiple or long-standing problems, the process of setting goals and establishing a focus necessitates prioritizing with respect to what is most immediate or most amenable to change or resolution. Sometimes the selection of a circumscribed aspect of the total problem constellation may be indicated. Breaking the problem down into smaller elements engenders hope and a sense of greater control.

Borderline patients often seek immediate relief from their uncomfortable feeling states or from the negative consequences of their actions but do not identify what they are doing that is problematic, nor do they possess the motivation to alter their behavior. An important aspect of setting goals is to enlist their participation. They need to identify some positive value that derives from their involvement in treatment, even if the only benefit is to avoid negative consequences. Rather than use confrontation and interpretation in order to try to help the patient see and take responsibility for their problematic ways of functioning, it is preferable to use a non-judgmental and educative approach in which the therapist explains to the patient what aspects of his or her attitudes or behavior are creating difficulties and why. In this process, it may be helpful for the therapists to convey their understanding and acceptance of how and why patients have acquired these attitudes and behaviors. Additionally, therapists need to demonstrate in tangible ways their interest in and capacity to help patients even in some small area of their lives. Therapists' ability to partialize patients' difficulties in order to make them less overwhelming and more manageable and to arrive at an often concrete and readily attainable goal is essential in mobilizing patients' sense of hope and willingness to be more active participants in the interventive process. The achievement of modest goals engenders feelings of mastery and enhances motivation.

Together the therapist and patient establish clear goals, which they must keep in the forefront. The therapist helps to maintain the focus but this is not always an easy task with borderline patients who are likely to have difficulty staying on a subject in a session, display a lack of continuity from meeting to meeting, often bring up new concerns, and frequently experience new crises. Therapists need to show flexibility in addressing other issues that arise even if they initially seem unrelated to the identified problem or stated goals. They need to determine whether a particular line of discussion is connected to the treatment focus and find ways of bringing patients back to the main problem. For example, rather than always adhering to the principle of allowing patients to discuss whatever is on their mind for an entire session, it may be advisable for the therapist to comment non-judgmentally on the patient's digression or tangent and invite the patient to return to a more relevant topic or to articulate some connection between what the patient is saying and the issues on which they are working. Rather than only empathically relating to what a patient is expressing in a particular session when it contradicts what was said at an earlier time, it may be helpful to bring up material from the earlier meeting in order to clarify the patient's present communications.

Educative, Mirroring, Role-Modeling, and Interpretive Techniques

Therapists should utilize a range of techniques in their work that include a heavy reliance on educative, mirroring, and role modeling strategies as well as interpretive techniques that are more associated with insight-oriented approaches. It is important for therapists to bear in mind that change occurs at two different levels: the level of overt behavior and the level of personality structure. It is thought that supportive treatment improves patients' coping skills and functioning while more intensive treatment modifies the personality. But these goals and their associated techniques are not mutually exclusive. To the degree that short-term treatment of borderline patients may be supportive of current functioning does not mean that the process and outcome of the work has no greater effect on the patient's personality. Much can be achieved when there is a meaningful therapeutic relationship that can be internalized by the patient. For example, when there is a positive connection between therapist and patient, helping a patient to acquire an increased and more positive repertoire of ways of soothing themselves can increase their actual capacity for self-soothing.

Although cognitive-behavioral approaches make different assumptions about the origins and nature of borderline pathology and use a different set of technical interventions than are characteristic of psychodynamic approaches, there is much to be learned from them about breaking problems down into manageable parts and conceptualizing them in ways that are more accessible to the patient's ego. The ability to think, process information, problem-solve, and use other cognitive processes are important aspects of ego functioning. It can be argued that a patient's self-concept or way of viewing others reflects how that patient has learned to think as well as what the patient has experienced. One can translate psychodynamic concepts into cognitive-behavioral terms in order to make it easier for them to take hold of an issue. For example, one can help patients think about their defense of splitting by talking about their "black and white" thinking about themselves or others or their problems with self-soothing by talking about their not being able to identify their feelings, talk themselves through certain feelings, or find ways of relieving their feelings. Likewise, a psychodynamically oriented clinician may integrate certain aspects of these approaches, such as the use of educative, cognitive restructuring, modeling, task-oriented, and problem-solving interventions, into the armamentarium without becoming mechanistic.

Managing Countertransference

There is general consensus that therapists are especially vulnerable to problematic reactions that can obstruct their work with borderline patients because of the impact of patients' urgent needs, primitive defenses, angry, demanding, and provocative behavior, and intense transference reactions. There has been a tendency to say that borderline patients induce particular responses in therapists in order to rid themselves of uncomfortable feelings and that it is useful to focus on what is happening in the interaction between patient and therapist in order to help the patient understand his or her internal states and how these affect interactions with and perceptions of others. There is a risk, however, in always using this perspective because it tends to hold patients responsible for what therapists are feeling when it is the therapists who have contributed to the patients' reactions because of the therapists' lack of attunement, unintentional insensitivity, or overly harsh comment or due to a failure to respond accurately to patients' needs. Even if a patient is inducing a reaction in the therapist, it is important for the therapist to contain rather than act-out feelings. There are many instances in which the therapist's ability to take responsibility for frustrating the patient or for a disruption in the therapeutic relationship will repair whatever rift that has occurred and also can have a positive effect on the patient and the treatment process.

Emphasis on Patients' Strengths and Talents

It is especially important for the therapist to search out and work with patients' strengths and talents. It is not always easy to maintain a strengths perspective when patients are beleaguered by severe personality pathology. At the very least, however, the fact that patients seek help is a strength upon which to build. Even those who display long-standing and severe problems may have shown remarkable resiliency in coping with difficult circumstances. It is useful to convey to patients that some of their problematic attitudes and behavior may have helped them to survive. Because so many patients have not experienced validation of their strengths and talents, it is also important for the therapist to function as a new kind of object in the patient's life.

Collaboration, Linkage, and Advocacy

The therapist not only draws on the patient's strengths and talents but also marshals outside resources during the interventive process. Often the therapist must reach out and involve others who can be of assistance to the patient, including the family, self-help groups, and community agencies and services. Intra- and interprofessional collaboration and work with others in the patient's social network often are needed in linking patients to vital resources and support systems. In some instances, the patient will need an advocate to help him or her obtain what is needed. Collaboration, linkage, and advocacy have their own distinctive set of skills that must become part of the therapist's repertoire.

Acceptance of the Limitations of Treatment

There are many benefits to short-term treatment, particularly those that result from being able to help patients make circumscribed changes in their ways of coping or attain a more fundamental improvement in their ego functioning, self-concept and self-esteem regulation, and ability to relate to others. There also are some potential limitations, however, for both therapist and patient. Because not all of the problems that the patient may evidence can be alleviated, it is important that therapist and patient accept the concept of partialized goals and focus on what is most amenable to change. In such cases, therapists may feel that they are not doing enough to help patients, fear that the patient's problems will reoccur, and believe that more can be achieved through further treatment. The patient, too, may feel frustrated that more cannot be accomplished although it has been shown that in many instances patients are more satisfied with the outcome of short-term contact than is the therapist. In addition to both therapist and patient being able to recognize and appreciate what has been accomplished, it also is important to bear in mind that even small gains may lead to further growth, that work continues after treatment ends, and that patients can seek help again at a later date.

Although the short-term nature of treatment supports independence, a second possible limitation surrounds the issue of separation and loss because the treatment process is designed to come to an end at a specified time. Both therapist and patient may wish to prolong the contact either because of the meaning the relationship has to each, the feelings that are aroused in the process of separation, or because of the wish to experience the satisfaction and gratification of the beneficial outcomes of the work. There is no simple way to address this issue. Some patients may be affected quite negatively by having to stop treatment. Others may be able to use the experience of having to end the treatment relationship to deal with the effects of prior losses and to master the feelings associated with endings. Yet other patients will find ways of extending the treatment or returning at a later time. What is necessary is for the therapist and patient to be aware of the time limits of the treatment from the outset, to spend time discussing the meaning of termination in the ending phase, and to find ways of helping the patient make a transition to greater independence and ways of continuing the work outside of treatment.

REFERENCES

Adler, G. (1985). *Borderline psychopathology and its treatment.* New York: Jason Aronson.

Adler, G. & Buie, D. H. (1979). Aloneness and borderline psychopathology: The possible relevance of child development issues." *International Journal of Psychoanalysis*, 60, 83-96.

American Psychiatric Association. (1994). *Diagnostic criteria from DSM-IV,* Washington, D.C.: American Psychiatric Association.

Bacal, H. (1985). Optimal responsiveness and the therapeutic process. In A. Goldberg (Ed.), *Progress in self psychology,* Vol. 1 (pp. 202-227). New York: Guilford Press.

Baker, H. S. (1991). Shorter-term psychotherapy: A self-psychological approach. In J.P. Barber & P. Crits-Christoph (Eds.), *Handbook of short-term dynamic psychotherapy* (pp. 287-318). New York: Basic Books.

Blanck, G. & R. (1974). *Ego psychology in theory and practice.* New York: Columbia University Press.

Blanck, G. & R. (1979). *Ego psychology II: Psychoanalytic developmental psychology*. New York: Columbia University Press.

Brandchaft, B. & Stolorow, R. D. (1984a). The borderline concept: Pathological character or iatrogenic myth? In J. Lichtenberg, M. Bornstein, & D. Silver (Eds.), *Empathy II* (pp. 333-358). Hillsdale, New Jersey: The Analytic Press.

Brandchaft, B. & Stolorow, R. D. (1984b). A current perspective on difficult patients. In P. E. Stepansky & A. Goldsberg (Eds.), *Kohut's legacy: Contributions to self psychology* (pp. 117-134). Hillsdale, New Jersey: The Analytic Press.

Cornett, C. (1991). Selfobject intervention in brief treatment with patients inappropriate for traditional brief psychotherapy models. *Clinical Social Work Journal*, 19, 131-148.

Corwin, M. D. (1996). Early intervention strategies with borderline clients. *Families in Society: The Journal of Contemporary Human Services*, 77, 40-48.

Davanloo, H. (1978). *Basic principles and techniques in short-term dynamic psychotherapy*. New York: Spectrum.

Davanloo, H. (1980). *Short-term dynamic psychotherapy*. New York: Jason Aronson.

Davanloo, H. (1991). *Unlocking the unconscious*. New York: Wiley.

Dungee-Anderson, D. (1992). Self-nurturing: A cognitive behavioral treatment approach for the borderline client. *Clinical Social Work Journal*, 20, 295-312.

Goldstein, E. G. (1990). *Borderline disorders: Clinical model and techniques*. New York: Guilford.

Goldstein, E. G. (1994). Self-disclosure in treatment: What therapists do and don't talk about. *Clinical Social Work Journal*, 22 (Winter, 1994).

Goldstein, E. G. (1995a). *Ego psychology and social work practice* (2nd ed.). New York: The Free Press.

Goldstein, E. G. & Noonan, Maryellen (1999). *Short-term treatment and social work practice*. New York: The Free Press.

Gunderson, J. G. & Chu, J. A. (1993). Treatment implications of past trauma in borderline personality disorder. *Harvard Review of Psychiatry*, 1, 75-81.

Heller, N. R., & Northcut, T. B. (1996). Utilizing cognitive-behavioral techniques in psychodynamic practice with clients diagnosed as borderline, *Clinical Social Work Journal*, 24, 203-215.

Herman, J. (1992). *Trauma and recovery*. New York: Basic Books.

Herman, J. L., Perry, J. C., & van der Kolk, B. (1989). Childhood trauma in borderline personality disorder. *American Journal of Psychiatry*, 146, 490-495.

Kernberg, O. F. (1975). *Borderline conditions and pathological narcissism*. New York: Jason Aronson.

Kernberg, O. F. (1984). *Severe personality disorders*. New Haven: Yale University Press.

Kernberg, O. F., Selzer, M. A., Koenigsberg, H. W., Carr, A. C., & Appelbaum, A. H. (1989). *Psychodynamic psychotherapy of borderline patients*. New York: Basic Books.

Kohut, H. (1971). *The analysis of the self*. New York: International Universities Press.

Kohut, H. (1977). *The restoration of the self*. New York: International Universities Press.

Kroll, J. (1993). *PTSD/borderlines in therapy.* New York: W. W. Norton.

Linehan, M. M. (1993). *Cognitive-behavioral treatment of borderline personality disorder.* New York: Guilford.

Luborsky, L. (1984). *Principles of psychoanalytic psychotherapy: A manual for supportive-expressive treatment.* New York: Basic Books.

Mahler, M., Pine, F., & Bergman, A. (1975). *The psychological birth of the human infant.* New York: Basic Books.

Malan, D. (1963). *A study of brief psychotherapy.* New York: Plenum.

Malan, D. (1976). *The frontier of brief psychotherapy.* Cambridge, MA: Harvard University Press.

Mann, J. (1973). *Time-limited psychotherapy.* Cambridge, MA: Harvard University Press.

Mann, J. (1991). Time-limited psychotherapy. In P. Crits-Christoph & J. P. Barber (Eds.), *Handbook of short-term dynamic psychotherapy* (pp. 17-43). New York: Basic Books.

Masterson, J. F. (1972). *Treatment of the borderline adolescent.* New York: Wiley-Interscience.

Masterson, J. F. (1976). *Treatment of the borderline adult.* New York: Brunner-Mazel.

Masterson, J. F. & Rinsley, D. (1975). The borderline syndrome: The role of the mother in the genesis and psychic structure of the borderline personality. *International Journal of Psychoanalysis*, 56, 163-77.

Messer, S. B. & Warren, C. S. (1995). *Models of brief psychodynamic therapy.* New York: Guilford Press.

Sifneos, P. (1972). *Short-term psychotherapy and emotional crisis.* Cambridge, MA: Harvard University Press.

Sifneos, P. E. (1979). *Short-term psychotherapy: Evaluation and technique.* New York: Plenum.

Sifneos, P. (1987). *Short-term dynamic psychotherapy* (2nd ed.). New York: Plenum.

Stadter, M. (1996). *Object relations brief therapy.* Northvale, NJ: Jason Aronson.

Strupp, H. H., & Binder, J. L. (1984). *Psychotherapy in a new key: A guide to time-limited dynamic psychotherapy.* New York: Basic Books.

Wells, M. & Glickhauf-Hughes, C. (1986). Techniques to develop object constancy with borderline clients. *Psychotherapy*, 23, 460-468.

Chapter 4
Interpretation in Short-Term Therapy: The Role of Level of Patient Functioning

Carol Tosone
Paul Crits-Christoph
Lester Luborsky

SUMMARY. There is much theoretical and clinical literature on the role of interpretation in psychoanalysis, psychoanalytic psychotherapy, and brief dynamic psychotherapy, but little supporting research data. Using 112 audiotaped sessions from 38 patients in supportive-expressive time-limited treatment, the present study hypothesized that therapists would modify the object and temporal content and frequency of their interpretations in relation to the level of patient functioning. The results did not support this hypothesis. Therapists were not less active with more interpretations for higher functioning patients, nor were they more active with fewer interpretations for lower functioning patients. Therapists were more active and made more genetic interpretations with married patients, regardless of level of patient functioning. The findings are discussed in terms of their implications for supportive-expressive psychodynamic therapy. *[Article copies available for a fee from The Haworth Document Delivery Service: 1-800-342-9678. E-mail address: getinfo@haworthpressinc.com <Website: http://www.haworthpressinc.com>]*

Carole Tosone, PhD, is Assistant Professor, Shirley M. Ehrenkranz School of Social Work, New York University. Paul Crits-Christoph, PhD, and Lester Luborsky, PhD, are Faculty, Department of Psychiatry, University of Pennsylvania.
Address correspondence to: Carol Tosone, New York University Ehrenkranz School of Social Work, 1 Washington Square North, New York, NY 10003.

[Haworth co-indexing entry note]: "Chapter 4. Interpretation in Short-Term Therapy: The Role of Level of Patient Functioning." Tosone, Carol, Paul Crits-Christoph, and Lester Luborsky. Co-published simultaneously in *Psychoanalytic Social Work* (The Haworth Press, Inc.) Vol. 6, No. 3/4, 1999, pp. 113-129; and: *Comparative Approaches in Brief Dynamic Psychotherapy* (ed: William Borden) The Haworth Press, Inc., 1999, pp. 113-129. Single or multiple copies of this article are available for a fee from The Haworth Document Delivery Service [1-800-342-9678, 9:00 a.m. - 5:00 p.m. (EST). E-mail address: getinfo@haworthpressinc.com].

KEYWORDS. Interpretation, level of patient functioning, brief psychotherapy

Interpretation is generally held to be the major curative factor in psychoanalysis, psychoanalytic psychotherapy, and short-term dynamic therapy (Arlow, 1987; Freud, 1912; Luborsky, 1984; Strachey, 1934). Described by Bibring (1954) as the "supreme agent in the hierarchy of therapeutic principles," interpretation is regarded as a central activity of the therapist, around which other aspects of treatment are organized to maximize its effectiveness. Despite the consensus of its clinical import, there is no universally accepted definition of psychoanalytic interpretation.

Both the concept of interpretation and its relationship to the therapeutic process have evolved over time. For Freud (1900), interpretation referred to the translation of the manifest into the latent content, whether this involved dreams, associations, symptoms, or behaviors of the neurotic patient. As the scope of psychoanalysis broadened to include patients with preoedipal and narcissistic pathology, interpretation also acquired new dimensions. With such lower functioning patients, the intent of interpretation shifted in relation to resistance, transference, and reconstruction. In a revised developmental and relational psychoanalytic framework, some authors (Chrazanowski, 1987; Kohut, 1971; Ornstein & Ornstein, 1975; Pine, 1986a) view interpretation primarily as a contact rather than a content or an insight promoting agent. In sharp contrast to traditional psychoanalysis, the transference neurosis is avoided in favor of providing a "holding environment" with lower functioning patients (Winnicott, 1965). Such therapy typically is more active and supportive, as well as less intense and interpretive. Activity involves the extent of the therapist's speech, exclusive of interpretations.

Not all psychoanalytic authors would concur with this approach. In particular, Kernberg (1975) and Masterson (1976) subscribe essentially to models of conflict, not those of developmental deficit. In discussing their clinical approaches to borderline patients, both consider interpretation to be the most important means of bringing about basic and lasting change. They assert that these patients can benefit from interpretations, including transference interpretations, early in treatment. In addition to conceptualizations of pathology and treatment approaches to lower functioning patients, controversy also exists in the use of the term "interpretation" throughout the history of psychoanalytic theory and practice. It has had diverse meanings and has so far failed to attain a generally agreed-upon, precise meaning. In their review of the literature on interpretation, Ornstein and Ornstein (1975) note a prevalent theme: most psychoanalytic theoreticians and clinicians regard interpretation as a way of understanding and explaining the patient's experience, including the genetic meanings of those experiences, both in and outside of treatment.

In actual practice, most clinicians are reported to use a mixture of interpretive (expressive) and holding (supportive) techniques early in treatment and throughout its course (Luborsky, 1984; Waldinger, 1987). Drawing upon the psychoanalytic literature on how therapist interventions should be tailored to the patient's level of functioning, Luborsky (1984) presents a supportive-expressive model in which supportive interventions are implemented with patients at lower levels of functioning who need strengthening of defenses, while interpretive interventions are used more frequently with patients at higher levels of functioning. From a clinical point of view, the interpretive techniques Luborsky and others employ may run the gamut from tentatively offering a thought or an observation to the point of delivering an edict by confronting the patient with an "objective truth" (Chrazanowski, 1987).

While clinicians have believed most strongly in the power of interpretation, they have provided little in the way of research data to support their convictions. There are very few solid research studies on interpretation, and these studies have a range of aims, methods, and results. Studies of the role of interpretation in psychoanalysis, psychoanalytic psychotherapy, and brief dynamic psychotherapy have been in the following areas: (a) depth of interpretation (Dittman, 1952; Harway, Dittman, Raush, Borden & Rigler, 1955; Howe, 1962; Rausch et al., 1956; Speisman, 1959), (b) process studies of the immediate in-session responses of patients to interpretations (Garduk & Haggard, 1972), (c) outcome studies relating interpretation to treatment progress (Malan, 1976; Marziali, 1984; Marziali & Sullivan, 1980; Piper, Debbane, Bienvenu, de Carufel, & Garant, 1986), and (d) accuracy of interpretation (Crits-Christoph, Cooper, & Luborsky, 1988; Silberschatz, Fretter, & Curtis, 1986).

Two studies directly addressed dimensions analogous to the level of patient functioning and therapist interventions. Piper, Joyce, McCallum, and Azim (1993) investigated the relationship between two measures of therapist techniques and outcome of short-term dynamic psychotherapy: (a) the concentration of therapist transference interpretations (the proportion of therapist statements per session that referred to the therapist), and (b) the correspondence of therapist transference interpretations with the therapist's initial dynamic formulation of each case. Quality of object relations was rated by a clinician based upon an interview that examined life long patterns in relationships. Interpretations were identified for 64 patients treated in short-term dynamic psychotherapy. The main finding from this study was that high rates of transference interpretation were associated with poor outcome for patients who had a history of high quality of object relations.

Horowitz, Marmar, Weiss, De Witt, and Rosenbaum (1984) found another dimension similar to patient level of functioning (developmental level of self-concept) interacted with therapist techniques in predicting the outcome of brief dynamic therapy. Greater use of exploratory interventions was found to be associated with positive outcome for patients higher in developmental level of self-concept, while greater use of supportive intervention was associated with better outcome for patients lower in developmental level of self-concept.

Neither of the above studies, however, directly examined the correlation of level of patient functioning with therapist interventions. Investigation of the extent to which therapists modify their interventions depending upon level of patient functioning would potentially provide empirical validation of a common psychoanalytic concept and a central principle of Luborsky's (1984) supportive-expressive model. Moreover, recently it has been suggested that research on the process of psychotherapy in relation to outcome is inherently confounded by the tendency of therapists to respond to patients with varying amounts and types of interventions based upon patient needs (Stiles & Shapiro, 1994). To the extent that therapists routinely exhibit different types of "responsiveness," psychotherapy process-outcome research would need to steer away from designs that attempt to relate amount or frequency of various types of interventions to outcome. With a given patient, for example, a low level of a certain type of intervention (for example, transference interpretation) might be a function of an appropriate clinical response by a therapist to the patient's needs or level of functioning, rather than an indication of bad technique, and therefore no relation between frequency of this technique and outcome would be found across a sample of patients. Thus, studies examining the relation to level of patient functioning and therapist interventions can shed light on the possible design of psychotherapy process-outcome studies.

The current study was designed to test the treatment recommendations of Luborsky (1984) by examining whether therapists varied their frequencies of different interventions as a function of level of patient functioning. Based upon Luborsky (1984), we hypothesized that therapists will make fewer interpretations with lower functioning patients compared to higher functioning patients and that therapists will make more genetic interpretations with higher functioning patients compared to lower functioning patients. We also hypothesized, based on other clinical writings that, in an effort to be supportive, therapists will be more verbally active with lower functioning patients. Moreover, the current investigation explored the role of other patient factors (age, marital status, sex) in relation to frequency of different therapist interventions.

METHOD

Patients

The patient group consisted of 38 outpatients who were recruited for short-term dynamic psychotherapy through the University of Pennsylvania's Center for Psychotherapy Research. The descriptive characteristics of the patients are summarized in Table 1. Of the thirty-eight patients, 29 (76.3%) were women and 9 (23.7%) were men. The patients ranged in age from 22 to 60, with a mean age of 37.1 (Median = 37.0, SD = 9.6). Twelve (31.6%) of the patients were married or cohabitating for more than one year while 26 (68.4%) were not married. For statistical purposes, the categories of previously married and never married were combined. In regard to education, all of the 38 patients had at least a high school degree, with 11 (28.9%) having some college, 15 (39.5%) having a college degree, and 9 (23.7%) having a graduate degree. Thirty-four (89.5%) of the patients were white and 4 (10.5%) were black.

Treatment

All patients were seen in short-term individual psychotherapy for a period of sixteen weeks (one session per week). Using Luborsky's (1984) treatment manual, the therapists employed time-limited sup-

TABLE 1. Descriptive Characteristics of Patients

Demographic Variable	Number	Percentage
Age (Years)		
22-29	8	21.0%
30-39	1	39.5%
40-49	1	26.3%
50-60	5	13.2%
Sex		
Male	9	23.7%
Female	2	76.3%
Marital Status		
Married, cohabitating	1	31.6%
Not married	2	68.4%
Education		
High school degree/some college	14	36.8%
College degree	1	39.5%
Graduate degree	9	23.7%
Ethnicity		
White	3	89.5%
African-American	4	10.5%

portive-expressive treatment, an abbreviated version of psychoanalytic psychotherapy. Supportive-expressive psychotherapy was originally developed at the Menninger Foundation and later revised by Lester Luborsky at the University of Pennsylvania. Supportive-expressive therapy was particularly suited to this study, as it had applicability to a broad range of patients and a brief, finite length which enhanced its value for clinical research. Within the time-limited version of supportive-expressive therapy, the therapist is expected to make an accurate decision within the first few sessions about the main relationship theme. This theme then becomes the focus of the therapeutic effort.

Therapists

Four doctoral-level mental health professionals (3 female, 1 male) participated in this research project. All four were experienced psychoanalytic psychotherapists who received ongoing group supervision. Two of the therapists had previously participated in outcome and process studies of supportive-expressive psychotherapy. Each therapist treated several randomly assigned patients. The therapists were blind to the level of patient functioning as measured on the Health-Sickness Rating Scale. The therapists were not involved in the selection of patients for the project.

Measures

The Schedule for Affective Disorders and Schizophrenia (SADS). The SADS (Endicott & Spitzer, 1978) is a highly structured diagnostic interview that was used in the current project to select patients who had a diagnosis of major depressive disorder according to the DSM-III. The SADS involves a progression of questions, items, and criteria that systematically identify specific Research Diagnostic Criteria (RDC). The SADS was administered twice at baseline, with the second administration scheduled one week after the first. Patients needed to meet diagnostic criteria for major depressive disorder at both assessments to qualify for the study.

Health-Sickness Rating Scale. The Health-Sickness Rating Scale (HSRS; Luborsky, 1962) is an eight-item clinician-rated measure of mental health based on an interview. The reliability and validity of the HSRS has been investigated in numerous studies (see Luborsky & Bachrach, 1974). A trained doctoral level diagnostician administered the SADS and rated the HSRS immediately following the SADS interview. The scores from the second baseline assessment were used for analysis in the current study.

The average of the eight-item HSRS was used as a general measure of psychiatric severity and level of patient functioning. The scale of the HSRS ranges from 0 to 100. For purposes of the current study, patients with scores of 50 or below were classified as lower functioning and those with scores of 51 or above were classified as higher functioning. The obtained raw scores ranged from 36 to 60, with a mean of 50. Twenty-one patients were categorized as lower functioning; seventeen were categorized as higher functioning. There were no significant differences between higher and lower functioning patients in regard to age, race, gender, marital status, or education.

Sessions. All 16 treatment sessions were audiotaped. The current study examined therapist interpretations drawn from transcripts of three early-in-treatment treatment sessions (sessions 3, 4, and 5). For 37 patients, all three sessions were available and used; for one patient, only session 3 was used (sessions 4 and 5 were not audible). Thus, a total of 112 sessions were included.

Identifying Interpretations. A therapist response scheme was developed to help judges clearly differentiate interpretations from other therapist responses. The categories included (a) interpretations, (b) clarifying remarks, (c) questions, and (d) all remaining remarks. Three judges independently coded all therapist statements in the 112 sessions using this scheme. All judges were blind to level of patient functioning.

A response was considered an interpretation if it met at least one of the following criteria: (a) the therapist explained possible reasons for a patient's thoughts, feelings, or behaviors, (b) the therapist alluded to similarities between the patient's present circumstances and other life experiences (Crits-Christoph et al., 1988). Adhering to these criteria avoided problems in coding interpretations according to a classical psychoanalytic definition. Such a definition involves making the unconscious become conscious. To code interpretations using these criteria would require complex judgments about the patient's "unconscious processes" and the patient's perception of same.

An interpretation was distinguished from a clarifying remark, in that the latter involved the therapist's observations about the patient's thoughts, feelings, or behavior without providing reasons for its occurrence ("You seem to feel pretty angry"). Additionally, a response was coded as a question when the therapist asked a general question which did not meet the criteria for an interpretation or a clarifying remark ("What happened when you were with her last night?"). All other therapist comments that failed to satisfy the requirements of the preceding three categories were placed in a residual classification of responses. Interjudge agreement for differentiating interpretations from other comments was 93.5%. The average number of all interpretations per session for the 38 patients was 3.2.

Interpretations were further coded in terms of their objects (persons referred to in the interpretation), temporality (reference to childhood, past, present, or future), and frequency (number of interpretations per session per patient). Three types of interpretations were of special interest for this study: (a) genetic transference interpretations which involve linking the therapist, parents, childhood, and present. For example, "When I comment on your being late, it reminds you of the times when your mother scolded you as a child for being late." (b) Here-and-now transference interpretations which involve only the therapist and the present. For example, "You feel safe in sessions with me." (c) Extra-transference interpretations which involve all objects other than the therapist, either alone or in combination, and all types of temporality (childhood, past, present, and/or future). For example, "It sounds like you felt very hurt when your sister didn't invite you to her party." For the measures of genetic interpretations, transference interpretations, and extra-transference interpretations, the final score for each patient was the average frequency of these types of interpretations within the three sessions coded. In addition, the overall level of non-interpretative therapist activity during a session (a count of all therapist statements made during a session minus interpretations) was computed, averaging over the three sessions available for each patient.

In order to code object and temporal aspects of interpretations, statements which were already identified as interpretations were presented to three separate judges, all of whom were blind to level of patient functioning. The average frequency per session of each class of object and each time frame was computed, and the three session scores were then averaged to yield a final score for each patient on each category.

Reliability was calculated on the average number of each type of object (therapist, parents, significant others, self, siblings, none) and temporal (childhood, past, present, future) aspects per session. Based on the sample of 38 cases, the pooled interjudge reliabilities (intraclass correlation coefficients) were .85 for therapist, .99 for parents, .95 for significant others, .76 for self, .36 for siblings, .87 for none, .74 for childhood, .84 for past, .98 for present, and .56 for future. The low interrater reliability for siblings (.36) and future (.56) is based on their low frequency in the sample and were therefore dropped from analysis.

For the 38 patients, there was a mean of 122.9 non-interpretive therapist statements made per session (range = 56 to 277; SD = 49). While there were no genetic transference interpretations in any of the sessions, there was at least one genetic interpretation for fourteen of the patients. The average number of all interpretations per session for the 38 patients was 3.2 (SD = 1.9), with a range from 1 to 9 interpretations per session.

RESULTS

Relation of Demographic Factors to Therapist Interpretations

We were first interested in examining whether therapists varied their interventions depending upon demographic variables. Little variability on ethnicity and education existed within the sample, so these factors were not examined. The relation of age, gender, and marital status (currently married versus not married) to therapist interventions were examined via Pearson correlations between these variables and frequency of therapist interventions. The results are presented in Table 2. One finding emerged. Therapists made significantly ($p < .05$) more genetic interpretations with married patients than unmarried ones (see Table 2). There were also trends ($p < .10$) for therapists to be more verbally active (higher frequency of non-interpretive statements) in general with married patients than unmarried ones, to give more here-and-now tranference interpretations to female patients, and to give more extra-transference interpretations to younger patients. Thus, each of the demographic variables was related to one of the therapist intervention measures to some degree. Although the findings at the trend level are difficult to interpret substantively, these relationships do present possible confounds for examination of the relationship between level of patient functioning and therapist intervention. Age, sex, and marital status were included as control variables in subsequent analyses.

TABLE 2. Correlations Between Demographic Variables and Frequency of Therapist Interventions

Therapist Interventions	Marital Status	Age	Sex
Non-Interpretations	$-.33$	$-.19$	.01
Interpretations	$-.11$	$-.25$	$-.12$
Here-and-Now Transference Interpretations	$-.08$	$-.03$	$-.32$
Extra-Trasference Interpretations	$-.10$	$-.27$	$-.11$
Genetic Interpretations	$-.35^*$	$-.06$	$-.16$

Marital Status coded as 1 = married, 2 = not married. Gender coded as 1 = male; 2 = female.
$^*p < .05$

Relation of Level of Patient Functioning to Therapist Interventions

Table 3 presents the results of partial correlation analyses, relating the HSRS to measures of therapist interventions, controlling for age, sex, and marital status. The central hypothesis that the therapist would modify the content and frequency of interpretation based on the level of patient functioning was not supported. Therapists did not make more interpretations with higher functioning patients, nor did they exhibit a higher level of verbal activity with lower functioning patients. There was a near significant trend for therapists to make more here-and-now transference interpretations with lower functioning patients than higher functioning ones ($p = .06$; two-tailed).

DISCUSSION

In considering the effect of demographic factors such as age, sex, and marital status on the content and frequency of therapist interpretation, one must taken into account the factor of attractiveness for treatment. The research literature suggests that therapists tend to view younger patients as more attractive and more suitable for psychotherapy than older patients (Hamberg et al., 1967; Luborsky, Crits-Christoph, Mintz, & Auerbach, 1988). These studies showed consequently that younger patients profited more from therapy. While the present study did not address psychotherapy outcome, it may suggest that therapists are more active and interpretive with younger patients because

TABLE 3. Partial Correlations of Level of Patient Functioning (HSRS) to Frequency of Therapist Interventions

Therapist Interventions	HSRS
Non-Interpretations	− .13
Interpretations	.04
Here-and-Now Transference Interpretations	− .32
Extra-Transference Interpretations	.10
Genetic Interpretations	.11

Note. Age, sex, and marital status partialled out.
HSRS = Health Sickness Rating Scale.

they are more interested in them. This could also indicate support for the "YAVIS" concept; that is, that therapists prefer working with patients who are young, attractive, verbal, intelligent, and successful. Age, coupled with similarities of therapists and patients, has been found to facilitate the formation of the patient's experience of the working alliance and to lead to better outcome (Lesser, 1961; Luborsky et al., 1988).

In the present study, all four therapists were married. While patients were not aware of the marital status of their therapists, the similarities between them may have been sensed. These therapists were more active and made more genetic interpretations with married patients. Similarities in demographic qualities, interests, values, and orientation toward interpersonal relations have been found to facilitate close working relationships. In the Penn Psychotherapy Project (Luborsky et al., 1988) the presence of patient-therapist demographic similarities related to patient improvement.

Elkin et al. (1989) found that marital status was a significant prediction of outcome in short-term treatment for depression. In the present study, married patients and therapists may have seen each other as having shared backgrounds, as being alike and able to understand one another. Therapists may have taken more interest in, and therefore were more active with, their married patients. In regard to the frequency of genetic interpretation with married patients, there is no known clinical or research literature which specifically addresses this topic. One can only speculate that in their genetic interpretations, perhaps the therapists were making comparisons between the patients' childhood relationship to their parents and their present day relationship to their spouses. In other words, in their interpretative work, the therapists may have focused more on their shared experiences with the patients. However, it should be mentioned that the overall pattern of findings in regard to demographic variables was only one statistically significant ($p < .05$) finding out of 18 correlations examined. Thus, our finding with marital status awaits replication before any confidence can be placed in this result.

Turning to the larger question of why the level of patient functioning was not found to influence the content and frequency of therapist interpretation, several issues, including the limitations as well as the theoretical, clinical, and research implications of the study, must be taken into account. Limitations included those imposed by a homogeneous sample (all with major depression), a relatively small sample size, and the use of transcripts from early treatment sessions. Had these limitations not existed, perhaps more correlations might have reached statistical significance.

Despite the considerable evolution in theory regarding the use of transference, implementation in psychodynamic treatment may not follow as closely. Although theoreticians emphasize the importance of transference interpretation, clinicians do not necessarily follow their recommendations. The findings of the study seem to indicate that there are some discrepancies between theory and practice; that is, therapists do not always follow the recommendations in the literature, particularly in regard to the analysis of transference. Therapists conducting short-term dynamic psychotherapy are expected to address transference manifestations quickly, rather than allowing them to unfold gradually, as in traditional psychoanalysis. In our data, there was a trend ($p < .10$) for therapists to make more here-and-now transference interpretations with lower functioning patients than with higher functioning patients. Although the direction of this finding is contrary to our prediction, it is possible that such "here-and-now" statements on the part of the therapist are less inferential and less abstract compared to genetic interpretations. Therapists may feel that less inferential interpretations are more appropriate for lower functioning patients. They may indeed be altering their technique depending on patient level of functioning, but rather than decrease the amount of expressive interventions, therapists simply change the form and content of the expressive interventions. Further research, however, is necessary to see if this trend in our data is a reliable result.

The fact that the level of patient functioning does not in general predict the type of therapist intervention also raises the question as to whether therapists can adequately implement this aspect of Luborsky's (1984) treatment manual. It is unclear, however, whether this is a fault of the therapists or a fault of the manual and its associated training that did not teach therapists adequately how to vary interventions as a function of level of patient functioning. The fact that they should vary interventions depending on level of patient functioning is suggested by the studies of Piper et al. (1993) and Horowitz et al. (1984). It should be kept in mind, however, that their assessments of level of patient functioning differed from that used in the present investigation. Perhaps better training procedures need to be implemented.

In addition to resistances, other factors to consider in the interpretation of the data are that early treatment sessions are generally used to establish a working alliance and to educate the patient about treatment (Luborsky, 1984; Pine, 1986a; Sifneos, 1972). Additionally, Kohut (1971) has remarked that the stance of inhibiting one's responses may encourage the patient's perception of the therapist as a cold, distant figure, regardless of the transference predisposition. Clinically, the personality and style of the individual therapists should also be taken into account in the interpretation of the data. Therapists may work differently with each patient, in response to the patient's uniqueness and to one's countertransference (Storr, 1979).

In regard to the research implications, the present study has added to the operational dimensions of interpretation. In contrast to previous studies on object interpretation which focused on particular persons in the patient's life (Malan, 1976; Marziali, 1984; Marziali & Sullivan, 1980; Piper et al., 1986), the present study examined not only specific persons, but also the temporal aspects of interpretation. Whereas, in these previous studies, a transference interpretation was comprised of the therapist-parent link, the present study added the childhood-present link to describe a genetic transference interpretation, and a here-and-now transference interpretation. This study could distinguish between two types of transference interpretations, which previous object interpretation studies had not done.

As the results of this study seem to indicate, the research literature on interpretation has not reached a consensus on its essential aspects. Nor has the research literature indicated which dimensions of interpretation could impact most effectively on treatment outcome. Perhaps future research on interpretation will lead to such an accord.

CONCLUSION

The findings of this study have particular relevance to social work practitioners who traditionally have devoted themselves to the treatment of patients from all levels of functioning. With the current thrust toward short-term treatment in a managed care market, social work clinicians must adapt their techniques to meet these demands. This study raises an important question for the social work practitioner, which is whether interpretation is core to the treatment process. At present, one cannot make recommendations about clinical technique based upon this study's research results. Future research may eventually address the question of how therapists can vary their content and frequency of interpretation with different types of patients to provide positive treatment outcomes.

REFERENCES

Arlow, J.A. (1987). The dynamics of interpretation. *Psychoanalytic Quarterly, 56,* 68-87.

Bibring, E. (1954). Psychoanalysis and the dynamic psychotherapies. *Journal of the American Psychoanalytic Association, 2,* 745-770.

Chrazanowski, G. (1987). Psychoanalytic interpretation in modern, clinical perspective: A flight from history. *Contemporary Psychoanalysis, 23,* 469-482.

Crits-Christoph, P., Cooper, A., & Luborsky, L. (1988). The accuracy of therapists' interpretations and the outcome of dynamic psychotherapy. *Journal of Consulting and Clinical Psychology,* 56(4), 490-495.

Dittman, A. (1952). The interpersonal process in psychotherapy: Development of a research method. *Journal of Abnormal and Social Psychology, 47,* 236-244.

Elkin, I., Shea, T., Watkins, J.T., Imber, S.D., Sotsky, S.M., Collins, J.F., Glass, D.R., Pilkonis, P.A., Leber, W.R., Docherty, J.P., Piester, S.J., & Parloff, M.B. (1989). National Institute of Mental Health Treatment of Depression Collaborative Research Program: General Effectiveness of Treatments. *Archives of General Psychiatry, 46,* 971-982.

Endicott, J. & Spitzer, R.L. (1978). A diagnostic interview: The schedule for affective disorders and schizophrenia. *Archives of General Psychiatry, 35,* 837-844.

Freud, S. (1900). The interpretation of dreams. *Standard Edition, 4-5.*

Freud, S. (1912). Recommendations to physicians practicing psychoanalysis. *Standard Edition, 12,* 110-120.

Garduk, E., & Haggard, E. (1972). Immediate effects on patients of psychoanalytic interpretations. *Psychological Issues, 7* (Monograph 28).

Hamberg, D., Bibring, G., Fisher, C., Stanton, A., Wallerstein, R., Weinstock, H., & Haggard, E. (1967). Report of ad hoc committee on central fact-gathering of the American Psychoanalytic Association. *Journal of the American Psychoanalytic Association, 15,* 841-861.

Harway, N., Dittman, A., Raush, H., Bordin, E., & Rigler, D. (1955). The measurement of depth of interpretation. *Journal of Consulting Psychology,* 19(4), 247-253.

Horowitz, M. J., Marmar, C. Weiss, D.S., De Witt, K.N., & Rosenbaum, R. (1984). Brief psychotherapy of bereavement reactions. *Archives of General Psychiatry, 41,* 438-448.

Howe, E. (1962). Anxiety-arousal and specificity: Rated correlates of depth of interpretation statements. *Journal of Consulting Psychology, 26* (2), 178-184.

Kernberg, O. (1975). *Borderline conditions and pathological narcissism.* New York: Jason Aronson, Inc.

Kohut, H. (1971). *The analysis of the self.* New York: International Universities Press, Inc.

Lesser, W. (1961). The relationship between counseling progress and empathic understanding. *Journal of Counseling Psychology, 8,* 330-336.

Luborsky, L. (1962). Clinicians' judgements of mental health: A proposed scale. *Archives of General Psychiatry, 7,* 407-417.

Luborsky, L. (1984). *Principles of psychoanalytic psychotherapy: A manual for supportive-expressive treatment.* NY: Basic Books.

Luborsky, L., & Bachrach, H.M. (1974). Factors influencing clinicians' judgments of mental health: Experience with the Health-Sickness Rating Scale. *Archives of General Psychiatry, 31,* 292-299.

Luborsky, L., Crits-Christoph, P., Mintz, J., & Auerbach, A. (1988). *Who will benefit from psychotherapy?* NY: Basic Books.

Malan, D.M. (1976). *Toward the validation of dynamic psychotherapy.* New York: Plenum Press.

Marziali, E. (1984). Prediction of outcome of brief psychotherapy from therapist interpretive interventions. *Archives of General Psychiatry, 41,* 301-304.

Marziali, E. & Sullivan, J. (1980). Methodological issues in the content analysis of brief psychotherapy. *British Journal of Medical Psychology, 53,* 19-27.

Masterson, J.F. (1976). *Psychotherapy of the borderline adult.* New York: Brunner and Mazel.

Ornstein, A. & Ornstein, P. (1975). On the interpretive process in psychoanalysis. *International Journal of Psychoanalytic Psychotherapy, 4,* 219-271.

Pine, F. (1986). *Developmental theory and clinical process.* New Haven: Yale University Press.

Piper, W., Debbane, E., Bienvenu, J., de Carufel, F., & Garant, J. (1986). Relationship between the object of focus of therapist interpretations and outcome in short-term individual psychotherapy. *British Journal of Medical Psychology, 59,* 1-11.

Piper, W., Joyce, A.S., McCallum, M. & Azim, H. F. (1993). Concentration and correspondence of transference interpretations in short-term psychotherapy. *Journal of Consulting and Clinical Psychology, 67,* 586-595.

Rausch, H., Sperber, Z., Rigler, D., Williams, J., Harway, N., Bordin, E., Dittman, A. & Hays, W. (1956). A dimensional analysis of depth of interpretation. *Journal of Consulting Psychology, 20* (1), 43-48.

Sifneos, P.E. (1972). *Short term psychotherapy and emotional crisis.* Cambridge: Harvard University Press.

Silbershatz, G., Fretter, P., & Curtis, J. (1986). How do interpretations influence the process of psychotherapy. *Journal of Consulting and Clinical Psychology, 54* (5), 646-652.

Speisman, J. (1959). Depth of interpretation and verbal resistance in psychotherapy. *Journal of Consulting Psychology, 23,* 93-99.

Stiles, W.B. & Shapiro, D.A. (1994). Disabuse of the drug metaphor: Psychotherapy process outcome correlations. *Journal of Consulting and Clinical Psychology, 62,* 942-948.

Storr, A. (1979). *The art of psychotherapy.* New York: Methuen.

Strachey, J. (1934). The nature of the therapeutic action of psycho-analysis. *International Journal of Psychiatry, 15,* 127-159.

Waldinger, R.J. (1987). Intensive psychodynamic therapy with borderline patients: An overview. *American Journal of Psychiatry, 144,* 267-274.

Winnicott, D.W. (1965). *The maturational processes and the facilitating environment.* New York: International Universities Press, Inc.

Chapter 5

Development, Psychopathology, and Brief Psychotherapy

Erika Schmidt

SUMMARY. When using a developmental model to conceptualize curative factors in brief psychotherapy, the impact of the developmental process and the nature of the psychopathology presented by the patient must be taken into account. Both factors shape the therapeutic work. A case example of a young adult in the midst of developmental transition illustrates these issues. *[Article copies available for a fee from The Haworth Document Delivery Service: 1-800-342-9678. E-mail address: getinfo@haworthpressinc.com <Website: http://www.haworthpressinc.com>]*

KEYWORDS. Development, psychopathology, brief psychotherapy

INTRODUCTION

Among the proliferation of theoretical models of brief dynamic psychotherapy, those based on developmental theory have the least

Erika Schmidt, MSW, is Faculty Member, Institute for Clinical Social Work, Chicago; Clinical Social Worker, Student Counseling and Resource Service, University of Chicago; and maintains a private practice in Chicago.

Address correspondence to: Erika Schmidt, Institute for Clinical Social Work, 68 East Wacker Place, Suite 1400, Chicago, IL 60601.

[Haworth co-indexing entry note]: "Chapter 5. Development, Psychopathology, and Brief Psychotherapy." Schmidt, Erika. Co-published simultaneously in *Psychoanalytic Social Work* (The Haworth Press, Inc.) Vol. 6, No. 3/4, 1999, pp. 131-143; and: *Comparative Approaches in Brief Dynamic Psychotherapy* (ed: William Borden) The Haworth Press, Inc., 1999, pp. 131-143. Single or multiple copies of this article are available for a fee from The Haworth Document Delivery Service [1-800-342-9678, 9:00 a.m. - 5:00 p.m. (EST). E-mail address: getinfo@haworthpressinc.com].

clear organizing principles and the least specific guidelines for intervention. If the four "essential elements" of brief therapy include a time limit, specific criteria for patient selection, a well-defined focus or central theme, and a high level of therapist activity (Groves, 1996, p. xi; Strupp and Binder, 1984), then developmentally based brief therapy is characterized by selecting patients in the process of life-course transitions and by a therapeutic focus on the developmental challenges of the current situation. Accordingly, such an approach deemphasizes conflict, deficit, psychopathology, and character structure. Problems are defined in terms of an adaptive failure to a life stage or a life crisis, whether accidental, like a loss through death or divorce, or predictable, like leaving home at the end of adolescence. Because of the developmental urgency of their needs, a developmental focus is often used in work with children and adolescents, but can be applied across a wide range of life course issues over the life span (White, Burke and Havens, 1981; Basch, 1995; Messer and Warren, 1995; Schmidt, 1996). Highlighting the developmental aspects of brief psychotherapy raises the question of how to understand the curative factors in a time-limited therapeutic process.

The developmental process contains its own intrinsic motivation and momentum that can be utilized in therapeutic work (Emde, 1990). Clower (1980) states, "Development is characterized by an active and persistent striving for optimal adaptation–and it has a strong self-righting tendency" (p. 180). This progressive impetus has the potential to make brief therapy at a critical developmental juncture particularly effective. Researchers have identified periods of qualitative change in development during which organizational shifts across affective, cognitive, social and motor domains of functioning occur. The most prominent of these are 2-3 months, 7-9 months, 15-18 months, 3 years, 5-7 years, 11-13 years, 15-16 years, and 18-20 years. These shifts are propelled by maturational factors which are then followed by periods of reorganization and consolidation (Emde, 1980). The subjective experience is often one of discontinuity.

At these times of transition, there is some disruption of ongoing psychological functioning that allows for the integration of new information about the self. Stern (1995) refers to these times as "clinical windows" (p. 155) in which a person's previously established psychological equilibrium can no longer be sustained under the impact of new developmental experience. Because old modes of functioning no longer work and new modes are not yet in place, these transitional periods can be excellent opportunities for therapeutic work. Often, the anxiety associated with disruptions caused by developmental shifts is the underlying precipitant for requests for therapy. Winnicott (1971) calls these "sacred" moments in which the therapist has "a great opportunity for being in touch with the child" (p. 4). At the point of disruption, the therapist can intervene, offering assistance in the process of integration and consolidation that follows. Viewed from this perspective, brief therapy is a temporal format that conforms to the developmental process at times of change and transition.

In considering the way in which brief therapy works during such periods, many authors draw a sharp distinction between facilitating progressive development and addressing issues of psychopathology or character structure. In his description of brief, preventive work with adolescents, some with very significant pathology, Laufer (1975) endorses the use of brief treatment saying, "What it can contribute–and I do not think we should expect anything beyond this–is to help prevent the existing pathology from interfering with the ongoing developmental process; that is to say, it can make it easier for the adolescent to confront the specific developmental tasks, thereby enabling the developmental process to proceed" (p. 525). White, Burke and Havens (1981) make a similar point about work with adults in an article in which they suggest matching the model of brief treatment to the specific conflicted developmental task in adult life. They comment, "The effectiveness of short-term work can best be seen, perhaps, as helping patients over developmental impasses rather than 'curing' individuals or producing profound character changes, unless such changes are a function of development" (p. 244).

Winnicott's creative, incisive use of a single or short series of therapeutic consultations also highlights the impact of brief intervention on the developmental process. "Whereas a child was caught up in a knot in regard to the emotional development, the interview has resulted in a loosening of the knot and a forward movement in the developmental process" (1971, p. 5). He cautions that the child or adolescent must have access to the "environmental provision of the kind that is needed . . . I rely on an 'average expectable environment' to meet and to make use of the changes that have taken place in the boy or girl in the interview, changes which indicate a loosening of the knot in the developmental process" (1971, p. 5). An interference in development has been resolved, and the resources within the environment will sustain the forward progression. Basch (1995) makes a similar point in describing a developmental model of brief therapy with adults. However, he suggests that the resources, which Winnicott locates in the environment, are to be found by gaining access to the patient's strengths that are no longer functioning adaptively. He states, "My focus is not primarily on the origins of the patient's difficulties in childhood but on the reasons why the strengths the patient has developed no longer serve and what if anything I might be able to do to rectify that situation" (p. xxv). He tries to pinpoint the area within what he labels the developmental spiral where the patient has become derailed and in the therapy works to reinstate the previous level of functioning. In defining a developmental stance, Messer and Warren (1995) separate the current situation from its genetic origins and history: "The developmental context provides a means for understanding and addressing problems in their immediate context, bringing a here-and-now emphasis, a crisis intervention orientation, and suggesting therapeutic foci that do not require sustained exploration of early life" (p. 282).

This view offers some conceptual clarity, but the distinction between development and psychopathology may be easier to maintain in theory than in practice. Since interferences in development often reflect some underlying difficulty, therapy must address the problem in some form, if not directly, then derivatively. Stern (1995) and Schafer (1992) both suggest alternative approaches to understanding the way a developmental approach to brief therapy may work. Stern disputes the traditional idea of developmental phases that assigns certain critical periods to the establishment of phase-specific issues. Instead, he states, "The basic clinically relevant issues such as trust, attachment, dependence, independence, control, autonomy, mastery, individuation, and self-regulation are life course issues. They are not issues that are age- or phase-specific. No one early period of life is specially devoted to the indelible writing of a definitive version of any of these issues . . . Rather, they are being worked on all the time. Nonethless, the manner in which they get worked on and the forms these issues take change across developmental epochs. The battleground constantly shifts, but the war may stay the same" (p. 70). Because of the discontinuous nature of the developmental process, the impact of new experiences cannot be fully anticipated and areas of vulnerability are likely to reappear in new contexts. Stern applies lessons learned from parent-infant psychotherapy, proposing the notion of serial brief treatment to explain the way people may make use of psychotherapy briefly and episodically as they repeatedly confront the same challenges in new contexts. He recognizes that the "working through must be longitudinal in time" (p. 157) as life-span issues, such as attachment, trust, autonomy, and regulation, are confronted in the developmental medium of the moment.

Schafer (1992) enters the discussion of brief psychotherapy by addressing technical interventions. He advocates that therapists "speak personally" (p. 288) and directly to the patient to enhance the alliance. He also suggests that therapists hasten the understanding of therapy by "talking to patients pedagogically" (p. 283), providing an education about the therapeutic process and about psychological life. Such an active, authoritative therapeutic stance is designed to create an "exploratory or investigative atmosphere" (p. 293) and to facilitate an identification with the attitude of the therapist toward the internal world. His recommendations are consistent with the general rule in brief treatment that the therapist assume a more active role in guiding the treatment. In contrast to most models of brief treatment, Schafer does not organize the process around a certain theme or goal, but does "focus on the phenomenology of experience" (p. 299). He describes brief treatments as abbreviated versions of long-term therapies with patients who, but for circumstances or defenses, might well be in psychoanalysis. Schafer's view is not explicitly a developmental one and, in fact, he emphasizes insight and self-awareness, rather than resumption of the developmental process, as the curative elements of the treatment. However, his educative approach, coupled with an open-ended exploratory attitude, is compatible with a developmental model and with Stern's suggestion that patients avail themselves of brief treatments during certain clinical windows of opportunity in which problematic issues are revived in response to developmental challenges.

The following case report describes a brief, six-month therapy with a late adolescent woman as she completed her college education and prepared for the transition to young adulthood. According to conventional prognostic indicators, she was a poor candidate for brief intervention, given her chronic, pervasive depression and character pathology and the absence of hopefulness about the possibility of being helped. The developmental issues she faced created a crisis that permitted therapeutic entry into longstanding difficulties which then enabled her to move forward developmentally.

CASE REPORT

Toward the end of fall of her senior year of college, Sarah presented at the college counseling service with symptoms of depression. On the intake form checklist, she marked as her areas of concern self-esteem, crying, anxiety, depression, and intimate relationships and added that she is angry and irritable, has trouble eating and sleeping, and is afraid to be alone. She elaborated on this, writing, "Things just seem to be out of control. I have never felt particularly happy or stable . . . At times I feel like my world has fallen apart and there is nothing I can do to put it back together. I have also felt unusually unmotivated about school." In the initial interview with an intake worker, she told of an ambivalent relationship with her boyfriend, reported a depressive episode during her senior year of high school, noticed by the family doctor but not treated, and difficulty separating from her family. About her family, she said, "They tell me what to think and feel." She denied suicidal thoughts or intent and agreed with the recommendation for therapy. Between November and June, Sarah was seen for 20 sessions–with interruptions due to vacations, family crisis, and a planned trip to potential graduate schools.

In the initial session, Sarah began by saying that she feels differently than she did during the intake interview and therefore could not articulate her presenting problems in any meaningful way. She described herself as someone who never rebelled, who always did the right thing, and who planned her life carefully so that nothing unpredictable would happen to her. She spent most of this session describing various romantic and interpersonal entanglements in great detail, as if it all happened unwittingly to her. Throughout this monologue she barely looked at me, but smiled to herself as she recalled the men who were infatuated with her. I felt quite concerned about her peculiar constrained affect and noted that the good-girl persona seemed at odds with her struggle to contain strong wishes and feelings.

Sarah began the second session by discounting what she told me in our previous meeting, saying those were not the "real reasons" she came into therapy. As explanation, she said that she always wants to be something other than what she is. To my comment that this reflected dissatisfaction with herself, she replied in a withering tone of voice, "of course." This interchange, including her condescension toward me, came to characterize much of what occurred between us. While she acknowledged my ability to understand what she was telling me, often her tone implied something like, 'any fool could see that.' In fact, much of her distress reflected the childhood and current reality that few people recognized what was quite obvious about her, that she was extremely depressed and unhappy. Her parents repeatedly told her that she was the child they did not have to worry about. Not surprisingly, she was skeptical of the usefulness of talking but now found herself "in a hole and I don't know how to get out of it." She had been reading psychology books, trying to determine whether to diagnose herself as obsessive-compulsive, depressed or borderline.

Over the next several sessions, I learned more about her background and about her current situation. Sarah is the only girl and oldest of three children from an intact middle-class family whose parents are professionals. She grew up in the neighborhood surrounding the university. Her younger brothers had a variety of behavior problems, but she was the good child in the family. The extended family lived nearby and Sarah helped care for older relatives and young cousins. Though she was praised for her responsibility, she felt extremely guilty because of the intensity of her private resentment of these burdens. Her exceptional intelligence and talent also won her much recognition, though she took little pleasure in either her abilities or the praise. Against a background of chronic unhappiness, Sarah described two severe episodes of depression, one at age 12 and the other during her senior year of high school. She connected the later one to the terminal illness of a relative and she simply refused to discuss the earlier one, saying only that she was more depressed then than she is now. I understood her refusal to discuss it to represent her fear of opening up potentially overwhelming memories and did not push her. However, I was conscious of her general aura of secrecy and the care with which she chose what to reveal to me.

She had been admitted to several outstanding colleges, but opted to attend school close to home as the "path of least resistance." The ambivalent nature of her tie to her family was clear to us both. Sarah did well academically in college and was involved in a variety of social activities as well and she assessed her overall college experience as very positive, particularly in helping her overcome social inhibitions. For the past several years she had a boyfriend whom she had been very dependent upon, but now was beginning to feel a need to test herself apart from him. However, her current anxiety made it impossible for her to separate from him and she kept referring to him as her "quasi-ex-boyfriend." As she faced graduation, Sarah had gone through the process of applying to law school and she was confident she would be admitted to the top schools. But she became increasingly convinced that to attend law school next year would be a mistake. Both her boyfriend and law school could counteract her sense of being "ungrounded and directionless," but she was aware that using them for these purposes would continue to defensively mask her difficulties. Her plan was to defer law school and travel for a year, stopping to do factory work along the way. The underlying goal was to have the opportunity to see what she could learn about herself without structure and demands.

Sarah was painfully aware of the discrepancy between her innate talents and her longstanding self-hatred and low self-esteem. Coining a phrase that we used to capture the quality of her unhappiness, she diagnosed herself as suffering from a "basic sense of insufficiency." Because she was so bright and talented, her family and friends dismissed the possibility that she could have any problems, sometimes out of envy and sometimes out of an inability to respond to the degree of her depression. Sarah knew she was unusually smart, yet she felt unable to do anything with her intelligence. To underscore this point, she quoted a professor's comment on a paper in which he said, "good analysis, but where are your ideas?" She found his observation very apt, as she saw herself as lacking creativity or an ability to use her intelligence in a satisfying way.

As I listened to Sarah's story, I was impressed by the paucity of emotional warmth or closeness in her references to her family and by the harsh, negative tone of her self-assessment and self-recrimination. It was sad to witness this talented, observant young woman who felt so pervasively depressed and hopeless. I felt overwhelmed by the degree of her self-hatred and unhappiness and worried about the limitations of working on these issues in a brief time frame. Early on I raised the possibility of her entering long-term therapy to deal with the chronic depression, anxiety, and characterological features of the interferences in her functioning. She responded, "I won't preclude it, but not now." This did not stop me from suggesting it several times over the course of her treatment, but she remained adamant that the timing was not correct.

The severity of Sarah's depression and character pathology as well as her subjective distress presented a therapeutic dilemma. The optimal treatment seemed to be long-term intensive therapy or psycho-analysis, but she was unwilling to consider this. Her manner toward me remained fairly prickly and standoffish, so I did not feel confident about the strength of the therapeutic alliance. She did not seem to expect much from me, nor would she let me do very much. Yet Sarah seemed to have some sense of what she needed even if neither of us could articulate it. Her insistence on separating from her boyfriend and leaving next year open in order to create the possibility of discovering something about herself worried me but also struck me as a coura-geous stance. She may have been correct in refusing to explore deeply at this point in her life. Her history indicated that in the past she had particular difficulty at times of developmental transitions. She high-lighted age 12, entering adolescence, her last year of high school, and leaving home as periods when she experienced the most intense de-pression. Now she faced college graduation and the entry into young adulthood, with the attendant developmental demands of identity con-solidation, making a career choice, and establishing intimate relation-ships. The disruption associated with this transitional period left Sarah vulnerable, given her history and her character structure, and at the same time available for intervention.

In the eighth session Sarah announced that she realized that the concerns she had already presented to me were not really what she needs to work on; instead, she had to deal with her "terrible fear of being alone." She went on to describe her inability to be by herself even briefly because she becomes aware at those moments of her sense of "insufficiency." Recently this anxiety had escalated to almost panic proportions. Finally, at a point where many brief therapies would be terminating, Sarah defined an authentic and meaningful focus for the therapy. In this same session she acknowledged what she called a "paranoia" about what other people think of her and asked me directly what I thought about her. I answered her straightforwardly, addressing the depression that limits her in many ways including interpersonally, the intensity of her negative feelings about herself, and the interference in being able to use her talents effectively. Though I tried to be tactful, I did not minimize the severity of her difficulties or her suffering. Without elaborating, she responded by saying she agreed with my assessment. This session marked a turning point in Sarah's therapy. She still refused to discuss certain aspects of her experience, but generally she was much less guarded and more invested in our work. A few weeks later she returned from a trip to Florida with friends over spring break to report an upsetting incident and introduced it by saying that she thought of me when it occurred. The group of friends had made plans to go out to dinner, with the assumption that anyone who wanted to come would meet at the appointed time. Sarah was late and they went without her so she was inadvertently left behind. The voice inside her head repeatedly told her, of course, you're not worthy of them liking you or wanting to be with you, though she knew rationally that this was not the case. At that moment of panic her problem of being alone became crystal clear to her because she realized that when alone the voice inside her head begins berating her. In the midst of her anxiety, she thought of me and the discussions we have had about this problem. I was relieved to hear about this because it indicated the beginning representation of a different way of being alone, an emerging capacity to manage her anxiety, and an identification with a thoughtful attitude toward her internal life.

Sarah spent several sessions reviewing her college years, stating she felt she had "really come into my own." To her satisfaction, she became less self conscious and more able to speak up for herself, though she noted that sometimes the talk is just "to fill space, not connected to my real self." These changes reflected important movement for her. She expressed sadness about the ending of the relationship with her boyfriend whom she had seen as her "best hope to be ok" and now she would lose that opportunity. However, she also recognized that becoming "ok" could not be done through that relationship. Poignantly she described her reaction when he told her he found her beautiful or that he loved her. As pleasing as it was to hear that, she experienced a great sense of loss because he did not seem to know who she was and his view of her certainly did not match her own view of herself. Sarah could not use his appreciation of her to enhance her own feelings about herself, and instead felt painfully reminded of her loneliness.

As graduation approached, Sarah became increasingly anxious and preoccupied though in "less demonic" ways than in the past. She lived in a "cloud of self-hatred and self-loathing" but she noted that it was not as consuming as the "spiral of self-hatred" she sometimes got caught in. To protect herself, she would only talk about these emotional states for a limited time and without much detail because she knew the session would end and she would have to leave. As I had periodically been aware, there was obviously much going on that she would not discuss. In one of these sessions she mentioned watching an old Marilyn Monroe movie. Following my own association, I asked her directly if she was having suicidal thoughts. She was very slow to answer, explaining that in the past when she has been in pain she has been accused of using it as an "attention ploy" and she did not want me to construe her answer as such. Finally she stated she was not as suicidal as she had been at age 12, but she also did not mean to imply that she is actually feeling suicidal. The delicacy with which she let me know about her despair created a countertransference tension that brought my anxiety and concern for her into sharp focus. In her associations to this discussion and a dream following it, she acknowledged her conflict about directly expressing herself. I had been aware of the absence of responsive caregivers who could provide assistance with her troubling affective states. She now added the additional fear that, if she revealed her thoughts and feelings, she would be in danger of being hated for what she had to say.

With graduation and termination imminent, Sarah's mood improved and she looked forward to her explorations of the coming year. She continued to talk about her "core of unhappiness and unworthiness" and her fear that she would simply have to learn to live with it. Again I suggested ongoing therapy and offered to assist her in finding a referral once she was settled. Though acutely aware of the ending, she found herself "disconnected" from the experience of leaving. As we discussed termination, she frequently asked me what I thought of her and in the final session noted that she had not had a chance to inquire about me. In this final session she brought me a gift of a plant she had purchased several weeks earlier, explaining it was to express her appreciation to me for sitting with her over these months. She added that she had a hard time caring for plants, but she had managed to keep this one alive to give to me.

DISCUSSION

In her initial presentation, Sarah met many of the usual exclusion criteria for brief therapy. There was evidence of significant character pathology and serious depression, she was not forthcoming about herself or her history, she did not report supportive, positive caregiving relationships, she did not identify a focus for the therapeutic work, and she was not hopeful about the usefulness of therapy but rather saw it as a last resort. Yet she was able to communicate something affectively about the level of her distress that we both recognized as important and worth exploration. Sarah also conveyed a firm sense of knowing something about herself, most of which she was unwilling to share, but it was solid enough that I could respect and appreciate it, even if I did not know much about it. One of the things Sarah knew related to the time frame she established for her treatment, insisting that the brief format suited her current needs. Presumably she could not emotionally afford to explore more deeply her depression and her past experiences because of the developmental pressures facing her. The potential transference revival of unresponsive and unavailable caregivers posed a threat to her functioning.

This treatment produced a fair amount of countertransference tension within the therapist. Partly this resulted from the awareness of the degree of Sarah's characterological difficulty in contrast to the time constraints she imposed on the treatment. This can be understood and appreciated in terms of the age-appropriate developmental thrust that did not permit her to further explore these issues. More problematically, there was not a sense of collaboration and negotiation in determining the scope of the treatment. Throughout the treatment, she was guarded and secretive about certain aspects of her internal life, simply refusing to discuss some matters and making oblique allusions to others. Sarah's suicidal ideation came up only indirectly and she was clearly reluctant to reveal it. The gift of a plant that she "managed to keep alive" was her most direct statement about her suicidal feelings. Her reference to her new ability to keep the plant alive seemed to acknowledge what had been our unspoken therapeutic task, to find a way to permit her to grow at a critical point.

Sarah's treatment occurred at a time of developmental transition and the anxiety associated with this provided a "clinical window" that enabled her to search for help. The prospect of graduation from college, with its career and relationship implications, heightened her panic about being alone which, in turn, left her open to the accusatory voice of self-hatred. Her history indicates a similar intensification of depression at earlier times of change so the reappearance of old conflicts in this new context can be understood as her continuing effort to work through these issues. In fact, Sarah already had made her choices about the current developmental decisions regarding her boyfriend and schooling. What emerged in the treatment were chronically unmet developmental needs, for recognition, for validation, for sharing of emotional states, and for assistance in regulating these states. The therapeutic alliance was established around the willingness to talk with her directly and realistically about her difficulties, in contrast to the superficial idealization she received from family and friends. This enabled her to begin to ameliorate some of the harshness directed at herself, but more importantly to begin to think about her subjective experience differently. With a slightly more benign and more authentic attitude, Sarah did indeed loosen the developmental knot sufficiently to permit herself to move forward. Sarah's therapy paralleled the developmental process that we no longer understand to occur in a systematic linear progression, but rather in fits and starts, marked by both continuity and discontinuity, with periods of turmoil and change followed by times of reorganization and consolidation.

BIBLIOGRAPHY

Basch, M.F. (1995). *Doing brief psychotherapy.* New York: Basic Books.

Clower, V.L. (1980). Comments on the application of the developmental point of view in psychoanalysis. *Psychoanalysis and Contemporary Thought,* 3(1): 171-193.

Emde, R.N. (1980). Ways of thinking about new knowledge and further research from a developmental orientation. *Psychoanalysis and Contemporary Thought,* 3(1): 213-235.

Emde, R.N. (1990). Mobilizing fundamental modes of development: Empathic availability and therapeutic action. *Journal of the American Psychoanalytic Association,* 38: 881-913.

Groves, J.E. (ed.). (1996). *Essential papers on short-term dynamic therapy.* NY: New York University Press.

Laufer, M. (1975). Preventive intervention in adolescence. *Psychoanalytic Study of the Child,* 30: 511-528.

Messer, S.B. & Warren, C.S. (1995). *Models of brief psychodynamic therapy.* NY: Guilford Press.

Schafer, R. (1992). Narrating psychotherapy. In Roy Schafer, *Retelling a life,* pp. 281-304. New York: Basic Books.

Schmidt, E. (1996). Brief psychotherapy with children and adolescents: A developmental perspective. *Child and Adolescent Social Work Journal,* 13(4): 275-286.

Stern, D. (1995). *The motherhood constellation.* New York: Basic Books.

Strupp, H. & Binder, J. (1984). *Psychotherapy in a new key–A guide to time-limited dynamic psychotherapy.* New York: Basic Books.

White, H., Burke, J. & Havens, L. (1981). In Budman, S. (ed.), *Forms of brief therapy,* pp. 243-267. New York: The Guilford Press.

Winnicott, D.W. (1971). *Therapeutic consultations in child psychiatry.* New York: Basic Books.

Chapter 6

Developmental Perspectives in Brief Treatment of Gay Youth

Nancy Stone

SUMMARY. This report explores representative dilemmas of gay youth in the transition from late adolescence to young adulthood and shows how brief treatment may facilitate efforts to work toward greater authenticity in sense of self and identity, revise maladaptive relational patterns, and strengthen coping capacities. It presents the case of an 18-year-old male who was seen in supportive psychodynamic treatment for 13 sessions in a university counseling service. Developmental and relational deficits, rooted in a stigmatized identity, perpetuated problems in functioning. The relational functions and supportive elements of the therapeutic process are emphasized in discussion of curative factors. Establishment of the selfobject bond with the therapist strengthened self, facilitated coping, and improved social functioning. The author emphasizes the importance of considering the impact of internalized homophobia and self-alienation in assessment of functioning and establishment of treatment goals. *[Article copies available for a fee from The Haworth Document Delivery Service: 1-800-342-9678. E-mail address: getinfo@haworthpressinc.com <Website: http://www.haworthpressinc.com>]*

KEYWORDS. Brief psychotherapy, gay youth, development

Nancy Stone, MA, LCSW, is Supervisory Social Worker, Student Counseling and Resource Service, University of Chicago.

Address correspondence to: University of Chicago, Student Counseling and Resource Service, 5737 South University Avenue, Chicago, IL 60637.

[Haworth co-indexing entry note]: "Chapter 6. Developmental Perspectives in Brief Treatment of Gay Youth." Stone, Nancy. Co-published simultaneously in *Psychoanalytic Social Work* (The Haworth Press, Inc.) Vol. 6, No. 3/4, 1999, pp. 145-160; and: *Comparative Approaches in Brief Dynamic Psychotherapy* (ed: William Borden) The Haworth Press, Inc., 1999, pp. 145-160. Single or multiple copies of this article are available for a fee from The Haworth Document Delivery Service [1-800-342-9678, 9:00 a.m. - 5:00 p.m. (EST). E-mail address: getinfo@haworthpressinc.com].

INTRODUCTION

We can understand many problems in functioning as adaptive failures in the context of stage-related tasks and life circumstances, and developmental perspectives provide useful ways of focusing the therapeutic process in time-limited intervention. Although a growing number of writers have applied developmental concepts in formulations of brief treatment (see, e.g., Basch, 1995; Budman & Gurman, 1988; Schmidt, 1999), researchers continue to emphasize the need to consider the special concerns, problems, and requirements of vulnerable and underserved populations in elaboration of short-term approaches (Borden, 1999; Messer & Warren, 1995).

With the foregoing concerns in mind, I focus on representative dilemmas in the emergence of gay identity in late adolescence and show how developmental formulations may inform our understanding of problems in functioning and therapeutic tasks in brief intervention with young men. A case report, describing the treatment of an 18-year-old youth shortly after the start of his "coming out" process, demonstrates ways in which time-limited psychotherapy can facilitate efforts to consolidate an authentic sense of self and identity, renegotiate maladaptive relational patterns, and strengthen coping capacities. Developmental and relational deficits, rooted in a stigmatized identity, perpetuate maladaptive behaviors which often lead to problems in living. I emphasize the relational functions and supportive aspects of the therapeutic process in discussion of curative factors. Empathic interpretations, focused on selfobject needs, validate subjective experience. Establishment of a selfobject bond with the therapist potentially strengthens self, promotes coping, and improves social functioning over the course of time-limited treatment. More generally, it may help to restore the process of development, repair, and structure building (Gardner, 1999).

DEVELOPMENTAL PERSPECTIVES

Although review of the theoretical and empirical literatures on the transition from late adolescence to young adulthood is beyond the scope of this report, it will be useful to summarize representative themes and concerns emerging from study of gay youth that enlarge our understanding of needs, difficulties, and developmental tasks.

While the experience of coming out is increasingly supported by a growing tradition of gay culture, researchers are careful to emphasize the particular vulnerabilities and adverse conditions that youth face in their efforts to integrate sexual identity and renegotiate ways of being and relating in such varied contexts as family, friendship, school, and work (Herdt & Boxer, 1993/1996). The homophobic character of our culture, elaborated in family, religious, and ethnic domains, encourages conformity to heterosexual roles and norms. As results of research by Herdt and Boxer show, same-sex desire is a sign to the child that he has a "special nature" which many sense as bad or unnatural, and accordingly it must be hidden and remain secret (Herdt & Boxer, 1993/1996, p. 103). The gay youth, often having realized in childhood that he is different not only from peers but from his presumably heterosexual family, grows up feeling isolated from those around him. He is, with few exceptions, stigmatized and alone, unable to make use of support even from his own kin, while assuming that because he is different, he is deviant as well. During the pre-adolescent and adolescent years, when longings for inclusion and need for normative peer bonding are central concerns, the gay youth is often derailed by knowledge of his difference and the need to protect himself from discovery. Hetrick and Martin (1987) stress the intrapsychic cost of dissimulation for the gay adolescent. At a time when exploration of relationships and expansion of opportunity should be primary activities, he is hindered in development of friendships with same sex peers. In addition, he suffers from lack of access to accurate information about an essential aspect of his identity as well as to role models who potentially provide affirmative examples of viable and authentic ways of being. They note that "one lives separate from oneself; a member of, but still separate from, one's primary group," and that the sense of belonging to that group, by way of peer relationships or religious affiliation, is effectively denied (p. 37). If belonging is to be achieved, it will often be accomplished only at the cost of some measure of negation or repudiation of the authentic self.

Cornett (1997) describes the sense of personal alienation that follows from the development of internalized homophobia. Internalization of our culture's anti-homosexual bias over the course of childhood and adolescence perpetuates self-loathing and leads to a pervasive alienation from self and fragmented identity (see Cornett, 1997, pp. 600-601). Drawing on Kohut's self psychological formulations and Sullivan's interpersonal theory, Cornett describes typical manifestations of alienation from authentic self, including: difficulties in describing thoughts, feelings, or values; judgmental stance toward self and world; limited capacity for empathy with self or others; difficulties in maintaining self esteem; sense of emptiness or incompleteness; propensity for involvement in relational situations that are potentially harmful; and a general sense that one is unworthy of understanding, acceptance, or love.

Colgan (1987) addresses the particular difficulties encountered by the gay late adolescent in the interplay between identity and intimacy. He describes the ways in which positive identity and positive intimacy reinforce each other where there has been congruence between the personal construct of self worth and the responses of others. He notes that maladaptive relational patterns, precipitated by activation of negative introjects about homosexuality, can lead the gay youth to seek relationships that perpetuate negative views of self. He identifies "over separation" and "over attachment" as two basic types of dysfunction, the former characterized by emotional distancing and wariness, the latter by an incessant search for romantic attachment accompanied by excessive tolerance, avoidance of negative affect, and need for attention and affirmation.

In the course of my clinical work with gay youth in a university counseling service over the last decade, I have identified a particular series of dilemmas that emerge in their efforts to separate from family, accept and integrate sexuality into sense of self and identity, manage relational experience, and revise life goals and directions. I will briefly describe representative issues. First, as the youth leaves home, separating from family and childhood friends, we would expect him to anticipate the possibility of genuine acceptance amongst new peers in a new environment. The start of college would seem to offer opportunities to move beyond the secrecy and isolation of earlier years and to embrace more authentic and expressive ways of being and relating. However, the decision to come out and embrace sexual identity may be accompanied by unrealistic hopes that one will somehow suddenly feel better. There may be fantasies that external acknowledgement will resolve the lack of internal integrity, or that affirmation by others will lead to self-acceptance as well. The youth may engage in poorly mediated disclosures in efforts to realize such hopes, and the precipi-

tous or inappropriate nature of his efforts–rather than sexual orientation itself–may elicit negative reactions.

Second, defensive structures, coping strategies, and relational patterns, developed in the service of protecting a discreditable self-identi-
fication, may now prove limiting or defeating in emerging efforts to be
seen, known, and understood. Where denial has been used as a defense
against sexual orientation, the youth may have elaborated a false self
in attempts to maintain a sense of belonging and connection with
others. If, on the other hand, the youth has withdrawn, he may show
impoverished affect or marked constrictions in expression of emotion,
even appearing schizoid on first impression. Herdt and Boxer
(1993/1996) describe some youth as figuratively having "left home"
in response to extended periods of isolation, living more hospitably
through television, movies, or other avenues of fantasy. Alternatively,
other youth, encompassed within Colgan's concept of "overattach-
ment," may be engaged in promiscuous behavior that is often puzzling to them, or are serially inclined to pursue inappropriate and
unrewarding relationships in which they are perceived as clingy and
narcissistic.

Finally, initial efforts to identify with other gay men may create
feelings of unanticipated anxiety as the youth begins to experience
previously contained internalized homophobia. When initial efforts at
self-disclosure and intimacy founder, the youth may experience further confusion, demoralization, and a sense of helplessness and hopelessness. As he finds himself questioning the value of his attempt at
authenticity, he may once again be at risk for withdrawal and identity
foreclosure (Erikson, 1950).

In the context of normative models of late adolescent development,
clinicians may interpret the foregoing problems and patterns as signs
of character pathology. When the singular variable of a secret, stigmatized identity is figured into the equation, however, we realize that we
may understand many behaviors as adaptive strategies in efforts to
establish safety and security, manage interaction, and preserve self in a
hostile environment.

CASE REPORT

The following case, describing the brief treatment of an 18-year-old
youth shortly after the start of his first year in college, illustrates

representative dilemmas in the transition from late adolescence to young adulthood. The course of intervention shows how short-term treatment carries the potential to help gay youth negotiate discontinuity in the coming out process, revise ways of relating in social contexts, and continue to consolidate a sense of self and identity.

Presenting Problem. Nathan, age 18, initiated contact at the counseling service shortly after the start of his first year in college. In completing the application for services he checked "sexual issues," "crying," "self esteem," "loneliness," "stress," and "depression" as problems in functioning. He noted that he had not received psychotherapy previously. In the assessment interview, he described "unhealthy views" of himself and related difficulties in establishing connections with others. He reported that he felt "dirty" and "unnatural" because of his sexual orientation. He explained that he had known since childhood that he was gay but had never revealed it to anyone until recently, when he had told his brother and a female friend. He described his parents as "hyper-religious" Southern Baptists, and the church he had been raised in as "strict" and "unforgiving." He had attended a parochial primary and middle school, and dated the realization of his sexual orientation to a point in childhood when he learned he would "most likely be going to hell because of it." He explained that he had never had a gay friend or a gay sexual experience, that he felt uncomfortable and fearful around gay men, and observed that he "felt sick" when he saw gay couples; he could only focus on "how dirty" they were.

Following his arrival at college, he explained, he had reaffirmed his decision to "come out," but presently sought help because the process was "not going well" and because "things were not coming together" in the way he had hoped. Although he had received no overtly negative responses, he described an acute sense of "the limitations" of being gay.

Family History. He spoke of his family with wistful affection in the opening session. He described his parents as "naive" and conveyed the sense that he had long ago forgiven them for having been too taxed by their respective burdens to be present for him in any meaningful way. He believed they had long suspected he was gay, but had opted not to address it. He noted that their own families of origin were riddled with secrets and that they tended to employ euphemisms in order to avoid dealing with "unpleasant things." He described his father as a "Willie Lohman type character," a remote and defeated man who considered himself a failure. His paternal grandfather, a formidable patriarch, regarded his son as weak and ineffectual, and his father had confirmed this notion by selling the family business and squandering the profits on questionable real estate deals. His parents had nearly separated following this course of events, and he recalled his father talking on one occasion about the virtues of suicide. He viewed his father as a "mysterious" figure in his own life, largely unavailable, and most particularly to this child.

He spoke of his mother with affection, but it was apparent that he experienced her as vulnerable, unstable, and in need of protection. He explained that his alcoholic maternal grandfather had left his wife for another woman, leaving his two eldest children behind, while taking Nathan's mother and brother with him. When he remarried, Nathan's mother gained two older half-brothers, both gay. The eldest, a priest, was allegedly "caught in the act," and, the story goes, committed suicide as a consequence; the other owned a gay bar, became infected with HIV, and also committed suicide. One can only imagine the impact this story had on the young Nathan coming into awareness of his own sexuality.

Nathan related that his brother, a year older, remained at home and had been historically rebellious and hostile. He had dropped out of church and school, and now worked sporadically as a bouncer at a local club. He was often unemployed and had brushes with the law involving drugs and petty crime. Nathan noted that his parents were unceasingly loving toward his brother and forgiving of his infractions. He has a younger sister with an unremarkable profile. Nathan, intellectually gifted and a talented violinist and choral singer, emerged as the most accomplished of the three.

It is not surprising, in light of the foregoing circumstances, that Nathan viewed his sexual orientation as unacceptable and potentially dangerous in the contexts of his family, school, and church. He did not appear to have denied his sexuality, but rather to have consigned it to a split-off, secret region of the self in order to preserve safety and avoid discovery. He related that he had experienced several incidents of harassment in middle school, but never reported them. He chose instead to suffer humiliation silently, "trying to file it away and concentrate on other things," thereby protecting himself and his family from having to reckon with an essential aspect of his identity.

Course of Treatment. Nathan was pleasant, engaging, and forthcoming in our initial meeting with a kind of dreamy and gentle quality. He was tall and rangy, and appeared to reside rather uncomfortably within his body. He had curly red hair at the time of our first meeting, but the color and style would change frequently over the course of treatment as he attempted to arrive at a look that felt right for him.

In the opening session, he explained in a rather puzzled fashion that his initial efforts to come out had not yielded the satisfaction he had anticipated. When I explored his expectations, he related dichotomous fantasies in which he was, in one scenario, celebrated and bathed in acceptance, while in another he was spurned and despised. He had felt let down, he explained, when neither had occurred. We discussed the idea that, after waiting so long to reveal this central aspect of self, he had hoped for a "perfect moment," or, at the very least, a dramatic moment. The lukewarm responses he had received felt anti-climatic. I understood his reaction as evidence of his deep need for acknowledgement, validation, and understanding. He had come to the realization of his homosexuality in isolation, with no one to confide in, and no like other with whom to process the experience. His main concerns until this point had been self-preservation and protection of his family from himself. Now he longed for authentic recognition; even negative recognition would have been preferable to the impoverished low profile he had maintained. From a developmental perspective, I anticipated that brief treatment could potentially facilitate his efforts to accept his sexuality and foster the process of integration and consolidation at this critical juncture.

Shortly after the start of treatment, Nathan reported that he had developed a crush on Eric, a new, "straight" friend whom he suspected was gay. He described a vivid dream the night before our session in which this young man had been present at a hospital where Nathan was brought for treatment of knife wounds following a fight. He related the dream to a particular incident in middle school where he had been harassed by a student who had called him a fag. Nathan explained that he had halfheartedly chased him down the hall, realizing that he would be incapable of exacting any kind of revenge which might have called further attention to himself. He remembered having been filled with rage and a sense of helplessness during the pursuit. In the dream, however, he had engaged the enemy, and, oblivious to pain, had reveled in the fact that Eric was there to bear witness to his battle scars. We focused on his experience of power in the dream in having acted on his rage and suffered the wounds. He observed sadly that he seldom felt powerful in his real life.

His preoccupation with Eric became the central concern in the following series of sessions. He described his feelings as non-sexual but romantic, and said that he was in love. He noted also that the inability to express these feelings was causing him great unrest. I observed that, in describing Eric to me, he had in fact related little of a substantative nature. Instead, he had made references to popular songs and characters in coming of age films that evoked his sense of Eric. Nathan explained that Eric was "cool," "popular," and smart, but also "mysterious" and "hard to know." Increasingly, the question of Eric's sexuality became secondary to the question of whether Nathan should tell him that he loved him. I sensed the urgency of his dilemma and felt worried. He appeared ready to sacrifice his friendship with Eric and possibly risk public humiliation as well, since he had talked freely about his feelings with several peers in their circle. At the same time, he said he felt that there was "no other way" to relieve his increasing anxiety in the relationship. We explored the potential advantages and negative outcomes of sharing his feelings with Eric. I tried to model ways of negotiating ambiguity and uncertainty, and to help him slow down. He acknowledged the risks of disclosing his love for Eric at this point in their relationship, and decided to get some distance and reflect on matters during the winter break.

He returned from the break, however, with his determination intact. In an impulsive gesture, he went to Eric's dorm and told him of his love for him with others in earshot. Then, without waiting for a reaction, he left. He reported feeling a sense of relief and returned to his dorm in what he described as a "manic state," telling friends and "anyone else who might care" what had happened. The morning after the incident, at the time of our session, he began to experience anxiety about the consequences of his behavior. I worried that the outcomes of this impetuous act would create more difficulty than he had anticipated. His failure to remain for Eric's reaction showed me the extent to which he was consumed with the idea of Eric, rather than Eric himself, and it was increasingly clear that there was a connection between the inscrutable Eric and his father. Additionally, I understood Nathan's preoccupation with Eric as a kind of idealized transference (in the context of his narcissistic vulnerabilities and failure to consolidate a cohesive, authentic sense of self). He had invested Eric with the attributes he himself wished to possess; he was cool, admired, and, if only in Nathan's fantasy, gay. In the twinship, Eric would be the best possible version of himself, allowing Nathan to idealize him, merge, and potentially identify with him. I thought of his obsession with Eric as a function of his own lack of and longing for a positive sense of self rather than as an expression of healthy attachment. I was concerned about his reality testing and his seemingly impaired ability to gauge the responses he evoked in others.

As we processed the experience, Nathan came to relate his anxiety about Eric to feelings of loneliness and a more general longing to feel "part of something real." We talked about his needs as understandable and healthy, and began to explore them in the context of the long-standing loneliness and isolation he had experienced in his family, church, and school as someone different and apart from others. In a spontaneous reflection, he realized the connection between Eric and his father, making his own transference interpretation about their shared mysteriousness and unavailability. Exploring the relationship further, he acknowledged how painful he had found his father's inability to express affection for and receive affection from him in ways that he was able to do with his other children; Nathan attributed his father's difficulties in their relationship to the strong possibility that he had long ago sensed that his son was gay. He observed sadly that none of his good works in school or artistic accomplishments seemed to have made up for that single immutable fact.

Eric's reaction, which came several days later, was a shock to Nathan, even though we had anticipated it as a possible response. Eric was angry. He refused to accept Nathan's apology and chided him about taking responsibility for his actions. Nathan observed that, while he understood Eric's anger, he felt put off by his authoritative tone, and later, in this conversation with Eric he reported a sudden awareness of a sanctimonious, "unoriginal" aspect of him that he had not previously appreciated. At this point, he related, he found his powerful attraction wane and subside: "He was not who I thought he was." He acknowledged a sense of sadness and emptiness, following the shift in his feelings, but also reported a sense of relief.

Although Nathan was inclined to consign this episode to history, in the following session I pressed him to make sense of what had happened. Initially defensive, he speculated that Eric was blocked and unable to deal with emotion. As he continued to reflect on the series of events, however, he began to see that he had, perhaps, acted inappropriately, overwhelming Eric and making assumptions he had no right to make. Together, we came to see the experience as a reenactment of Nathan's historically failed attempts to engage his father, who had remained, like Eric, stolidly unavailable. He acknowledged that this understanding gave him ways of making sense of what had occurred.

We enlarged the focus on relational concerns in the next phase of intervention. The close friendships he was forming, almost exclusively with women, reflected patterns that had emerged in his relationship with Eric. He showed a tendency to form idealized attachments rapidly. He placed himself virtually at the disposal of the other, often compromising his own interests and better judgment in attempts to comply with perceived needs or demands. When these relationships inevitably foundered, he de-idealized the other and found himself feeling anxious, empty, and lost, questioning his capacity to be a good friend. We focused on one relationship in particular wherein he increasingly recognized his sense of vulnerability and fear that he would lose the friendship if he were to express his own needs or establish more reasonable boundaries in the relationship. Nathan traced his feelings of helplessness in addressing these issues to a chronic avoidance of conflict and reluctance to lobby on his own behalf. If was as if, he said, he didn't have the right, nor could he afford to do so. Recognizing this problem as a function of his compromised self-esteem, he was troubled by the idea that compliance and generosity might be the strongest currency in his relationships. He decided to discuss his concerns with the young woman in question. He was relieved to discover that she understood his dilemma, respected his needs, and did not withdraw from him as he had feared.

One day, between sessions, I received a call from Nathan's dormitory resident counselor who, with Nathan's permission, told me of an incident that had occurred several days earlier. Someone had placed a sign in a hallway which read: "Big Gay Nathan." The counselor explained that he had been visibly upset, and she had encouraged him to call me. He did not initiate contact, however, prior to our scheduled session. I expected him to relate the experience at the start of our next meeting. Instead, he announced that he had "no problems" to speak of that day. After a silence, he asked whether I had learned of the sign in the dorm. I acknowledged that I had, and that I had been concerned about him. He related that he had felt humiliated and particularly hurt by the wording of the sign. It was, after all, a stark statement of fact, he reasoned, and yet it was somehow more odious than slander. His female friend, who had been the focus of the preceding sessions, had come to his defense, tearing down the sign, and this had comforted him. I told him how sorry I was that this had happened, but I also wondered why he had not contacted me directly. He became dismissive of the incident, but added that he imagined I might have been upset by what had happened. I wondered privately whether he had been reluctant to share his hurt and embarrassment with me because he feared that, perhaps like his mother, I was too vulnerable to help him in his experience of need and distress. I reminded him that I wanted to and could be available to him in times of difficulty. He returned to the incident, describing it in greater detail and elaborating on his experience of hurt, embarrassment, and vulnerability in its wake.

Nathan appeared sobered and more reflective in subsequent sessions, and reported feeling mildly depressed. Nothing had happened the way he had thought it would. Even his academic performance, always in the past a "sure thing," had been a disappointment, diminished by the foregoing course of events. Now, in reviewing his experience, he spoke of a need to "regroup" and start over after having "made a mess" of his first term of college. He acknowledged earlier hopes that the experience of coming out would transform his life. He realized now that he had left home unaware of how deeply compromised he felt by his sexuality: "I'm still coming out to myself," he reflected. Now he acknowledged that transformation was going to be more complicated than he had anticipated, and that real change would involve more than simply an announcement.

We began to explore ways in which he felt he could resume efforts to give shape and direction to his life, not simply through his relationships, but by forging a more authentic and fully realized relationship with himself. Shortly thereafter he reported that he was considering a year's leave from school. He would live and work at home and possibly do some traveling as well. He explained that he wanted time to focus on himself and his family, and to get some perspective on his life. Although we explored other options, Nathan felt increasingly determined to proceed with his plan, not so much because this was the "right" decision, but because it would be his idea, his choice. I understood him as assuming greater control and acting as the agent of his own destiny. I came to support him in the plan, but urged him to regard his experiences of the preceding months, while painful and disappointing, as carrying the potential to help him move forward. He acknowledged an enhanced capacity to make sense of his thoughts, feelings, and actions and growing ability to express his real feelings in interaction with others. He said that he understood, however, that success in accepting and integrating his sexuality, coming out, and realizing more authentic ways of being and relating would occur only over time. Two months after his return home, he wrote to relate that he had come out to his parents. They had handled the disclosure reasonably well, he reported, but they had not mentioned it at all since he had told them. He wanted to discuss the matter with them and was not inclined to settle for their silence. He was trying to think of how to raise the issue again in a way that would encourage dialogue.

DISCUSSION

Nathan's intake assessment provided a profile of a young man who had grown up with a discreditable identity that was, in effect, confirmed as such in virtually every significant domain of his life. There were clear indications of strong internalized homophobia and resulting failure to have integrated his sexuality into sense of self and identity. Accounts of family experience suggested that his parents' capacities for emotional investment were sorely compromised by their own deficits and that they were not reliably available as selfobjects to meet mirroring needs, confirm his sense of worth, or to offer idealizable strength and wisdom. Further, it seemed likely that his ability to recruit their support was limited by the secret they tacitly agreed not to know.

Having come of age with a fundamental aspect of his identity split off and reviled, it was inevitable that he would experience varying degrees of fragmentation and difficulties in regulating affect, self-esteem, and morale. Lacking an internal cohesion, he showed a pronounced tendency to merge with aspects of others' personalities and proclivities and to move from person to person in search of safety, security, and wholeness; in essence, he longed for others to do for him what he had not been able to do for himself. The fear and disgust that he felt for other gay men had isolated and insulated him. Indeed, a collateral aspect of his romantic obsession with Eric may well have been the safety it offered in its impossibility, and the way it served to maintain his state of immobilization in regard to the reification of his sexuality. He had no gay friends and was resistant to my efforts to engage him in any exploration of opportunities for involvement in the gay community.

Balanced against his narcissistic vulnerabilities and difficulties in negotiating relational experience, Nathan showed considerable strengths, including a generous and expansive nature, a sense of humor, and an appreciation of the ironic that reflected an underlying resilience. His intellectual and musical gifts were sources of esteem and pleasure, which garnered external affirmation as well. Nathan realized that he was having difficulty shortly after his arrival at college, but he did not know why. He had come to college with an ambitious agenda of which he was not fully aware. He sought nothing less than to experience himself as authentic and real in ways that he had not previously felt. But he had no language with which to articulate years of unacknowledged need and longing and make sense of his experience. I think that this is what our work began to provide for him. The task of treatment, as I understood it, was to (a) help him process his experience of coming out, within the context of his own history, (b) support him in negotiating immediate problems in functioning, and (c) strengthen his capacities for further growth and development. The internalized homophobia that perpetuates alienation from self occurs in relational contexts over the course of development, and formulations of the therapeutic endeavor emphasize the critical role of relational processes in efforts to reinstate growth and individuation (Cornett, 1997). Here, establishment of a selfobject bond and empathic interpretations focused on need and longing legitimized subjective experience and increasingly helped him to (a) recognize and accept need and desire; (b) regulate feeling, self esteem, and morale; and (c) work toward more authentic and adaptive ways of being and relating–what Kohut (1987) would describe as a sense of "hanging together, of feeling real" (p. 42). While Nathan remains vulnerable and at risk for negative outcomes, the course of treatment appeared to have helped him establish another beginning at a critical juncture in development. Sometimes, as Gardner (1999) emphasizes, developmental processes mobilized in the course of brief intervention may continue following end of treatment–a correction in course rather than a completed journey.

BIBLIOGRAPHY

Basch, M. F. (1995). *Doing brief psychotherapy.* New York: Basic Books.

Borden, W. (1999). Comparative perspectives in brief dynamic psychotherapy. In Borden, W. (Ed.), *The therapeutic endeavor in brief dynamic treatment: Theory, research, practice and commentary.* Binghamton, NY: The Haworth Press, Inc.

Budman, S. & Gurman, A. S. (1988). *Theory and practice of brief psychotherapy.* London: Hutchinson.

Colgan, P. (1987). Treatment of identity and intimacy issues in gay males. In Coleman, E. (Ed.), *Psychotherapy with homosexual men and women: Integrated identity approaches for clinical practice,* pp. 101-123. New York: The Haworth Press, Inc.

Cornett, C. (1997). Clinical social work practice with gay men. In Brandell, J. (Ed.), *Theory and practice in clinical social work,* pp. 599-617. New York: Free Press.

Erikson, E. H. (1950). *Childhood and Society.* New York: W. W. Norton.

Gardner, J. (1999). Using self psychology in brief treatment. In Borden, W. (Ed.), *The therapeutic endeavor in brief dynamic treatment: Theory, research, practice and commentary.* Binghamton, NY: The Haworth Press, Inc.

Herdt, G. & Boxer, A. (1993/1996). *The children of Horizons.* Boston: Beacon Press.

Hetrick, E. S. & Martin, A. D. (1987). Developmental issues and their resolution for gay and lesbian adolescents. In E. Coleman (Ed.). *Psychotherapy with homosexual men and women: Integrated identity approaches for clinical practice,* pp. 25-41. New York: The Haworth Press, Inc.

Kohut, H. (M. Elson & E. Kohut, Eds.) (1987). *The Kohut seminars.* New York: W. W. Norton.

Messer, S. & Warren, S. (1995). *Models of brief psychodynamic psychotherapy: A comparative approach.* New York: Guilford.

Schmidt, E. (1999). Development, psychopathology, and brief psychotherapy. In Borden, W. (Ed.), *The therapeutic endeavor in brief dynamic treatment: Theory, research, practice and commentary.* Binghamton, NY: The Haworth Press, Inc.

Chapter 7

The Gay Therapist's Response to a Gay Client Practicing Unsafe Sex: A Dilemma in Brief Psychotherapy

Bertram J. Cohler

SUMMARY. The significance of psychoanalytic perspectives for brief psychotherapy is discussed in the report of a gay man practicing unsafe sex (known colloquially as "barebacking."). The paper focuses both on understanding transference and counter-transference issues in work with this man. *[Article copies available for a fee from The Haworth Document Delivery Service: 1-800-342-9678. E-mail address: getinfo@haworthpressinc.com <Website: http://www.haworthpressinc.com>]*

Bertram J. Cohler is William Rainey Harper Professor of the Social Sciences, The College and the Departments of Psychology (The Committee on Human Development), Psychiatry and General Studies in the Humanities, The University of Chicago and Acting Director, The Evelyn Hooker Center for Gay and Lesbian Mental Health, The University of Chicago.

Address correspondence to: Bertram J. Cohler, 5730 South Woodlawn Avenue, Chicago, IL 60637-1603.

This chapter is dedicated to the memory of Andrew Boxer, Founding Director of the Evelyn Hooker Center, Board Member, Horizons Community Services and a pioneer in the study of psychodynamic and life-course perspectives regarding gay and lesbian lives.

The assistance and support of Horizons Psychotherapy Service, Bruce Aaron, Former Director, and Mark Contorno, Present Director, together with our student interns, is gratefully acknowledged.

[Haworth co-indexing entry note]: "Chapter 7. The Gay Therapist's Response to a Gay Client Practicing Unsafe Sex: A Dilemma in Brief Psychotherapy." Cohler, Bertram J. Co-published simultaneously in *Psychoanalytic Social Work* (The Haworth Press, Inc.) Vol. 6, No. 3/4, 1999, pp. 161-201; and: *Comparative Approaches in Brief Dynamic Psychotherapy* (ed: William Borden) The Haworth Press, Inc., 1999, pp. 161-201. Single or multiple copies of this article are available for a fee from The Haworth Document Delivery Service [1-800-342-9678, 9:00 a.m. - 5:00 p.m. (EST). E-mail address: getinfo@haworthpressinc.com].

162   *COMPARATIVE APPROACHES IN BRIEF DYNAMIC PSYCHOTHERAPY*

KEYWORDS. Brief psychotherapy, gay mental health, countertransference

Recent literature on psychoanalytic psychotherapy emphasizes the importance of the unique collaboration of therapist and client (Gill, 1994; Hoffman, 1991).This follows several decades of debate regarding the working or therapeutic alliance as a significant source for realizing change (Greenson, 1965; Friedman, 1988; Zetzel, 1958a). Clearly, Freud understood the importance of the real relationship between analyst and analysand in his work with men and women living in a world similar to his own and with whom he shared a ready empathy (Gay, 1988). He saw psychoanalysis as a particular kind of conversation between two persons sharing common background and interests rather than simply as a medical procedure (Lipton, 1977).

During the post-war period, and with the rise of ego-psychology, much of Freud's distinctively personal approach was eclipsed by emphasis on an approach to psychotherapy focusing on presumed mechanisms and functions of a psychic apparatus founded on a "scientific" psychology which shared little with the initial view of psychoanalysis as a human science (Gill, 1976; G. Klein, 1976). Over the past two decades, however, there has been renewed focus on psychoanalysis and psychoanalytic psychotherapy, including both long-term and brief treatment, as a distinctive collaboration within a two-person psychology rather than a scientific psychology focusing on intra-psychic functions and mechanisms (Gill, 1994).

Clinical perspectives all point to the importance of the therapist's role in the therapeutic situation (Gardner, 1983; Kohut, 1959; Winnicott, 1972). There is an appreciation of the therapist's distinctive power position (Foucault, 1961, 1975, 1976), an understanding of the extent to which any therapeutic outcome inevitably reflects a narrative or story co-constructed by therapist and client (Ricoeur, 1977; Schafer, 1981, 1982, 1992), and an appreciation of the therapist's contribution of a safe and empathic environment in which the client, feeling understood and appreciated, may be able to relax to self-criticism. This perspective on psychotherapy as a real relationship between two persons emphasizes the therapist's continuing self-exploration, reciprocal to the client's own personal struggle. This is essential in order to maintain an empathic listening stance which is curative to the extent that it fosters the client's experience of being understood and facilitates an enhanced sense of coherence, vitality, and personal integrity (Basch, 1983e; Kohut 1984).

Regardless of the therapist's own sexual orientation, psychotherapeutic work with gay men and women poses unique challenges for the therapeutic collaboration and is likely to elicit particularly strong personal responses which potentially limit therapeutic progress unless the meaning of work with lesbians and gay men becomes the focus of the therapist's own self-exploration. The gay client comes to psychotherapy with the cumulative experience of anti-gay prejudice endemic within our society which limits realization of personal integrity. Regardless of the client's avowed commitment to a gay identity, self-criticism learned over a lifetime, even if presently disavowed, may make it additionally difficult for the gay client to acknowledge warded-off wishes and fears (Herek, 1995, 1996). Inevitably, the gay therapist has experienced similar anti-gay prejudice and may even continue to do so in his professional life (Blechner, 1995; Drescher, 1995).

The gay therapist's own continuing self-criticism or "internalized homophobia" (Malyon, 1982), reciprocal to that of the client, is one of the most complex dynamics in psychotherapy with gay men; clinical work with gay men who continue to practice unsafe sex may sharpen the intensity of the gay therapist's own self-criticism, with the client's unsafe sexual practices all too resonant with the anti-gay sentiments of the larger community, and may also interfere in the effort to understand the reasons and causes of this personally dangerous behavior. The straight therapist is likely to harbor similar feelings of criticism and, unless comfortable with his or her own sexual identity, may experience the gay client's life-style as reprehensible.

The therapist's own reluctance to recognize personal feelings reciprocal to work with gay clients may compromise the positive facilitating alliance which creates particular problems in brief psychotherapy. With a limited number of sessions, realization of a working alliance at the outset of psychotherapy is critical in moving forward, but particularly difficult when recognizing the extent of potential self-criticism when issues related to sexual orientation are a part of what lead the gay man to seek psychotherapy. Additional concerns may compound this intricate dynamic of self-criticism and self-hatred shared by gay therapist and client, including attaining enhanced personal comfort with sexual identity; making decisions regarding disclosure of sexual identity within family, community, and work place; and mourning the loss of partners or close friends through the AIDS pandemic (Blechner, 1997; Hildebrand, 1992; Shelby, 1994b). While these issues may be tangential to those which lead the gay client to seek psychotherapy, they inevitably influence therapeutic work.

This paper explores the foregoing concerns in a report on a 25-session psychotherapeutic treatment of a gay man practicing unsafe sex in a gay bath house where there is a high possibility of HIV infection. In many ways, the therapeutic situation is akin to that of Freud in Vienna working with analysands from his own social circumstances. A gay man concerned with issues similar to those of my client in seeking to maintain an intimate relationship, a part of a small community of gay men and women sharing the same gay spaces, and with a number of friends who are HIV positive, I was uniquely familiar with my client's own personal struggles and at times painfully aware of issues which I had tried to avoid in my own life while I attempted to remain empathic with my client's effort to realize his goals. I did experience particular anxiety about my client's apparently nonchalant attitude regarding his sexual practices. The client had a penchant for anal intercourse without using condoms (the colloquial term is "barebacking"). I was unable to intervene effectively in this activity, which I viewed as life-threatening but which my client viewed as necessary in order to maintain a sense of being alive and as possibly promising the prelude of an intimate relationship.

PSYCHOTHERAPY AND GAY SEXUAL EXPRESSION IN THE TIME OF AIDS

One of the most important contributions of the systematic study of lives over time to the mental health literature has been emphasis upon the interplay of particular lived experience in the midst of particular social and historical changes which are distinctive to those persons who are consociates, traveling together as a cohort across the course of life from earliest childhood to oldest age (Elder, 1995, 1997; Plath, 1980). While such social changes as the civil rights movement of the 1960s affected everyone alive, these events have different impacts on the lives of younger and older groups (Boxer & Cohler, 1989). For example, the generation of middle-aged gay men at the time of the social ferment of the period 1965-1975 was little affected by the emergence of enhanced public acceptance of same-gender sexual orientation. These men already had settled upon careers for which sexual orientation mattered little. It was impossible to be "out" at work, nor did these men see any reason to make public their own sexual orientation. However, the social changes accompanying this decade of social discord had quite different significance for a cohort of younger people who seized upon the model of the civil rights movement and demanded equal protection under the law for all persons regardless of sexual orientation. These younger women and men wanted to bring their private and public lives together in order to realize a life less fragmented than in the older cohort of largely closeted gay men and women.

In a similar manner, the emergence of the AIDS pandemic a decade later had a different impact for cohorts of older adults, many of whom enjoyed lasting long-term relationships with other older men and had fewer acquaintances within the cohort of younger and middle-aged men more sexually active within the community but unaware that at the same time they were becoming infected with HIV. Within each cohort, the AIDS pandemic assumed different meanings as a consequence of such factors as living in a large city where social networks fostered rapid spread of knowledge regarding the gay plague, or living a more socially isolated life in a small town (Settersten & Hägestad, 1996; Settersten & Mayer, 1997).

THE SOCIAL ORGANIZATION OF THE GAY COMMUNITY AND SEXUAL EXPRESSION

Using the Civil Rights movement of the preceding decade as an example, in the decade following patrons' resistance to arrest in a police raid on New York's Stonewall Inn in June, 1969 (Duberman, 1993; Young, 1995), the following decade witnessed grudging public acceptance of gay and lesbian lives as non-normative (Schafer, 1995), but also as non-psychopathological (Cohler, Galatzer-Levy, & Shelby, 1998). With new-found public indifference to sexual orientation as dimensions relevant to personal adjustment or morality, gay culture became public in ways which previously had not been possible. Anti-discrimination laws were passed in many American cities, eliminating much of previous legal interference and fostering such visible institutions as the gay press and gay legal defense organizations.

Among gay men, the new sexual freedom accompanying the emergence of a gay rights movement was expressed in such institutions as bars, bookstores, and movie theaters, many of which had back rooms facilitating anonymous sex, together with the new visibility of the gay bath house. Chauncey (1994) has noted that the bathhouse was a firm part of gay culture in New York at the turn of the century. Generally free from police harassment, the gay bathhouse fostered recreational sex among men without the fear of reprisal (although, as Cohler (1998) has observed, not without a sense of stigma). Tragically, this decade of new-found sexual freedom for men previously secretive about their sexuality spawned the pandemic which is now known as AIDS. Seroconversion, which marks initial infection with the virus (HIV), leads to manifest symptoms of the illness over varying periods of time, often a decade or more.

It was clear by the early 1980s that gay men were developing unusual medical conditions which over the ensuing decade were carefully charted. Shilts (1987) has provided the classic discussion of this pandemic and the basis for reluctant public acceptance of what came to be known as the "gay plague." Many of the first generation of gay men succumbing to AIDS were unaware that seroconversion had taken place until the emergence of specific AIDS symptoms. A second cohort of men born in the late sixties and seventies, becoming young adults in the late eighties and early nineties, grew up with the awareness of the gay plague and were carefully coached from elementary school on the risk attending exchange of bodily fluids such as semen, particularly in anal intercourse. In the absence of any vaccine and lacking any effective cure, public health efforts stressed condom use as the most effective means of avoiding infection.

PSYCHOTHERAPY WITH GAY MEN IN THE AGE OF AIDS

There is a large literature focusing on issues of technique with lesbians and gay men in long-term dynamic expressive psychotherapy (Herron, Kinter, Sollinger, & Trubowitz, 1993; Isay, 1993; Krajeski, 1984; Stein, 1988, Stein & Cabaj, 1996, Stein & Cohen, 1984, 1986) and several valuable works on therapeutic technique with gay men (Alexander, 1996; Cabaj & Stein, 1996; Cornett, 1993; Hetrick & Stein, 1984; Gonsiorek, 1982; Stein & Cohen, 1986; Silverstein, 1991). This literature examines such issues as the disclosure of the therapist's own sexual orientation to the client, the implications of the therapist's sexual orientation for the therapeutic process, the gay client's feelings of worthlessness as a consequence of sexual orientation, and the reciprocal feeling shared by the gay or lesbian therapist of a similar "internalized homophobia" (Malyon, 1982) or self-criticism as a consequence of being gay or lesbian.

This literature also has explored issues related to the client's relationship with the parental family, particularly when the family is aware of the client's sexual orientation; issues posed for the client by disclosure of sexual orientation to family and friends and, if appropriate, within the workplace; realization of intimacy with partners, and the particularly complex issues posed for the lesbian or gay parent. Much of the literature addresses problems of adolescent or young adult development, or work with men and women across the years of "settled adulthood," relying on a developmental course whose sequence of entrance and exits from major adult roles is too often assumed parallel to that among straight adult counterparts (Boxer & Cohler, 1989).

Social and historical changes over the past three decades have been so rapid that reports published only a decade ago regarding issues in psychotherapy with gay and lesbian people seem dated. Increasing acceptance of same-gender sexual orientation within urban centers has changed the focus of discussion of sexual identity. Gay and lesbian clients most often seek out therapists who are themselves active in the gay community in the sometimes misguided belief that a gay or lesbian therapist will be better able to empathize with their situation than a straight therapist. Drescher (1997) has cautioned that such assumptions may serve as a cover for the client's difficulty in talking about feelings. The assumption that the therapist must either have had a shared experience or must know about the client's situation simply because both are gay or lesbian needs to be carefully examined.

THE THERAPIST AND THE GAY CLIENT IN THE TIME OF AIDS

Beyond the issue of complementarity of sexual orientation among gay clients and their therapists, anti-gay prejudice is so pervasive in contemporary society, regardless of the therapist's own sexual orientation, that the clinician inevitably harbors internalized homophobia (Malyon, 1982). Further, while we might suppose that the gay therapist would carry less anti-gay prejudice and feelings of stigma than the straight therapist, having experienced the pain of approbation for sexual identity since childhood, the gay therapist may experience even more such internalized self-criticism than a straight therapist. Criticism of the client's life-style, preferred sexual practices, and choice of partners may be experienced either implicitly or explicitly in the therapeutic encounter (Blechner, 1997; Forstein, 1986; Hetrick & Stein, 1984, Stein & Cabaj, 1996; Stein, 1988). Indeed, the gay therapist's feelings about his own sexuality and sexual identity may be a more significant source of countertransference response than might be experienced by a straight therapist. The gay therapist's own often disavowed self-hatred at being gay might lead to unreasonable expectations about what might be attained in psychotherapy or regarding the client's choice of partner or occupation.

Psychotherapy with men who participate in unsafe or risky sex poses countertransference issues above and beyond these more general concerns in work with gay clients. Over the past decade, with increased understanding of the mechanisms leading to seroconversion and the course of HIV to AIDS symptoms and, most recently, the presumed promise of multiple retrovirus medicine (the AIDS "cocktail") in turning an almost certain death notice into increased quality of life for an indefinite term, medical advances in the treatment of HIV have changed the terms of working with gay men with HIV (Borden, 1989; Herek & Greene, 1995; Shelby, 1995).

Most recently, two collections of papers reporting on psychotherapy with gay men have discussed the issues raised for therapist and client alike as a consequence of this life-threatening illness spread almost exclusively through particular sexual practices that have long been a source of satisfaction among gay men (Cadwell, Burnham, & Forstein, 1994; Blechner, 1997). Two reports have focused explicitly on the therapist's own reflexive response to the client's serostatus, sexuality, and sexual practices (Fishman, 1994; Petrucelli, 1997). Fishman writes as an openly gay man who is a member of that generation of now middle-aged men who have lost friends and clients to AIDS. He notes that, following the death of a client, he developed both survivor guilt and even counterphobic responses (if AIDS is inevitable, then it might be best to get it over with). Personal grief first mounted then turned to numbness as clients and friends succumbed to the illness. Fears of abandonment led Fishman to withdraw from his clients with AIDS when working in San Francisco at the time when men with AIDS began to die in large numbers. Fishman's report of continuing feelings of grief, resentment at abandonment and, ultimately, numbness is echoed in Odets' (1995) reflections on remaining HIV negative and a therapist in the Bay Area during the emergence of the epidemic, and adds further to Fishman's poignant account. Across the first decade of the epidemic, those who remained "negative" for HIV often regarded themselves as lucky. Since little had been known about HIV or mode of transmission and, since the concept of "safer" sex had not yet appeared, many men felt that their survival was due to chance.

A second report (Petrucelli, 1997) concerns a client's continuing, compulsive, unsafe sexual practices even after testing HIV positive. Even among HIV positive persons, further infection with a different strain of the virus is possible and raises ethical issues for the therapist. Unsafe sex (primarily anal intercourse without condoms, or receiving semen while performing fellatio) poses particular risk for HIV infection and other sexually transmitted diseases. Sexually active men who do not periodically determine their HIV status and men aware that they are HIV positive but who fail to disclose their own HIV status, and who fail to take appropriate measures to ensure safer sex run the risk of infecting another person. While the partner clearly shares responsibility and should seek such information and, in any event, take appropriate precautions, unprotected sexual contact with another on the part of an HIV positive client may lead the therapist to feelings of anger and even disgust with the client's actions. These feelings of disgust or even rage with the client's careless sexual practices may be intensified when the therapist has lost a friend or lover to AIDS.

The story of Petrucelli's relationship with her HIV positive client and her response to her client's unsafe sex practices is unique in its candor (Petrucelli, 1997). She portrayed her role, as being her client's Wendy, the ever watchful, somewhat practical oldest sister in the family seduced by Peter Pan into traveling to Never-Never Land. Her client was particularly flamboyant in his pursuit of sexual partners as enactment of complex transference responses and in his lurid descriptions of these encounters, designed to interest and seduce his woman therapist with explicit tales of his exploits. She was both aware of and interpreted these maneuvers, while also mindful of the extent to which the client's HIV positive status served to organize his own behavior. At the same time, she took a strong stance against the client's compulsive, unsafe sexual practices which posed a danger of infecting a partner.

Petrucelli (1997, p. 149) reports feeling angry at the fact that her client was potentially infecting others, but also aware of his vulnerability. Over the course of their work, as therapist and client came to recognize the extent to which anonymous sexual encounters just prior to or following sessions represented a complex set of feelings towards the therapist, the stories became more lurid but the client's actions shifted as he attempted to find and maintain a steady relationship with a lover. Petrucelli reports that her client, a Hispanic-American man growing up in the midst of poverty and both sexually and physically abused from early childhood, was particularly sensitive to her words and her responses to his stories.

The therapist and client both attended to this issue of seduction and stimulation; these sessions seemed to arouse the client in complex ways which often resulted in an anonymous sexual encounter on the way home after the session, Petrucelli wonders whether she was too much interested in the sex talk for her own reasons and whether her concern about her client's sexual enactments reflected a sadomasochistic relationship which she and her client each needed for quite different reasons. Recognizing both the intensity of the underlying depression and also the extent to which sexual enactments served to organize the client's life, she maintained that early intervention in the client's compulsive sexuality would lead either into a flight into health or else to enhanced feelings of depletion.

COMPLEMENTARY AND CONCORDANT IDENTIFICATIONS IN PSYCHOTHERAPY

Petrucelli writes as a presumably straight woman serving as a supportive but not naive source of support for her vulnerable client. Her capacity for empathic listening is evident in her report. This sustained capacity for vicarious introspection which permitted Petrucelli to remain attuned to her client, even at times when she could not support his activities which potentially endangered others, is one of two modes of the therapist's response to the therapeutic relationship. Initially termed counter-transference by Freud (1910), referring in a more limited manner to the extent to which the analysand's experience of self and others stimulates anew unresolved aspects of the analyst's own transference neurosis, this term has too often been used to refer to all aspects of the therapist's personal response to the analysand, such as in

Petrucelli's experience of herself as Wendy, guiding an irresponsible and mischievous but lovable and ever-boyish Peter Pan.

What Freud (1910) referred to as the analysand's influence upon the analyst's unconscious feelings includes both the analysand's presentation of material which touches upon the analyst's own personal struggles and the analysand's reports of thoughts, feelings and actions which are likely to elicit a variety of dysphoric feelings in the listener, such as anxiety evoked by the analysand's presentation of self, or concern for the analysand's well being. Either of these responses, evoked reciprocal to the client's own narrative of lived experience, could be sufficient to lead to disruption of the therapeutic relationship and to the therapist's disengagement from empathic listening. What is distinctive about psychoanalysis as a means of study of lived experience in both brief and longer-term psychotherapeutic intervention is recognition of the implicit meanings present in all relationships, including the therapist's capacity for recognizing response to the client so that empathic listening is not disrupted by the therapist's all-too-understandable human response of wishing to withdraw from experiences likely to evoke anxiety and other dysphoric feelings (Greenson, 1960, 1965; Kohut, 1959, 1984; Schafer, 1959; Zetzel, 1958a, 1958b).

Discussion of countertransference in the years since Freud's preliminary comments regarding the possibility of a therapist's erotic response to the analysand has challenged both his insistence upon therapeutic neutrality (Lipton, 1977; Mann, 1997) and also his claim that it is possible to eliminate the therapist's own experience of the client as an element of the psychoanalytic situation (Fliess, 1953; Kohut, 1959; Racker, 1968). Over the past three decades, inspired at least in part as a result of the impact of child development study upon psychodynamic theories of personality development, clinical theory has emphasized the similarity between the child-caretaker tie and that of therapist and client as a metaphor for the curative aspects of psychotherapy (Apprey & Stein, 1993; Mahler, Pine, & Bergman, 1975; Stern, 1985; Tolpin & Kohut, 1980).

Positing that the experience of diminished sense of personal vitality and integrity leading to sense of personal depletion is the outcome of the client's sense of failed attunement of caregiver and offspring early in the client's own life, the excitement and pleasure of sexuality could be used by the client in an effort to feel once more alive in a world otherwise experienced as psychologically barren (Shelby, 1994a;

Tolpin, 1997). Discussion of therapeutic technique has focused on the importance of the clinician's emotional attunement to the client's present emotional state, reflected in part by the meanings which the client provides for the experience of sexuality, as critical for positive outcome of psychotherapy (Burke & Cohler, 1992; Cohler, 1976; Flarsheim, 1975).

Particularly important in this discussion has been consideration of those aspects of the therapist's own personality which might facilitate, or interfere with, attunement between therapist and client. From initial accounts by English analysts (Winnicott, 1949; Heimann, 1950; Little, 1951) to Abend's (1989) review of the countertransference literature, recognizing the analytic relationship as one between two persons requires a consideration of sentiment and wish among both participants in this relationship (Gill, 1994). Current perspectives on countertransference, understood as not only those erotic wishes stimulated by such work, but also the totality of the therapist's experience of the client and their relationship, emphasize the significance of the therapist's experience of the client as a ubiquitous and even necessary element of the therapeutic relationship. Indeed, problems posed by the many and often pejorative uses of the term countertransference suggest that there might be more useful terms for portraying the therapist's experience of the client and their relationship.

The concept of countertransference may refer either to the experience of the patient, which serves mainly to inform the therapist regarding the patient's previously disavowed wishes and sentiments, or to those sentiments evoked within the therapist which contain information particularly relevant to understanding the patient, and which are experienced reciprocally, empathically and intersubjectively as the experience of the client's own lived experience (Casement 1986, Kohut, 1959; Grayer & Sax, 1986; Stolorow, Atwood, & Branchaft, 1994). In addition, the concept of countertransference is sometimes used to refer to responses reflecting the specific phase of the treatment in which therapist and client find themselves (Vaslamatzis, Kanellos, Tserpe, & Verveniotis, 1986). Other theorists have suggested that the concept of countertransference portrays the therapist's position within the treatment situation, the unique content of the patient's own life history, or the analyst's personal emotional response to those of the patient (Missenard, 1989).

Racker (1968) notes that the concept of countertransference refers both to complementary identifications (most closely approaching Freud's initial use of this term) and concordant identifications (most closely allied with recent focus on the therapist's emotional resonance with the client's own lived experience). Complementary identifications include the range of the therapist's responses, which are a consequence of the evocation of unresolved elements of the therapist's own psychopathology, silent but continuing sources of distortions in the therapist's attunement to the client's present struggles. These complementary identifications include the therapist's own unrecognized and disavowed erotic responses evoked by the therapeutic situation. Being with the client during times of personal turmoil may evoke other salient but unresolved issues within the therapist's own life history which may also interfere in maintenance of an empathic listening attitude.

Concordant identifications refer to those potentially disruptive responses on the part of the therapist, which are reciprocal to the client's report of embarrassing, painful or even self-endangering experiences which would quite naturally cause a person otherwise unaware of the impact of this conversation to withdraw from the relationship. It is the therapist's own personal analysis which offers the best hope for dealing with the possible disruptions imposed by being with clients expressing painful feelings and thoughts, or reporting those actions which are threats to the client's well-being or potentially life-threatening (Fliess, 1944, 1953; Kohut, 1959).

Recognition that the therapist's dysphoric feelings represent the vicarious experience of the client's own present world of lived experience, apart from the therapist's life, leads to the therapist's enhanced capacity to bear such painful feelings without emotional withdrawal or subtle punishment of the client for having evoked these feelings. As a result of being able to be emotionally with the client even as vicariously experiencing these painful feelings (cf. Winnicott's (1962c, 1972) concept of the "holding environment" of both infancy and psychotherapy), the therapist gains important clues regarding the client's experience of self and others and also enhances the client's capacity for integrating these painful thoughts and feelings within a life story providing greater personal vitality and integrity than was possible at the outset of psychotherapy.

It is important to distinguish countertransference or complementary identifications from counter-resonance or concordant identifications with the patient's own lived experience (Casement, 1986; Grayer & Sax, 1986; Boyer, 1989). It is also important to differentiate the analyst's empathic, reciprocal experience of the patient's feelings of emptiness and terror from the analyst's own unresolved wishes and sentiments evoked counter to the analysand's enactments of wish and sentiment. The analyst's own unresolved wishes and sentiments may interfere in the process of a deepening and enlivening therapeutic relationship, and may make it additionally difficult for the analysand to achieve greater self-understanding. The analyst's own capacity for continuing self-inquiry is important in facilitating the analysand's capacity for enhanced self-understanding (Gardner, 1983).

Emergence of unrecognized wishes within the therapist, whether parallel, counter or reciprocal to those of the analysand, may compromise the effectiveness of psychoanalytically oriented treatment. The task of self-inquiry regarding the therapist's own understanding of the analysand's distress is further compromised by the assumption, based on a misreading of Freud's papers on technique (1910, 1912a, 1912b, 1914, 1915), that the ideal therapeutic stance is akin to that adopted by the surgeon. Psychotherapy is a relationship between two persons, and it is the very humanity of this relationship which is so essential for therapeutic change. Success in assisting the analysand to make implicit wishes and sentiments explicit, to develop additional perspectives on the presently remembered life history, and to realize solace and capacity for personal integrity, depends in large part on the therapist's own prior capacity for self-inquiry.

Empathic resonance, facilitated by continuing self-inquiry, which fosters increased understanding of the analysand and appropriate therapeutic intervention, must be differentiated from enactment of sentiments and intentions which are not in awareness and not accessible to the therapist's own self-inquiry. Counter resonance is facilitated by continuing self-inquiry, and must be differentiated from the therapist's effort, counter to the evocation of the analysand's enactments, to provide protection from reenactment of aspects of the therapist's own unresolved nuclear neurosis or psychologically primitive wishes and sentiments. Precisely because they are not accessible to self-inquiry, issues in the therapist's own life may interfere in the therapeutic process, mitigating against effective therapeutic change.

Following Freud's (1912, 1914) discussion of the significance of the facilitating positive transference, apart from the analyst's experience counter to the analysand's reenactment of the nuclear conflict of early childhood, this here-and-now relationship between the therapist and client represents what may be the single most important element facilitating the interpretive work of psychoanalysis and dynamic-expressive psychotherapy (Kohut, 1984), and may also be the aspect of the therapeutic situation most likely to be disrupted by the therapist's experience of the client's narrative of lived experience.

THE THERAPIST'S PERSONAL RESPONSE TO A CLIENT'S REPORT OF "BAREBACKING"

Evocation of complementary and concordant identifications are ubiquitous elements in psychotherapy, but perhaps nowhere as significant as in the treatment of the more troubled patient. More difficult patients elicit more powerful and more psychologically primitive personal responses on the part of the therapist and require particularly courageous and continuing self-scrutiny on the part of the therapist working with these patients. Failure to help the patient recognize wishes and sentiments evoked anew within the therapeutic relationship presents serious problems for the vitality of psychoanalytic intervention with the more troubled client. Continued awareness of frustration and rage, reciprocally experienced in response to the intensity of the analysand's demands, taxes the capacity for self-inquiry of even the most personally integrated therapist.

Perhaps it is for this reason that there is agreement in the literature that these patients are particularly likely to elicit intense countertransference feelings which may be expressed as therapeutic pessimism or even premature termination of psychotherapeutic work (Renik, 1986; Thoma, H., Kachele, & Jiminez, 1986). Countertransference responses appear to be more prominent (Denis, 1990), more difficult to manage (de Urtubey, 1989), and more integral to the therapeutic encounter (Shectman, 1989) among clients for whom psychologically primitive or archaic personality characteristics are predominant. Psychotherapeutic perspectives informed by psychoanalysis appear to be particularly relevant in work with the more troubled client.

The client described in this report, Mr. B., was a particularly troubled young man who elicited both complementary and concordant identifications as a result of his suicidal ruminations and self-destructive unsafe sexual activities. He initially called a gay community social and psychological services agency, seeking help for two problems described as recent difficulties in resolving a relationship, abruptly broken off by his partner of a year-and-a-half, and concern that having passed his 35th birthday, an important milestone for gay men often assumed to mark the transition from younger to older adulthood (Harry & DuVall, 1978), he would no longer be regarded as appealing as he had been before, and would no longer be able to attract the beautiful young partner he hoped to engage. The client was seen mostly at weekly intervals for a period of nearly a year; the extended length of time was due to his continuing suicidal wishes, and in order to help the client cooperate with his psychiatrist and the medication regime which had been prescribed and to which he often did not adhere. When the client decided that he no longer wished help, and that he was not making progress in his goal of finding what he termed a "husband," he was referred to an agency post coming-out group; he has chosen not to follow up on this recommendation.

BRIEF PSYCHOTHERAPY
WITH THE MORE TROUBLED CLIENT

A number of perspectives on brief psychotherapy founded on the psychoanalytic model of personality development and change have been described (Crits-Cristoph & Barber, 1991). Many of these accounts advocate particular innovations in technique in order to facilitate expression of the client's distress and characteristic mode of engaging others as early as possible in a time-limited therapeutic situation. There has been much less explicit focus on the significance of the therapist's experience of self and others, including evocation of complementary identifications which might interfere in the client's experience of that empathic mode of listening which is so central to an effective psychotherapeutic outcome (Kohut, 1984).

The model of short-term psychotherapy which I followed in working with this man is founded on the concept of anxiety-suppressive brief psychotherapy portrayed by Basch (1995), Sifneos (1971), dynamic supportive psychotherapy (Pinsker, Rosenthal, & McCullough, 1991) and short-term supportive-expressive psychoanalytic psychotherapy (Luborsky & Mark, 1991). Common to these perspectives is the assumption that, particularly in work with the more troubled client, a major focus of intervention is development of coping strategies and return to prior levels of functioning. This restoration of self is facilitated both by provision of a therapeutic environment maximally responsive and designed to reduce anxiety leading to enhanced capacity for self-reflection and understanding, and enhanced experience of personal integrity and coherence.

Luborsky and Mark (1991) are more explicit than Sifneos (1971) in their attention to the therapeutic relationship, although neither of these perspectives addresses in detail the therapist's complementary and concordant identifications which are essential both in understanding the client's response to the therapist and in facilitating the therapist's capacity for empathic listening which is deepened when the therapist is aware of his or her own experience of the client. Work with the more troubled client, perhaps optimally not the ideal candidate for brief psychotherapy, is likely to elicit both complementary identifications not previously in awareness (Kantrowitz, 1996), and discomforting concordant identifications evoked reciprocally to the client's personal disorganization and terrors (Burke & Cohler, 1992; Cohler, 1976; Flarsheim, 1975).

This perspective on psychotherapy is founded on concepts of optimal educational environment (Winnicott, 1960; Bettelheim, 1974; Cohler & Galatzer-Levy, 1992) for both classroom and psychotherapeutic process as one which reduces rather than enhances anxiety which inevitably interferes both in learning and feelings of personal safety. Luborsky and Mark (1991) note additionally that the therapist should function as a supportive ally in the client's effort to master self-defeating actions, a concern particularly important in work with gay men and women who often believe that they should punish themselves for their non-normative desire (Lynch, 1998). Observations of these self-destructive enactments with the therapist may become an opportunity for using an emerging transference in the service of such enhanced self-understanding. It is especially important in brief psychotherapy to understand the client's reasons for asking for help at the particular time, and to agree upon goals which might be realistically met in a process necessarily time-limited. Most often, a personal crisis leads to the need to seek help (Sifneos, 1971).

A LIFE MADE DESOLATE

The client described in this report sought help following the end of a relationship. He is the second of three offspring in a middle-class Jewish family presently living in a nearby suburban community. He has an older sister and a younger brother. He portrayed his older sister as someone who can't keep a job even though trained as a nurse. The younger brother works in the financial service industry, and is portrayed as moderately successful. The client recalls his growing up as uneventful, a classic Jewish middle class upbringing. He described his mother as a "typical Jewish mother," a warm, caring woman who enjoys making him things to take back to his apartment when he comes each week or so for dinner. He recalls his mother as always having been understanding, available for her three children and as not playing favorites. His father is a "typical Jewish father," hard working but not terribly warm or interested in the lives of his children. His father has a small business which provides the family with a decent, moderate life-style. The client complied with my interest in knowing something about his life as we began our work together. At the same time, he made it clear that his concerns were not with his family, all of whom were supportive of his gay identity. His concerns were much more focused on the present and his goals for brief psychotherapy: getting over his feelings of loss from a just-ended relationship and support in his efforts to realize a lasting relationship. His wish was for a committed life-partner and a "suburban home with a white picket fence."

Presently the client works in the world of fine arts where he spends two-thirds of his time in the administration of a gallery, and free-lances on web-site designs the rest of his time. The world of the arts provides little income but permits flexible hours, which is an important asset since the client spends much of the night on a search for prospective sex partners. The client portrays himself as having led a sheltered adolescence in a traditional family and community; he first became aware of his sexual orientation as gay during his second year at college when he was approached by a somewhat older student for coffee and conversation, which turned into mutually acceptable sex play.

A tall, thin, nice-looking man with a trim, athletic build who appears about his stated age in his mid-thirties, the client dresses in the manner of the fine arts—mostly trendy black-on-black clothes. He is worried about his complexion which shows some after-effects of problematic adolescent acne, his thinning hair, and his facial features which he is sure will be a turn-off for anyone desiring to know him better. The client arrived at appointments at the stated hour, usually carrying a tattered black bag and a soft drink which disappeared by the end of the hour. Other times, he had a bottle of water at the ready.

The client appeared for his first hour complaining that he was nearing his birthday and felt old. This approaching birthday was terrifying for him, since having been abandoned by his boyfriend of the past year-and-a-half, he had been unable to meet another man and begin a relationship. He was clearly depressed, reporting problems of being preoccupied with the loss of this relationship. At one point, describing his experiences at an annual celebration within the gay community when he had first met his boyfriend, he broke into tears describing the exact spot where the two had first exchanged glances and then agreed to meet for a drink which led to a mutually satisfying sexual encounter. This "husband" had been the third longer term relationship he had enjoyed. His first partner, whom he met at a bar while in college, had been a somewhat domineering person who compromised the client's feeling of a need for space. The conclusion of this relationship led to his decision to move back to Chicago from the east coast.

A second relationship of more than six years had begun after the client's return to Chicago. He had met his partner at a bar, had found initial sexual intimacy a source of pleasure, and had suggested that they see each other again. Over the next weeks, the two men became increasingly close and eventually the client moved in with his newly found partner. However, over time, initial ardor cooled, particularly on the part of his partner who began seeing other men and telling the client about these affairs. The couple decided that there was little in the relationship to hold them together, and agreed together to break up. After this relationship, the client found himself somewhat at loose ends and began to frequent the bars. As chance would have it, he soon met his most recent boyfriend and began a passionate affair. However, his boyfriend was nearly ten years younger than he, and soon began to disappear for days at a time when he would be involved in short-term, passionate relationships with other men whom he had met casually while the client was at work.

The client found his new-found friend very attractive and described him as a cute, sexy, young Hispanic man. He savored their sexual intimacies and was desolate when, after periods of time when his boyfriend disappeared only to return, the boyfriend proclaimed his need for freedom and moved out. The client spent days roaming the neighborhood looking for his lost lover and became increasingly depressed. After a time of about three months when he was tearful, increasingly lethargic, and, unable to concentrate on his work, he called the agency for help. Listening to the client, his depression was pronounced; further inquiry revealed that while he had contemplated suicide, he would never actually follow through because of the hurt it might cause his mother, the one constant, caring person in his life.

Having seen the client for a diagnostic evaluation, I recommended that in addition to psychotherapy he seek psychiatric intervention for his depression. The client was a member of an HMO plan and consulted me about the choice of a psychiatrist to see regarding anti-depressant medication. Eventually he found a psychiatrist who placed the client on Prozac. However, since this medication began to affect his sexual functioning, the client was switched to Welbutrin which he has continued to take to the present time.

Following his abandonment by his most recent partner, the client has led a rather solitary, lonely life. Somewhat shy and reclusive, he finds it increasingly difficult to meet new friends. Indeed, other than his parents and his older sister, also somewhat at loose ends, he has few contacts with others. He lives in a studio apartment and works irregular hours depending upon gallery activities. He finds it difficult to take initiative and feels at a loss regarding the problem of finding a new boyfriend. His last boyfriend had told the client about a local bath house for gay men where anonymous sexual contacts are possible. Following the break-up, the client began frequenting the bath house.

The client finds himself compulsively at the bathhouse about four nights a week. He tends to arrive after midnight, stays until dawn, and then either goes home to sleep or goes off to work. His daily round is rather consistently one of spending some time at the gallery, return home from work for dinner and an evening spent watching television or sleeping. Sometime before midnight, he has two martinis, then ventures forth to one of two or three bars or a favorite dance club. When he goes to the bar, he usually stands apart, watches the videos, and reports that he is too self-conscious and shy to approach anyone else. On some nights he starts by visiting a dance club where he enjoys the music and the ambiance, while on other nights he starts by visiting one of the local bars.

Sometime after midnight, often after 2:00 a.m. when the bars close, the client will head for a bathhouse. Over the next 6 hours he seeks sexual contacts, often as many as five in a night. The client's principal interest in going to the bathhouse is his hope that he might find a partner there. Twice he has been able to interest another man sufficiently that he believed he had been successful. The first was from Puerto Rico, visiting in the city. The two of them went home to his apartment for two days of intensive and highly satisfying sexual experience, after which the man had to return to Puerto Rico. Another potential partner was someone he had known from frequenting the bathhouse.

Having wasted more than a decade after college searching for partnership, he felt desperate about both his age and his inability to find a man willing to make a commitment to a relationship. While he knew he was possessive, he also felt he couldn't stop himself. Another relationship founded on a chance meeting at a bar went a similar way. After a period of intense and pleasurable sexuality, his newly found friend felt overwhelmed and pressured by the client's demands for an exclusive relationship and backed away from the intensity of this contact. There is a sense of looking for something to make up for the feeling of desolation and emptiness which this man experiences. He seeks nurturance; although his childhood was, as he portrays it, uneventful, there is a sense that some need for affirmation was not met within his family. His family's acceptance of his sexual orientation may belie more continuing indifference towards him than a genuine appreciation and understanding of his unique needs.

UNDERSTANDING DESPERATION: THE COURSE OF BRIEF PSYCHOTHERAPY

At the time he entered treatment, the client was in a desperate way. He had seen his former partner at the bathhouse but this companion of five years told him to disappear. The client found himself immensely attracted to what he termed his former "husband" once again, and desperate about recovering the intense and sexually satisfying relationship which they had initially enjoyed. His trips to the bathhouse were now organized around the search for his former partner who had disappeared after the initial contact.

Meeting me for the first time, the client shook hands and began narrating his present distress and its antecedents. His life story was one of desperation, afraid that being alone upon reaching what he presumed was mid life portended being alone in later life, not being able to find partnership, as well as grief following all his past relationships which had gone sour. From the outset, I felt the intensity of this client's sense of disappointment in life and his fear that things would never change. At the same time, the client found it difficult to reflect on the significance of his distress. Although the anti-depressant medication took the edge off his inability to mobilize his resources, or even to get up the energy to talk in more than a mumble in our times together, the medication could not effect relief from his sense of desperation about his circumstances. Hour after hour he would intone that psychotherapy could provide little help for his problems and that the only thing that would help would be finding a partner at the bathhouse.

We talked about his sense of himself when going out to a gay bar in his neighborhood, possible messages about himself he was giving to others by his posture and difficulty making small talk, and about strategies he might use in finding friends. Although working in a hip and gay friendly environment, the client had little use for his gay co-workers. I began to see his diffidence and his preoccupation with his looks as a protection against feelings of vulnerability. Terribly isolated and fearful about his inability to realize partnership, his entire life had become organized around the search. At the same time, the client had particular difficulty understanding his contribution to the situation or the manner in which his possessiveness, which was so central in driving away potential friends, might stem from his feelings about himself.

Suicidal preoccupations disappeared after the medication was stabilized, but the underlying sense of desperation showed little change across the course of treatment. Hours became repetitive with the client settling into his chair, sipping his soft drink, and complaining that little had changed since our last meeting. He still had not been able to find a prospective partner and saw little hope of doing so. His daily round had not changed, with four-night-a-week late encounters at the bathhouse following an earlier round of bar visits. My efforts to help him experience his feelings about these disappointing experiences were usually met with refusal even to think about his feelings.

I attempted to help the client think through strategies alternative to the round of bar and bathhouse visits. I tried to explore with him his problems with low self-esteem and his feelings of disappointment that others inevitably let him down because of his intensity and his possessiveness. I tried to relate these feelings to our work together, wondering if he felt I would let him down, and his wondering whether I could stand his intensity. The client had great difficulty talking about his feelings towards me, insisting that he knew I was doing all that I could for him and that his was surely a hopeless situation. What he wanted was a "husband," a cute, younger, Hispanic man, well-read in contemporary literature and sophisticated in the arts, and was disappointed in me for not helping him realize that goal.

In an effort to help him be able to find some greater sources of satisfaction in his life and move beyond his preoccupation in finding the ideal partner, I attempted to explore his talents, including his artistic sensitivity and his interest in literature and the arts. The client had provided me with the address of his web home-page where I could leave messages about schedule changes. The client also had a telephone answering machine. The home page reflected interests of a person deeply involved in the fine arts. I observed in our work together that he talked almost exclusively about his worries about aging and partnership, but that I seldom heard about his accomplishments. Again, the client shrugged off such efforts at helping him see his many talents and persisted in his goal of using our work in order to find the ideal "husband." We talked about his disappointment that I couldn't help him find the man of his dreams.

As our work progressed, I became increasingly concerned about the client's refusal to practice safer sex during his visits to the gay bathhouse. At that time, an editorial in the local gay newspaper which he and I both read had discussed the newly labeled phenomenon of "barebacking." Although the AIDS pandemic had led to heightened concern regarding safer sex, there was growing concern that some gay men had grown weary of this focus on safer sex and had once more resorted to unprotected and risky practices in recreational sex. The client made mention of the newspaper editorial which condemned this practice of "barebacking." He scoffed at the editorial and, in response to my question, proceeded to tell me in greater detail than before about his nights at the bathhouse. Leaving his bathhouse cubicle door open, and displaying his trim, well formed body, it is clear that he is an inviting partner for a sexual encounter. If the prospective partner is young and good looking he invites them in. However, he is afraid that asking his partner to use a condom will be a turn-off and will discourage the partner who could be the source of a relationship. He also maintains that the condom hurts when he is the receptive partner.

Much further discussion revealed that the only time when he doesn't feel disappointed and depressed is during the few minutes when he is participating in anal intercourse as either partner, although his preference is for receiving his partner's penis and, particularly his semen, as the receptive partner. At those moments, he is able to push away disappointment and enjoy the pleasurable sensation of his climax. After that, he is once again hurled into a sense of disappointment and despair, makes it clear that he wishes for his partner to leave, and begins to prepare for the next visitor. We talked about the many personal implications of barebacking, of his certainty that his life can't get better anyway, and of the manner in which barebacking might insure a suicidal outcome. First, since he believes that there is nothing to live for, he says the specter of AIDS doesn't frighten him. Although the bathhouse goes to great effort to educate members regarding safer sex, including nightly demonstrations of condom use, these efforts have little impact upon those men such as my client who feel futile about life. Second, the client presumes that in any event he must already be HIV positive, so that there is little reason for concern regarding his penchant for unprotected anal sex. The element of danger to health inherent in barebacking with its implications for danger only increases his excitement of the encounter. Finally, my client insisted in response to my questions that there was little reason in getting tested for AIDS since taking medication too early in the course of the illness only reduces the effectiveness of later medical intervention. I attempted again to work on the factors leading to the sense of depletion which might lead to the lack of motivation in protecting his health. The client consistently refused to acknowledge this issue. My role was to help him find a partner and little else was relevant.

THE THERAPIST'S DILEMMA IN RESPONDING TO THE CLIENT'S REPORTS OF UNSAFE SEX

I felt both anger and concern for my client's well-being. Not only was he possibly infecting others (he steadfastly refused to get an HIV test), but he posed an increased risk for himself either in becoming infected or becoming infected with an additional strain of HIV which would further comprise any possibility of treatment. I was also aware, however, that my feelings about my client's unsafe sexual practices were compounded by my own self-criticism as a gay man. My own ethnographic work (Cohler, 1998) had supported observations reported by Bolton and his colleagues (Bolton, 1995, 1996; Bolton, Vince & Mak, 1994) and Henriksson (1995) that the gay bathhouse actually promoted safer sex as a venue where education could take place; I had observed little unsafe sex in my own ethnographic study of gay bathhouses (Cohler, 1998). I was confronted by the paradox between my client's actions which seemed stereotypic of criticism leveled at the gay community as preoccupied with sex and doing little to curb the AIDS pandemic, and the reality that responsible elements of the gay community had in fact accepted the challenge to create an environment fostering safer sex.

Unlike Petrucelli (1997), I felt unable to take an explicit stance against barebacking. In the first place, the client made it clear that approbation would lead him to leave therapy (a threat which we discussed at some length in terms of its meaning for each of us). Further, he looked to me for affirmation and admiration, which I understood as a mirroring transference reflecting the lack of appreciation of his talents and skills elsewhere in his life (Kohut, 1977; Kohut and Wolf, 1978). We talked about the importance of my continuing admiration for him and his talents. I believed that taking a more critical position than I had regarding his practice of unsafe sex would be experienced by him as an empathic failure. Consultation with colleagues led to divided opinions. Some maintained that I should take a strong stand about the client's refusal to engage in safer sex and maintained that as a therapist I had an educational responsibility. There were, however, problems in maintaining the therapeutic alliance as a consequence of taking a strong stand regarding the client's practice of unsafe sex. Also the reality was that as a graduate of a prestigious Ivy League college, and long active in the gay community, my client certainly knew the means for practicing safer sex.

Clearly, I could be of more help to him if he continued to see me, even if still practicing unsafe sex, than if he quit psychotherapy. I might be able to help him find the reason for his unwise decision. Indeed, I hoped that our relationship would lead to development of a

more consolidated self-structure; as he became capable of experiencing growing personal integrity, the client would be able to resolve his
need for compulsive and unsafe sex. However, feeling guilty about not
having been more active in confronting him about his practice of
unsafe sex, I took this issue up with him. The client's response was
much as I expected. He was furious. He assured me he knew the risks
and expected me to be understanding and supportive of his struggles,
and not to confront or condemn him, as he was sure everyone would if
they knew of his unsafe sexual practices. He once again threatened to
leave psychotherapy, complaining anew that I was of little help to him
in realizing the two goals that he had in seeking help, mourning the
loss of his most recent relationship, and finding a "husband."

The problem was one of lowered self-esteem; he believed himself
to be so boring and unattractive that he could not imagine any of these
potential partners would be interested in him; his only hope was that
some appropriate partner would be attracted to his body and begin a
relationship on the basis of this attraction. At any rate, he hadn't met
anyone who engaged him at work or in the artistic circles in which he
moved. I noted this irony to him–that he was unusually fortunate in
being able to know other gay men in circumstances other than gay sex
venues, where there was a chance that he could form a satisfying
relationship. The client did not see these as preferable alternatives to
his own solution of the nearly nightly trips to the bathhouse. A man
who had two prior satisfying relationships of some duration, I remained puzzled why it was now so difficult for him to find satisfying
partnership. What I didn't fully appreciate was the extent of his self-
hatred which I believed propelled him to act in ways which were
self-destructive. Following Kris (1990), Lynch (1998) has discussed
the issue of self-criticism in therapeutic work with gay men. This
self-criticism is consistent with Malyon's (1982) initial formulation of
"internalized homophobia," but emphasizes the extent to which client
and therapist are mutually involved in struggle with this issue. While I
was able to be empathic with my client's search for a relationship, my
own unresolved self-criticism as a gay man, together with my own
fear that I could end up old and alone, made it difficult for me to be
responsive to my client's concerns. I recalled a high-school essay in
which I had portrayed an "old woman" of 35 and only wished that I
was 35 again. I also recalled a less than empathic remark by a younger

colleague that it would be real hard to be 50 and have to find partnership, since older men are not sexy.

While our work together did help the client mourn the loss of his most recent relationship, it did little to change the client's practice of unsafe sex or the desperation which led him into the bathhouse four nights each week. He did acknowledge some sense of shame; once he observed that "nice" boys didn't frequent the bathhouse. While at a local gay bar one night my client did meet one possibly eligible partner who met his criteria: young, good looking, very sexy and enjoying sex, and also bright and able to talk about ideas. Unfortunately, this new friend also had a group of other friends important to him and once again my client became preoccupied with feelings of jealousy and possessiveness which repelled his new-found friend. This new-found friend was also planning to return to the west coast which created a situation of uncertainty that my client found difficult to bear.

One night, when his new-found friend did not arrive at the bar as he had expected, he went by his apartment. He rang the buzzer but there was no answer. Certain that his friend was there but had not heard the buzzer, the client attempted to open the front window and crawl into the apartment. Just at that moment, a police car came down the street, saw him attempting to enter the apartment and was on the verge of arresting him when his friend came to the window, helped him in, and reassured the police. However, his friend was very critical of his effort to break in and severed all ties with him. As we reviewed this incident, I tried to help the client to see how his possessiveness might interfere in getting for himself what he sought but the client was reluctant to even consider the basis of this possessiveness.

During much of this time, the client had occasional company from a younger Hispanic man, a hustler who used the client's apartment as a place to stay between clients. At these times he slept in the client's bed; on some occasions he would permit the client to have sex with him, while on other occasions he was less interested in the client's sexual overtures. I attempted to focus on the uncertainty, and the effect of this uncertainty in the young hustler's whereabouts, as a factor leading to the client's present sense of desperation. However, the client insisted that as they had no real relationship there was little reason for jealousy. In any event, as the client noted in a dismissive tone, the young hustler was hardly his equal in anything save sex.

Towards the end of our scheduled work together, there were several brief absences, mine for a meeting, and his due to changes in his work schedule. Most important, the client was approaching his dreaded 35th milestone birthday on what would have been a regularly scheduled appointment during the week when I would be away at a meeting. Although I attempted to talk with him both before and after this birthday, it was clear that my absence was a disappointment for him. While he readily acknowledged that being a year older made him feel even more desperate than before to find a partnership before he was too old, he was unable to acknowledge his anger towards me for being away at such a difficult time. His response was to take a trip back East to visit an old college friend. He reported that this friend seemed to be in a situation very much like his own, which he thought might be typical for his generation. He seemed unable to forgive me for having disappointed him, but also found it difficult to acknowledge this disappointment.

Mr. B. maintained that since I couldn't help him find a partner, our work together was of little use to him and that he was glad it was nearing the time to end. The client said that he thought we might as well stop before the end of the scheduled appointments. He said that he wanted little more from treatment and that he was not interested in learning more about himself. I suggested that he was angry with me and disappointed that I could not further extend our previously agreed upon limit of twenty-five sessions. I also observed that he wanted me to feel the desperation and frustration which he felt in his own life, and that he was leaving me before I would abandon him. He noted that he had been to see his psychiatrist, who refused to increase his Welbutrin prescription even though he felt more desperate about his life situation. We talked about his possible disappointments with both his psychiatrist and myself. Just as our first work together had begun about the time of his birthday, now our work together was ending around this important event which highlighted his fear of getting older and not being able to attract a partner.

The client reiterated that he felt bored, that he must indeed be frustrating me. I acknowledged my own disappointment that he wanted to act and not think about reasons and causes. Over the last few hours of our work, the client was particularly closed off, merely repeating anew the now all-too-familiar details of his daily round and complaining that he did not yet have a boyfriend. I asked if he was trying to see whether I would get bored and leave him as he had so often been left. I also wondered if he had been disappointed that I had not been present on the day of his birthday, which would have been one of our scheduled appointment times. On one occasion he said he was sure I was bored, that there was little sense in going further, and he walked out of the room about three-quarters of the way through the session.

At our next meeting, when I asked the client about his response to the preceding hour, he said that he just didn't want anything more than to figure out how he could succeed in getting a "husband." Since I couldn't give him the answer to that problem, he might as well stop. He said that he wanted this to come to an end. I again suggested that he was angry at me that our work had to conclude, that he had left me before I could leave him, and suggested that we take another time or two to say good bye and review our work together. I noted that we had been successful in one regard: his initial feelings of loss and grief regarding his past losses seem to have been resolved and he was now ready to go forward unencumbered by that grief. He agreed to continue with his medication.

The client agreed that he would contact me if he needed someone to talk with. We ended our work together in mutual disappointment; he that I had not helped him find the right partner, and I that I had not been able to help him understand the basis of the present urgency he felt, which only deepened his problems in being able to realize partnership. We talked about a group as the next step in seeking help. Some months after concluding psychotherapy, the client responded to an agency survey, noting that things were much the same as before and that he still felt moody and frustrated in not being able to realize a relationship with the man of his dreams.

THE THERAPIST'S OWN PERSONAL RESPONSE TO THE CLIENT'S PRACTICE OF UNSAFE SEX

Therapeutic work with Mr. B. raised important issues regarding the clinician's own response to his possibly self-destructive activities. The first issue was approached from the perspective of self psychology (Kohut, 1971, 1977, 1984). Most recently, Shelby (1994a) and Tolpin (1997) have urged reconsideration of the significance of sexuality for lived experience. Rather than viewing sexuality in terms of interpersonal relationships (earlier termed "objects" in traditional psychoanalytic drive theory), self psychology suggests that sexuality be understood in terms of the search for personal coherence and integrity. From this perspective, Mr. B.'s sexual behavior represented a search for admiration and connection with another which might replace his experience of being unappreciated. This sense of appreciation was reflected in his enjoyment of a sexual partner's admiration of his athletic body and his capacity to participate in mutually satisfying sexuality. He believed, however, that he had little to offer apart from his body; he was in his element in the bathhouse where he could show his trim, athletic body. The problem was that such satisfaction from admiration was short-lived. Within minutes following the sexual encounter, Mr. B. was once more on the prowl for a partner who could provide the missing function of admiration.

The client's desperate search for admiration posed a problem in our therapeutic work. Mr. B. was a talented and creative artist whose work had received a certain amount of critical acclaim. As with many artists, his own self-criticism was so great that he found it difficult to accept any positive notice of his work. His response to my suggestions that he had difficulty in accepting admiration and enjoying it led to angry renunciation of this acclaim and of my effort to foster understanding of the importance to him of this search for affirmation. His sensitivity obviously extended to his failure to manage safer sex. From his perspective, he had only one goal, that of finding a partner, and only a single resource to bring to bear, his body and his capacity to satisfy others sexually. Efforts to consider his unsafe sexual practices threatened to interfere in what he believed to be his only asset in being able to find a lover. He connected unsafe sex with being psychologically alive, while safer sex–using condoms in anal intercourse–with being psychologically dead.

Following Racker's (1968) distinction regarding complementary and concordant identifications as two aspects of the therapist's personal response in psychodynamic psychotherapy, I related complementary identifications to my own fears, as a middle-aged gay man, of growing older and no longer being regarded as attractive within the gay community. While aware of my concern about aging, I have not been able to feel comfortable with the reality of changes in appearance, such as balding; this fear of aging plays some part in my career-long study of aging and life course. Concordant identifications were reflected in my appreciation for my client's sense of desperation with his life. Fliess (1944, 1953) has well portrayed the experience of "tasting" or living with an analysand's personal terror, loneliness, or sense of personal depletion.

There were times when I felt an enormous pessimism regarding the possibility of helping Mr. B. negotiate his terrible sense of loneliness. I was able to realize that these feelings were reciprocal to the client's own self-state and that I was being permitted to experience the world as he experienced it. Recognizing this source of distress, I was able to be empathic with the client's sense of desperation, but without withdrawal; that would have been experienced as an empathic break and would have compromised any additional possibility of being of help to him. While I was able to be empathic with the client's preoccupation with his sexuality as a means of finding partnership, I was less successful in helping him have the courage to try safer sex while still being able to use his sexual prowess as a means of attracting a prospective partner. He was convinced that unless his partner specifically asked for safer sex, such a request on his part would be a "turn-off" for prospective sexual partners.

CONCLUSION

The therapist's own response in work with clients practicing unsafe sex has seldom been discussed in the psychotherapy literature. The one report which most closely approximates the present account (Petrucelli, 1997) portrays a Peter Pan-Wendy transference in which the woman therapist provides understanding and support which helps to contain the unsafe sexual practices of her mischievous, multiply abused client. The present report reviews my own experience of frustration in brief psychodynamic psychotherapy with a gay man whose personal concerns lead to unsafe sexual practices. Growing up in a well-meaning and stable family, the client realized a gay identity while in college and maintained two stable relationships before the present crisis, brought about by the break-up of his relationship with a lover of several years. Fearing that as a result of what he perceived as his aging he might no longer be able to attract a partner, the client sought compulsively to reassure himself regarding his youthful attractiveness. He hoped that he might be able to continue to realize the admiration which he so desperately needed through near-nightly forays at a local gay bathhouse where at times in the past he had been able to attract multiple partners over an evening of sexual encounters which often involved unsafe or risky sex.

The client expressed his concern that demand for safer sex might "turn off" prospective sexual partners, and also the discomfort which he felt when a partner penetrated him using a condom. Underlying this unsafe sexual practice now known as barebacking, was a sense of self-hatred expressed in possibly self-destructive activity consistent with the transmission of HIV, and a momentary experience of psychological aliveness. This man, feeling psychologically depleted, was excited and stimulated by the fleeting sexual encounter and particularly his partner's admiration for his body and sexual responsiveness. Ultimately, this client's experience of personal depletion made it difficult for him to sustain any sense of satisfaction derived from the admiration of his sexual partners regarding his body or his sexual potency.

My client's fears of growing older and concern that he might no longer be able to attract sexual partners, presently an organizing force in his life, had increased his depression and sense of futility. As my client's 35th birthday unfortunately coincided with my absence, this disappointment became the final unbearable frustration since he presumed that my absence was due to my experience of boredom with his recitation of his round of activities at the bathhouse. Together with the reality of approaching the end of treatment, this absence at such a critical juncture for him became an unbearable disappointment and my client ended the psychotherapy before I would have to remind him that our time together was up.

While able to foster some resolution of a recently failed relationship, one of the two goals for which the client sought help, I was unable to help him deal with his anticipation of his own aging as he turned thirty-five. My fear of my own aging and its implications for remaining attractive to possible partners, a complementary identification, led at one point to an empathic break in our relationship which I was later able to recognize. While recognizing my own concerns reciprocal to those of my client, I was not able to help him with his feelings of anger and frustration at being able to find the relationship which he sought with a man significantly younger than himself. He viewed me as a magician able to reverse what he believed to be his aging and able to make him sufficiently attractive that he might be able to form a tie with one of his sexual partners.

I was aware of my client's intense need for admiration, together with his problems in being able to sustain this admiration over time. Indeed, this issue had been explored in our work together when I noted that my admiration for his web site and telephone answering message provided only the most fleeting enhancement of self-esteem, and that even the admiration of his co-workers for his many talents provided him with little lasting satisfaction, As I reciprocally experienced his desolation and desperation about his life, I was able to use this concordant identification as a means of helping my client to recognize the many meanings involved in his near nightly bathhouse trips and, ultimately, the significance for him of unsafe sex, which I understood as self-destructive but which he experienced as a source of sensation and as necessary for his survival in a world otherwise experienced as depleted. In this paradox, however, the realistic element of his self-destructive activities, which reflected his intense self-hatred, resonated with my own complementary identification as a gay man experiencing anti-gay prejudice of our society over a lifetime. I felt frustrated at not being able to help my client find other sources of admiration, but did not fully appreciate the many meanings which he attached to this activity.

From a public health perspective, this report shows the extent to which less safe sexual practices are motivated, often by a sense of personal depletion in which the risky sex provides the person with some sense of remaining psychologically alive. From the perspective of psychotherapy with gay men, particularly when practicing unsafe sex, the present report highlights the importance of the therapist's own response to the client's reliance on unsafe sexual practices as a factor relevant to the client's experience of self and sexual practices and, ultimately, to the client's motivation for realizing safer sexual practices. Following Kohut (1959) and Racker (1968), I understood my own contribution in terms of concordant identifications founded on vicarious introspection with the client's efforts to realize enhanced sense of personal vitality from sexual encounters posing a risk to his health, but also recognized the role of complementary identifications stemming from my own concern, shared in common with my client, regarding the fear of growing older and remaining able to attract other men for lasting intimate partnership.

REFERENCES

Abend, S. (1989). Countertransference and psychoanalytic technique. *Psychoanalytic Quarterly, 58*, 374-395.

Abramowitz, S., Cohen, J. (1994). The psychodynamics of AIDS: A view from self psychology. In. Cadwell, S.A., Burnham, R.A., Forstein, M. (Eds.), *Therapists on the front line: Psychotherapy with gay men in the age of AIDS*. Washington, DC: The American Psychiatric Association Press, 205-221.

Alexander, C.J. (1996). (Ed.) *Gay and lesbian mental health: A sourcebook for practitioners*. Binghamton, NY: Harrington Park/The Haworth Press, Inc.

Apprey, M., Stein, H.F. (1993). *Intersubjectivity, projective identification and otherness*. Pittsburgh, PA: Duquesne University Press.

Basch, M. (1983a). The perception of reality and the disavowal of meaning. *Annual for Psychoanalysis, 11*, 125-153.

Basch, M. (1983b). Empathic understanding: A review of the concept and some theoretical considerations. *Journal of the American Psychoanalytic Association, 31*, 101-126.

Basch, M. (1995). *Doing brief psychotherapy*. New York: Basic Books.

Bettelheim, B. (1974). *A home for the heart*. New York: Alfred A. Knopf.

Blechner, M. (1995). The shaping of psychoanalytic theory and practice by cultural and personal biases about sexuality. In. T. Domenici and R. C. Lesser (Eds.), *Disorienting sexuality: Psychoanalytic reappraisals of sexual identities*. New York: Routledge, 265-288.

Blechner, M. J. (1997). Psychodynamic approaches to AIDS and HIV. In. M. J. Blechner (Ed.), *Hope and mortality: Psychodynamic approaches to AIDS and HIV*. Hillsdale, NJ: The Analytic Press, 3-62.

Bolton, R. (1995). Sex talk: Bodies and behaviors in gay erotica. In. W. Leap (Ed.), *Beyond the lavender lexicon: Authenticity, imagination, and appropriation in lesbian and gay languages*. Luxembourg: Gordon and Breach, 173-203.

Bolton, R. (1996). Coming home: The journey of a gay ethnographer in the years of the plague. In. E. Lewin and W.L. Leap (Eds.), *Out in the field: Reflection of lesbian and gay anthropologists*. Urbana, IL: The University of Illinois Press, 147-170.

Bolton, R., Vince, J., Mak, R. (1994). Gay baths revisited: An empirical analysis. *GLQ, 1*, 255-273.

Borden, W. (1989). Life review as a therapeutic frame in the treatment of young adults with AIDS. *Health and Social Work, 14*, 253-259.

Boxer, A., Cohler, B. (1989). The life course of gay and lesbian youth. An immodest proposal for the study of lives. In. G. Herdt (Ed.), *Gay and lesbian youth*. New York: Harrington Park Press, 315-355.

Boyer, L. B. (1989). Countertransference and technique in working with the regressed patient, Further remarks. *International Journal of Psychoanalysis, 70*, 701-714.

Burke, N., Cohler, B. (1992). Countertransference and counter-resonance in the Psychodynamic psychotherapy of eating disorders. In. J. Brandell (Ed.), *Countertransference in child and adolescent psychotherapy*. New York: Aronson, 163-169.

Cabaj, R.P., Stein, T.S. (1996). *Textbook of homosexuality and mental health.* Washington, DC: American Psychiatric Association Press.

Cadwell, S.A., Burnham, R.A., Forstein, M. (Eds.) (1997). *Therapists on the front line: Psychotherapy with gay men in the age of AIDS.* Washington, DC: The American Psychiatric Association Press.

Casement, P. J. (1986). Countertransference and interpretation. *Contemporary Psychoanalysis, 22,* 548-559.

Chauncey, G. (1994). *Gay New York: Gender, Urban Culture and the Making of the Gay Male World, 1890-1940.* New York: Basic Books.

Cohler, B. (1976). The significance of the therapist's feelings in the treatment of anorexia nervosa. *Adolescent Psychiatry, 5,* 352-384.

Cohler, B. (1998). Saturday night at the tubs: Age, cohort and the social life of the urban gay bath house. Unpublished manuscript, the Committee on Human Development and the Evelyn Hooker Center for Gay and Lesbian Mental Health, The University of Chicago.

Cohler, B., Galatzer-Levy, R. (1992). Psychoanalysis and the classroom: Intent and meaning in learning and teaching. In. N. Szajnberg (Ed.), *Educating the emotions: Psychoanalysis in American culture.* New York: Plenum Publishing Company, 41-90.

Cohler, B., Galatzer-Levy, R., Shelby, D. (1998). *Gay and lesbian lives: Developmental course, life-story and psychoanalysis.* New York: The American Psychoanalytic Association.

Cornett, C. (1993). Dynamic psychotherapy of gay men: A view from self-psychology. In. C. Cornett (Ed.), *Affirmative dynamic psychotherapy with gay men.* New York: Arsonson, 45-76.

Crits-Cristoph, P., Barber, J.P. (1991). Introduction and historical background. In. P. Crits-Cristoph and J.P. Barber (Eds.), *Handbook of short-term dynamic psychotherapy.* New York: Basic Books, 1-16.

Denis, J. F. (1990). Personality disorders in psychiatry. *Canadian Journal of Psychiatry, 35,* 208-14.

Drescher, J. (1995). Anti-homosexual bias in training. In. T. Domenici and R.C. Lesser (Eds.), *Disorienting Sexualities.* New York: Routledge, 227-242.

Drescher, J. (1996). Psychoanalytic subjectivity and male homosexuality. In. R. Cabaj and T.S. Stein (Eds.), *Textbook of Homosexuality and Mental Health.* Washington, DC: The American Psychiatric Press, 173-190.

Drescher, J., (1997). The analyst's authority and the patient's sexuality. Unpublished manuscript, The William Alanson White Foundation.

Duberman, M. (1993). *Stonewall.* New York: St. Martin's Press.

Elder, G.H., Jr. (1974/1999). *Children of the Great Depression: Social change in life experience (25th Anniversary Edition).* Boulder, CO: Westview Press/Harper Collins.

Elder, G. (1995). The life-course paradigm: Social change and individual development. In. P. Moen, G.H. Elder, Jr., and Kurt Lüscher (Eds.), *Examining Lives in context: Perspectives on the ecology of human development.* Washington, DC: American Psychological Association, 101-139.

Elder, G. J., Jr. (1997). The life-course and human development. In. R. M. Lerner

(Ed), *Handbook of Child Psychology. Volume I: Theory.* (General Editor W. Damon). New York: Wiley, 939-991.

Elder, G.H., Jr. (In Press,b). Human Lives in changing societies: Life course and developmental insights. In. R. Cairns, G.H. Elder, Jr., and E. Costello (Eds.), *Developmental Science: Multiple Perspectives.* New York: Cambridge University Press.

Epstein, S. (1996). *Impure science: AIDS, activism, and the politics of knowledge.* Berkeley, CA: The University of California Press.

Fishman, J.M. (1994). Countertransference, the therapeutic frame, and AIDS: One psychotherapist's response. In. Cadwell, S.A., Burnham, R.A., Forstein, M. (Eds.), *Therapists on the front line: Psychotherapy with gay men in the age of AIDS.* Washington, DC: The American Psychiatric Association Press, 497-516.

Flarsheim, A. (1975). The therapist's collusion with the patient's wish for suicide. In P. Giovacchini (Ed.), *Tactics and techniques in psychoanalytic psychotherapy.* New York: Arsonson, 155-195.

Fliess, R. (1944). The metapsychology of the analyst. *Psychoanalytic Quarterly, 11,* 211-227.

Fliess, R. (1953). Countertransference and counteridentification. *Journal of the American Psychoanalytic Association, 1,* 268-284.

Forstein, M. (1986). Psychodynamic psychotherapy with gay male couples. In. T. S. Stein and C.J. Cohen (Eds.), *Contemporary perspectives on psychotherapy with lesbians and gay men.* New York: Plenum Medical Book Company, 103-138.

Foucault, M. (1961/1988). *Madness and civilization: A history of insanity in the age of reason* (Trans. R. Howard). New York: Random House/Vintage Books.

Foucault, M. (1975). *Discipline and punishment.* New York: Pantheon.

Foucault, M. (1976/1990). *The history of sexuality: Volume 1: An introduction.* (Trans. R. Hurley). New York: Random House.

Freud, S. (1910/1957). The future prospects of psycho-analytic therapy. In *Standard Edition of the Complete Psychological Works of Sigmund Freud.* London: The Hogarth Press, *11,* 141-161.

Freud, S. (1912a/1958). Recommendations to physicians practicing psychoanalysis. In J. Strachey (Ed. and Trans.), *The standard edition of the complete psychological works of Sigmund Freud, 12,* 109-120. London: Hogarth Press.

Freud, S. (1912b/1958). The dynamics of the transference. In J. Strachey (Ed. and Trans.), *The standard edition of the complete psychological works of Sigmund Freud, 12,* 97-108. London: Hogarth Press.

Freud, S. (1914/1958). Remembering, repeating and working through: Further recommendations on the technique of psychoanalysis. In J. Strachey (Ed. and Trans.), *The standard edition of the complete psychological works of Sigmund Freud, 12,* 146-156. London: Hogarth Press.

Freud, S. (1915/1958).Observations on transference-love: Further recommendations on the technique of psycho-analysis III). In. J. Strachey (Ed. And Trans.). *The Standard Edition of the Complete Psychological Works of Sigmund Freud.* London: The Hogarth Press, *12,* 159-171.

Friedman, R. (1988). *The anatomy of psychotherapy.* Hillsdale, NJ: The Analytic Press.

Gardner, R. (1983). *Self-Inquiry.* Boston: Little-Brown and Atlantic Monthly Press.

Gay, P. (1988). *Freud: A life for our times.* New York: Norton.

Gill, M. (1976). Metapsychology is not psychology. In M. Gill & P. Holzman (Eds.), *Psychology versus metapsychology.* New York: International Universities Press.

Gill, M. (1994). *Psychoanalysis in transition: A personal view.* Hillsdale, NJ: The Analytic Press.

Gonsiorek, J. C. (1982/1985). *A guide to psychotherapy with gay and lesbian clients.* Binghamton, NY: Harrington Park Press/The Haworth Press, Inc.

Grayer, E. D. and Sax, P. (1986). A model for the diagnostic and therapeutic use of countertransference. *Clinical Social Work Journal, 14,* 295-309.

Greenson, R. (1960). Empathy and its vicissitudes. *International Journal of Psycho-analysis, 41,* 418-424.

Greenson, R. (1965). The working alliance and the transference neurosis. *Psychoanalytic Quarterly, 34,* 155-181.

Greene, L. R., Rosenkrantz, J & Muth, D. Y. (1986). Borderline defenses and countertransference, Research findings and implications. *Psychiatry, 49,* 253-264.

Harry, J., DuVall, W. (1978). Age and sexual culture among homosexually oriented males. *Archives of Sexual Behavior, 7,* 199-202.

Heimann, P. (1950). On countertransference. *International Journal of Psycho-Analysis, 31,* 81-84.

Henriksson, B. (1995). Risk factor love: Homosexuality, sexual interaction and HIV-prevention. Göteborg Sweden: Göteborgs Universitet Institutionen för socialt arbete Skriftserien.

Herek, G. (1995). Psychological heterosexism in the United States. In. A. R. D'Augelli and C. Patterson (Eds.), *Lesbian, gay, and bisexual identities over the life span.* New York: Oxford University Press, 321-346.

Herek, G. (1996). Heterosexism and homophobia. In. R. Cabaj and T.S. Stein (Eds.). *Textbook of Homosexuality and Mental Health.* Washington, DC: The American Psychiatric Association Press, 101-113.

Herek, G.M., Greene, B. (1995). (Eds.). *AIDS, identity, and community: The HIV epidemic and lesbians and gay men.* Thousand Oaks, CA: Sage Publications (Psychological perspectives on lesbian and gay issues).

Herron, W.G., Kinter, T., Sollinger, I. Trubowitz, J. (1993). Psychotherapy for homosexual clients: New concepts. In. C. Cornett (Ed.), *Affirmative dynamic psychotherapy with gay men.* New York: Arsonson, 1-22.

Hetrick, E.S., Stein, T.S. (1984). *Innovations in psychotherapy with homosexuals.* Washington, DC: American Psychiatric (Association) Press.

Hildebrand, P. (1992). A patient dying with AIDS. *International Review of Psycho-analysis, 19,* 457-469.

Hoffman, I.Z. (1991). Discussion: Toward a social-constructivist view of the psychoanalytic situation. *Psychoanalytic dialogues, 2,* 287-304.

Isay, R. (1993). In. C. Cornett (Ed.), *Affirmative dynamic psychotherapy with gay men.* New York: Arsonson, 23-44.

Kantrowitz, J.L. (1996). *The patient's impact on the analyst.* Hillsdale, NJ: The Analytic Press.

Klein, G. (1976). *Psychoanalytic theory: An exploration of essentials.* New York: International Universities Press.

Kohut, H. (1959/1978). Introspection, empathy, and psychoanalysis: An examination of the relationship between mode of observation and theory. In P. Ornstein (Ed.), *The search for the self (Vol. 1).* New York: International Universities Press, 205-232.

Kohut, H. (1971). *The analysis of the self.* Madison, CT: International Universities Press.

Kohut, H. (1977). *The restoration of the self.* Madison, CT: International Universities Press.

Kohut, H. (1979). The two analyses of Mr. Z. *International Journal of Psychoanalysis, 60,* 3-27.

Kohut, H. (1982). Introspection, empathy, and the semi-circle of mental health, *International Journal of Psychoanalysis, 63,* 395-407.

Kohut, H. (1984). *How does analysis cure?* Chicago: The University of Chicago Press.

Kohut, H., Wolf, E. (1978). The disorders of the self and their treatment: An outline. *International Journal of Psychoanalysis, 59,* 413-425.

Kooden, H. (1991). Self-disclosure: The gay male therapist as an agent of social change. In. C. Silverstein (Ed.), *Gays, lesbians, and their therapists.* New York: Norton, 143-154.

Krajeski, J. (1984). Psychotherapy with gay and lesbian clients. In. E. S. Hetrick and T.S. Stein (Eds.), *Innovations in psychotherapy with homosexuals. Washington, DC: The American Psychiatric Association Press,* 75-88.

Kris, A. O. (1990). Helping patients by analyzing self-criticism. *Journal of the American Psychoanalytic Association, 38,* 605-636.

Lipton, S. D. (1977). The advantages of Freud's technique as shown in his analysis of the Rat Man. *International Journal of Psychoanalysis, 58,* 255-273.

Little, M. (1951). Countertransference. *International Journal of Psychoanalysis, 32,* 32-40.

Luborksy, L., Mark, D. (1991). Intensive short-term dynamic psychotherapy. In. P. Crits-Cristoph and J.P. Barber (Eds.), *Handbook of short-term dynamic psychotherapy.* New York: Basic Books, 110-136.

Lynch, P. (1998). Debasement in the sphere of homosexual love as understood through Freud's formulation of the universal tendency to debasement. *Journal of the American Psychoanalytic Association* (in press).

Mahler, M., Pine, F., Bergman, A. (1975). *The psychological birth of the human infant.* New York: Basic Books.

Malyon, A. (1982). Psychotherapeutic implications of internalized homophobia in gay men. *Journal of Homosexuality, 72,* 59-69.

Mann, D. (1997). *Psychotherapy: An erotic relationship.* London: Routledge.

Meissner, W. (1996). Empathy in the therapeutic alliance. *Psychoanalytic Inquiry, 16,* 39-53.

Messer, S., Warren, C.S. (1995). *Models of brief Psychodynamic therapy: A comparative approach.* New York: the Guilford Press.

Missenard, A. (1989). Contre-transfert et processus analytique (1). (Countertransference and analytic process: (I). *Topique: Revue Freudienne, 19*(44), September, 295-315.

Odets, W. (1994). Seronegative gay men and considerations of safe and unsafe sex. In. Cadwell, S.A., Burnham, R.A., Forstein, M. (Eds.), *Therapists on the front line: Psychotherapy with gay men in the age of AIDS.* Washington, DC: The American Psychiatric Association Press, 427-452.

Odets, W. (1995). *In the shadow of the epidemic: Being HIV-Negative in the Age of Aids.* Durham, NC: Duke University Press.

Petrucelli, J. (1997). "Playing with fire": Transference-countertransference configurations in the treatment of a sexually compulsive HIV-Positive gay man. In. M. Blechner (Ed.), *Hope and mortality: Psychodynamic approaches to AIDS and HIV.* Hillsdale, NJ: The Analytic Press, 143-162.

Pinsker, H., Rosenthal, R., McCullough, L. (1991). Dynamic supportive psychotherapy. In. P. Crits-Cristoph and J.P. Barber (Eds.), *Handbook of short-term dynamic psychotherapy.* New York: Basic Books, 220-247.

Plath, D. (1980). Contours of consociation: Lessons from a Japanese narrative. In P.B. Baltes and O.G. Brim, Jr. (Eds), *Life-Span Development and Behavior, Volume 3.* New York: Academic Press, 287-305.

Racker, H. (1968). *Transference and Countertransference.* New York: International Universities Press.

Reich, A. (1951). On countertransference. *International Journal of Psychoanalysis, 32,* 25-31.

Renik, O. (1986). Countertransference in theory and practice. *Journal of the American Psychoanalytic Association, 34,* 699-708.

Ricoeur, P. (1971). The model of the text: Meaningful action considered as text. *Social Research, 38,* 529-562.

Ricoeur, P. (1977). The question of proof in Freud's psychoanalytic writings. *Journal of the American Psychoanalytic Association, 25,* 835-872.

Schafer, R. (1959). Generative empathy in the treatment situation. *Psychoanalytic Quarterly, 28,* 342-373.

Schafer, R. (1981). *Narrative actions in Psychoanalysis.* Worcester, Mass: Clark University Press (Volume XIV of the Heinz Werner Lecture Series).

Schafer, R. (1982). The relevance of the 'here-and-now' transference interpretation to the reconstruction of early development. *International Journal of Psychoanalysis, 63,* 77-82.

Schafer, R. (1992). *Retelling a life: Narration and dialogue in psychoanalysis.* New York: Basic Books.

Schafer, R. (1995). The evolution of my views on non-normative sexual practices. In T. Domenici and R. C. Lesser (Eds.), *Disorienting Sexuality: Psychoanalytic reappraisals of sexual identities.* New York: Routledge, 187-202.

Settersten, R. A., Jr., Hägestad, G. (1996). What's the latest? Cultural age deadlines for family transitions. *The Gerontologist, 36,* 178-188.

Settersten, R. A, Jr., Mayer, K. U. (1997). The measurement of age, age structuring, and the life-course. *Annual review of sociology, 23,* 233-261.

Shectman, F. (1989). Countertransference dilemmas with borderline patients, The contribution of psychological testing. *Bulletin of the Menninger Clinic*, *53*, 310-318.

Shelby, D. (1994a). Homosexuality and the struggle for coherence. In. A. Goldberg (Ed.), *Progress in self psychology*, *10*, 55-78. Hillsdale, NJ: The Analytic Press.

Shelby, D. (1994b). Mourning within a culture of mourning. In Cadwell, S.A., Burnham, R.A., Forstein, M. (Eds.), *Therapists on the front line: Psychotherapy with gay men in the age of AIDS*. Washington, DC: The American Psychiatric Association Press, 53-80.

Shelby, R.D. (1995). *People with HIV and those who help them*. New York: Harrington Park Press/The Haworth Press, Inc.

Shelby, R.D. (1998). About cruising and being cruised. Unpublished paper, The Library of the Institute for Psychoanalysis (Chicago).

Shilts, R. (1987). *And the band played on: Politics, people, and the AIDS epidemic*. New York: St,. Martin's Press.

Sifneos, P.E. (1971). Two different kinds of psychotherapy of short duration. In. H.H. Barton (Ed.). *Brief therapies*. New York: Plenum Publishing Company, 82-90.

Silverstein, C. (1991) (Ed.) *Gays, lesbians, and their therapists*. New York: Norton.

Stein, R. (1997). The shame experiences of the analyst. In. A. Goldberg (Ed.), *Progress in self psychology*. Hillsdale, NJ: The Analytic Press, 109-123.

Stein, T. (1988). Theoretical considerations in psychotherapy with gay men and lesbians. *Journal of Homosexuality*, *15*, 75-96.

Stein, T.S., Cabaj, R.P. (1996). Psychotherapy with gay men. In. R.P. Cabaj and T.S. Stein (Eds.), *Textbook of homosexuality and mental health*. Washington, DC: The American Psychiatric Association Press, 413-432.

Stein, T.S., Cohen, C. J. (1984). Psychotherapy with gay men and lesbians: An examination of homophobia, coming out and identity. In. E.S. Hetrick and T.S. Stein (Eds.), *Innovations in psychotherapy with homosexuals*. Washington, DC: The American Psychiatric Association Press, 59-75.

Stern, D. (1985). *The interpersonal world of the infant*. New York: Basic Books.

Stolorow, R., Atwood, G., Branchaft, B. (1994). (Eds.) *The intersubjective perspective*. New York: Jason Aronson.

Strachey, J. (1958). Editor's note. In. Freud, S. (1915/1958), Observations on transference-love: Further recommendations on the technique of psycho-analysis III. In. J. Strachey (Ed. and Trans.) *The Standard Edition of the Complete Psychological Works of Sigmund Freud*. London: The Hogarth Press, *12*, 160-161.

Thoma, H. Kachele, H. and Jiminez, J. P. (1986). La contratransferencia en una perspectiva historico-critica. *Revista de Psicoanalisis*, *43*, 1237-1272.

Tolpin, M. (1997). The development of sexuality and the self. *The Annual for Psychoanalysis*, *XXV*, 173-187.

Tolpin, M., Kohut, H. (1980/1989). The disorders of the self-the psychopathology of the first years of life. In. G. Pollock and S. Greenspan (Eds.), *The course of life*. (Volume II). Madison, CT: International Univrsities Press, 229-253.

de Urtubey, L. (1989). Contre-transfert et interpretation freudienne ou kleinienne *Revue Francaise de Psychanalyse*, *53*, 873-883.

Vaslamatzis, C., Kanellos, P. Tserpe, V. & Verveniotis, S. (1986). Countertransference responses in short-term dynamic psychotherapy. *Psychotherapy and Psychosomatics, 46*, 105-109.

Weinberg, M. S. (1970). The male homosexual: Age-related variations in social and psychological characteristics. *Social Problems, 17*, 527-538.

Winnicott, D. W. (1949). Hate in the counter-transference. *International Journal of Psycho-Analysis, 30*.

Winnicott, D. W. (1960). The theory of the parent-infant relationship. *International Journal of Psychoanalysis, 41*, 585-595.

Winnicott, D.W. (1962). Dependence in infant-care, in child-care, and in the psychoanalytic setting. *International Journal of Psychoanalysis, 44*, 339-344.

Winnicott, D. W. (1972/1986). *Holding and interpretation: Fragment of an analysis.* London: Hogarth Press.

Young, I. (1995). *The stonewall experiment: A gay psychohistory.* London: Cassell.

Zetzel, E. (1958a/1970). Therapeutic Alliance in the analysis of hysteria. In E. Zetzel, *The capacity for emotional growth.* New York: International Universities Press, 182-196.

Zetzel, E. (1958b/1970). The analytic situation and the analytic process. In E. Zetzel, *The capacity for emotional growth.* New York: International Universities Press, 197-215.

Chapter 8

On Learning to Learn Again

Dennis L. McCaughan

We don't have that sort of absolute knowledge about human
living, and therefore, we shall remain eternally young.

–Harry Stack Sullivan

KEYWORDS. Sullivan, psychotherapy, interpersonal, brief, treatment

INTRODUCTION:
PORTRAIT OF THE YOUNG PSYCHOTHERAPIST

As a young psychotherapist in training, I had the good fortune to be
educated at one of those now long gone state supported facilities
devoted to training, research, and service. A large monolithic structure
located in a larger medical complex, the institute supported several
nationally recognized programs in adolescent treatment and the

Dennis L. McCaughan, PhD, is Clinical Assistant Professor of Psychology and
Psychiatry, University of Illinois at Chicago; Faculty, Program in Advanced Psychodynamic Clinical Practice, School of Social Service Administration, University
of Chicago; and maintains an independent practice in Chicago.
Address correspondence to: Dennis L. McCaughan, 55 East Washington, Suite
2302, Chicago, IL 60602.

[Haworth co-indexing entry note]: "Chapter 8. On Learning to Learn Again." McCaughan, Dennis L.
Co-published simultaneously in *Psychoanalytic Social Work* (The Haworth Press, Inc.) Vol. 6, No. 3/4,
1999, pp. 203-217; and: *Comparative Approaches in Brief Dynamic Psychotherapy* (ed: William Borden)
The Haworth Press, Inc., 1999, pp. 203-217. Single or multiple copies of this article are available for a fee
from The Haworth Document Delivery Service [1-800-342-9678, 9:00 a.m. - 5:00 p.m. (EST). E-mail address:
getinfo@haworthpressinc.com].

psychopharmacology of the major mental disorders as well as an active outpatient clinic. The practice of psychotherapy was dominated by psychoanalysis although an imaginative and articulate neo-Piagetian formed an active opposition. The reigning paradigm was the analyst and the analyzed, the observer and the observed, with the psychotherapist's participation generally viewed as directed toward understanding the patient's psychic life or, if that was obscured, then the patient's behavior as a reflection of that inner world.

This idea of the patient as an object to be understood suffused theory with a certain promise, if not magic. The term "object" suggested something one could observe at a safe theoretical distance rather than the "live creature," in John Dewey's phrase, of actual clinical practice. Theories of objects offered me the promise of a correct, if not final understanding. Encounters with live creatures in psychotherapy were real, changing, and uncertain. In my quest for certainty, I would come to see, I undervalued an interaction that both restricts and potentially liberates the awareness of both participants. I later diagnosed my suffering as stemming from what Edgar Levenson (1972) called the "fallacy of understanding." At the time, I searched for understanding apart from active participation in the doing of therapy. While I was often cautioned against being seduced by the patient, I was never warned against the seduction of theory. Despite the guidance of several creative and supportive supervisors, I found that my learning was overshadowed by the anxiety I felt in working with a group of severely disturbed and disturbing adolescents (McCaughan, 1985). A certain intellectualization of the process of therapy came all too easily to those like myself who had spent years in various graduate programs and professional schools. I sought refuge in the distant and academic writings of Heinz Hartman's elegant extensions of ego psychology. Anna Freud's analysis of the concept of neutrality–a position equidistant between the various psychic agencies–seemed equally Olympian. Some of us had been reading the work of the English psychoanalysts as well. Melanie Klein's idiom captured what many of us felt with our patients: they were often rude, uncivil and at times painfully toxic. The work of Heinz Kohut was slowly gaining recognition, and I found that his ideas sounded very much like the Winnicott I was reading. Kohut offered a rationale for adapting to the patient's demands and needs: clinical necessity became theoretical virtue. Merton Gill was forcefully arguing his view that the essence of the therapeutic relationship was to be found in the analysis of the transference. For several years, a group of us sat around and played supervisor to Gill's therapist. Even an analyst of Gill's stature appeared uncertain and confused, a fact largely absent from the conventional clinical and theoretical literature. One can only admire someone like Gill who in my days as a student of psychotherapy made his clinical work transparent. Increasingly, Gill found that the interpersonalists had all along been sympathetic to his views. Gill, however, remained true to the Freudian paradigm, perhaps to square himself theoretically (if not spiritually) with Freud. As powerful as the concept of transference was in Gill's hands, it remained in my own understanding still tied to an expression of the patient's private experience apart from the social field of the therapeutic encounter in which both participants were equally engaged. It was the idea of a two-person psychology and its experience that eluded me. Looking back, it might have been more useful if I had considered the question of how learning takes place in psychotherapy rather than what could be understood of the patient's individual experience.

My own awareness of the interpersonal tradition came through my interest in studies of the psychiatric hospital pioneered by people like Alfred Stanton and Morris Schwartz (1954) who themselves had been influenced directly by the work of Harry Stack Sullivan. I began a rather unsystematic reading of his journal, *Psychiatry,* and found my way to the related journal, *Contemporary Psychoanalysis,* and then to the work of Frieda Fromm-Reichman (1950). Her work was the basis for the storied account of standing as engaged witness to a patient's heroic struggle and remains a significant document in the history of psychotherapy (Green, 1964). Harold Searles (1979) received a thorough reading as well. He described with great candor a clinical situation both personally disturbing and conceptually confusing. What I felt I knew best was the anxiety of my own participation in the therapeutic process. I began to formulate my experience in less formal terms posing questions, "Who is doing what to whom and why?" I became less concerned with what Will (1970, p. ix) calls "the supposedly private economy" of the other, a concern that often results in highly speculative, theoretically driven assumptions about the inner world of the patient. The result was a greater awareness of my own participation in the relationship with the other and the inevitable tensions that often characterize the psychotherapeutic interaction. It occurred to me that theory, in my hands at least, served as a kind of antidote in that it seemed to have a direct relationship to the anxiety that I often experienced in my work. As Friedman (1988) playfully observes, "Therapists function in a sea of trouble and they talk as though they don't" (p. 6). That is, a theoretical understanding of the inner workings of the other allowed me to talk about the patient's experience without having to give equal attention to my own. The experience of a two-person psychology gave way to a preoccupation with the psychology of the other. Dyrud (1979) has argued that our theoretical and clinical language remains very much the language of individual psychology despite the recent emphasis in the literature on a "two-person" psychology. This observation remains true today.

SULLIVAN'S CHALLENGE: THE "MOTHER OF ALL ILLUSIONS"

In mulling over the contribution of Sullivan to our understanding of human relatedness and its problems, what remains essential in my understanding is the participation between therapist and patient and the awareness that comes from such an encounter. That this seemingly simple observation continues to challenge us defines Sullivan's legacy and his continuing relevance to the practice of psychotherapy. It is clear in reading Sullivan that he struggled as well with a perspective that challenged the one-way direction of therapeutic interaction and influence. Although Sullivan himself did not fully embrace the implications of his own contribution for the practice of psychotherapy, it seems clear that he did formulate the problem of mutual influence by translating George Herbert Mead's concept of "reflected appraisals" into the psychopathology of self-other relations. For this reason, Sullivan remains of vital concern to what we often consider our now common understanding of interpersonal processes and psychotherapy.

I want to argue that many of us moved beyond Sullivan before having fully engaged his views and struggled with his challenge. I will try to address Sullivan's continuing relevance to our work as psychotherapists, whether we practice the short or long form of this uncertain yet compelling encounter. I have begun with an account of my own early experience as a psychotherapist as a way to convey what I think to be the assumptions that continue to influence our work and, however fascinating and necessary, distract us from the immediacy of our relationship with the other person. At this point I will discuss what Sullivan called the "mother of all illusions" as a useful introduction to his work and then consider his now classic work, *The Psychiatric Interview* (1954/1970). And finally, I want to suggest ways in which our understanding of short-term interventions can benefit from a continuing struggle with Sullivan's legacy.

In "The Data of Psychiatry," his inaugural paper in *Psychiatry* in 1938, Sullivan writes:

> The individuality of a particular electron is of no concern to the physicist; the individuality of the biologist's dog is not apt to confuse his biology of the dog. It is quite otherwise, however, with the traditionally emphasized individuality of each of us, "myself." Here we have the very mother of illusions, the ever pregnant source of preconceptions that invalidate almost all our efforts to understand other people. (p. 121)

The study of interpersonal phenomena, the domain of psychiatry in Sullivan's view, requires a revolutionary shift in perspective. And it is the mythic, heroic "me" that must be engaged if we are to understand ourselves and others. This, to paraphrase Sullivan, is a real "mother" of a paradigm shift. The idea that our private self (or selves) should not be the central preoccupation of what it means to be human is a blow to all of us who have been reared in a culture that so clearly prizes the individual. The task of psychotherapy is often seen as focused on freeing the "true self" from the bondage of the past and its claims upon the present. Sullivan's great friend, Clara Thompson, whose own work owes much to Sullivan's influence and who, in turn, tutored Sullivan in psychoanalysis based on her own analysis and training with Sandor Ferenczi, offers a useful clarification of this somewhat puzzling position. In a style of thinking that was simple and direct, Thompson (1958/1964) argues that the private self was not rejected by Sullivan as much as he saw it as existing outside his theoretical system. The fantasy life of a person may well exist but it is of no concern to the psychotherapist until it finds expression in the interpersonal moment. Sullivan's view of language led him to be suspicious of efforts to know what the other was thinking until there was clarification as to what was said and what was meant by what was said. Formulations based on our ideas about the other reflect our prized individuality in that it is this very individuality that leads us to assume an understanding of the other apart from what we can directly observe. Theorizing about events taking place in the steamy intrapsychic hothouse was for Sullivan no substitute for the direct heat of the interaction and its observable consequences for the persons involved. In the *Interpersonal Theory of Psychiatry* (1953), Sullivan writes that " . . . we will not study people as such, but what they do, and what can be fairly inferred as to why they do it" (p. 26).

Levenson (1982), in contrasting the Freudian and interpersonal perspectives, captured the essence of this view in a memorable phrase as the difference between the "detoxification of fantasy and the demystification of experience" (p. 127). The use of the term psychoanalytic to describe Sullivan may be of questionable value in that it evokes a continental view of the speculative person rather than an American and pragmatic one which seems more in keeping with Sullivan's vision. The result has been to view Sullivan as something of a minor player within the larger psychoanalytic tradition, as a psychoanalytic theorist in a new suit of common clothes cut from a more formal and elegant fabric. That was certainly true at the time I was in training–no one I knew was engaged with his ideas concerning personality development, much less psychotherapy. (A brief visit by the late John Schimel from the William Alanson White Institute in New York was the exception in my experience and I remember his consultation as playful and engaged.) Many psychoanalytically trained clinicians knew relatively little about the social science tradition (e.g., the Chicago School of sociologists and the anthropological work of Edward Sapir and his student Ruth Benedict) that so influenced Sullivan, a tradition that orthodox psychoanalysis found suspect, given its concern with the social field of behavior as contrasted with the psychic depths of the isolated person. In some important respects, Sullivan's vision has more in common with Dewey than Freud. Further it is worth noting that while many of us seemed to know at least something about the geographically distant Winnicott and Klein, we knew relatively little about a way of thinking within driving distance of many American cities. Obviously, there were then and are now many reasons why we remain relatively uninformed about the various psychoanalytic schools of thought. The very idea of a school naturally suggests certain requirements for matriculation and a commitment to one vision as opposed to others. Schafer (1983), in discussing the problems of a comparative psychoanalysis, has argued that the problems of comparing the various psychoanalytic schools is that theories are elevated to the level of myths with all the attendant emotional investments. To see theories as fictions, as stories told about our understanding of ourselves and others, is to recognize more fully what Harold Bloom (1973) in describing the dynamics of English poetic creation called the "anxiety of influence." It is often exceedingly difficult to appreciate the novel contribution of a rival school without lapsing into defensive justification or simplistic dismissal. The tendency to idealize our intellectual origins blinds us to their continuing and often unacknowledged influence. We are, however, fortunate that in the last 15 years we work in an intellectual environment in which a comparative psychoanalysis is increasingly possible. This is due in large part to the work of Greenburg and Mitchell (1983) who themselves developed in a tradition that sought to marry Sullivan's contributions with the contemporary psychoanalysis of Clara Thompson.

The emergence of a vital comparative study of psychoanalytic contributions over the last decade has allowed us to see Sullivan's essential position more clearly, as Sullivan himself would have predicted. It was, after all, Sullivan who recognized the potential for new learning in drawing comparisons between our own experience and that of others. By locating the observer's position squarely at the center of the human encounter, in the evolving space between self and other, Sullivan cleared the way for recognizing our participation in the therapeutic process and made possible the many recent developments in psychoanalytic studies including the constructivist critiques of therapeutic interaction. From this position, Sullivan's clinical contributions, his way of working, can be more fully appreciated.

SULLIVAN AT WORK: THE PSYCHIATRIC INTERVIEW

A contemporary reading of Sullivan's clinical text, *The Psychiatric Interview* (1954/1970), will suggest what might have helped this young therapist of 20 years ago, but more importantly will clarify Sullivan's continuing relevance to our work today. Sullivan's psychotherapeutic program concerns itself with increasing awareness of interpersonal experience and the corresponding development of flexibility in characteristic patterns of relating. Anxiety, Sullivan argues, increases when my version of me and you is at odds with your version of me and you. In many ways, *The Psychiatric Interview* is a fascinating albeit idiosyncratic manual on the management of anxiety. As Dyrud (1979) observes in his trenchant essay on Sullivan's contribution, it is this capacity that defines "expertness" in the field of interpersonal relations. When read this way, Sullivan's own personality makes real the clinical encounter and the tensions and uncertainties that go with it. The fact that these pages were delivered originally as lectures before finding their way into the present form gives the reader a sense of Sullivan's presence and allows one to imagine Sullivan actually speaking with an audience before him. Sullivan's lectures in written form are often thought of as difficult to read, probably because they require listening, a conversational kind of engagement. It is possible to feel in these pages the flow of an encounter with both a challenging personality and a challenging clinical and theoretical account. It is this, the therapist's presence, that defines the therapeutic situation: the therapist for better and for worse, and a patient, for better and for worse. It is what these participants do together, and do to and with each other, and the awareness that comes from such an encounter that can lead to a more satisfying way of living. Obviously, it is the therapist who must guide this process but it remains *this* therapist and not some version of a therapist as so much of our clinical dogma would suggest. Here is Sullivan describing his work. In this example Sullivan is interviewing a young man "sinking into schizophrenic illness" who had "spent a good deal of time in the kitchen with his mother making dirty cracks at her."

> . . . I undertook to discover what was so surprising to him about this business of his hostile remarks to his mother, and he made it quite clear that the surprising thing was that she had never done him any harm, and had actually enfolded him in every kind of good. To all this I thought, "Oh yeah? It doesn't sound so to me. It doesn't make sense. Maybe you have overlooked something."
>
> By that time I was actually able to say something like this: "I have the vague feeling that some people might doubt the utility to you of the care with which your parents, and particularly your mother, saw to it that you didn't learn how to dance, or play games, or otherwise engage in the frivolous social life of the people your age." And I was delighted to see the schizophrenic young man give me a sharp look. Although he was seated where I didn't have to look directly at him. I could see that. And I said,

"Or was that an unmitigated blessing?" There was a long pause, and then he opined that when he was young he might have been sore about it.

I guessed that that wasn't the whole story–that he was still sore about it, and with very good reason. Then I inquired if he felt any disadvantage in college from the lack of these social skills with which his colleagues whiled away their evenings, and so on. He recalled that he had often noticed his defects in that field, and that he regretted them.

With this improvement in intelligence, we were able to glean more of what the mother had actually done and said to discourage his impulse to develop social techniques. At the end of an hour and a half devoted more or less entirely to this subject, I was able to say, "Well, now, is it really so curious that you're being unpleasant to your mother?" And he thought that perhaps it wasn't. (p. 21)

There are many things to say about this exchange that speak to Sullivan's sense of the interview and the assumptions behind it. Again, what is noteworthy is Sullivan's use of language. It is the language of interpersonal relations, the vernacular of everyday speech. When Sullivan reports his reaction to the patient's paean to his mother, he thinks to himself "Oh yeah? It doesn't sound so to me. It doesn't make sense. Maybe you have overlooked something." There is no speculation about the patient's inner life; there is no further mystification of the patient's seemingly mystifying account. His response is simple and direct: let's find out. Here we see the patient's anxiety concerning his hostility towards his mother as disruptive to the awareness of his interpersonal experience. His experience of his mother must exclude his hostility and once it begins to be expressed he finds himself increasingly disorganized and fearful. What Sullivan calls "security operations" restrict the patient's awareness in the interview itself and the patient's "sharp look" indicates that Sullivan is now threatening the patient's stance in that the patient acts as if he must hold to the position that his anger towards his mother is unjustified. This is an example of the operation of "selective inattention" in that the basis for the patient's hostility is kept out of awareness in order to preserve a particular pattern of relating.

Sullivan's manner suggests that the patient's hostility must have some basis particularly given the patient's claim that, as Sullivan wryly puts it, his mother had "enfolded him in every kind of good." Out of the corner of his eye Sullivan carefully observes the patient's response to his comment that the young man might indeed have had reason to be angry with his mother and ties that to rather specific kinds of satisfying social experiences from which the patient was apparently protected. The patient's response, the "sharp look," delights Sullivan because he recognizes the anger as an increase in the patient's anxiety and therefore the potential for an increase in awareness. At this point Sullivan wonders, "Or was that an unmitigated blessing?" The movement of the interview, from the patient's view of his saintly mother to Sullivan's reflection on the social pleasures and necessities of growing up, establishes an interpersonal situation in which the patient's hostility is now plausible. Further, he locates the patient's complaint not in some toxic fantasy about his mother but in the observable reality that certain social experiences that we all require in some measure growing up might have been denied him. Sullivan wonders if the patient might not still be "sore" about his early experience and then moves to the present, inquiring about the patient's current experience as a college student. The young man acknowledges his social limitations and there is, as Sullivan notes, a corresponding increase in the patient's "intelligence." This leads to further exploration of the actual relationship between mother and son and the social "defects" which keep him in the kitchen "making cracks at her." At the end of the ninety minutes, Sullivan offers the possibility that his behavior towards his mother might make sense after all.

Nowhere in this exchange is there any specific "interpretation," rather Sullivan seems to work at clarification through questions that explore the patient's contemporary interpersonal experience. How could it be, Sullivan wonders, that the patient's hostility is directed toward someone he describes as so loving and committed. Sullivan's approach to the anxious patient is not, as he says, to " . . . do magic with reassuring language. The magic occurs in the interpersonal relations, and the real magic is done by the patient, not by the therapist. The therapist's skill and art lie in keeping things simple enough so that something can happen; in other words, he clears the field for favorable change, and then tries to avoid getting in the way of its development" (p. 216). Once Sullivan put the question of the patient's relationship to his mother at the moment of the "sharp look," "the field for favorable change" had been cleared for the moment and Sullivan could get out of the way of its development as the patient described the specifics of his troubled social relationships. We can also see the establishment of a gradient of hope in that the patient might now suspect that his problems in establishing adequate and satisfying social relationships were not a function of his defects but of his inability to recognize what was happening in his relationship with others as reflected in his relationship with his mother. That is, the interview allowed the patient to gain some purchase on what was happening to him as Sullivan became aware of what the patient's anger was all about. Here again, Levenson's distinction between "demystification of experience" and the Freudian "detoxification of fantasy" is relevant. Sullivan attempts to provide the patient with a better story, a story that accounts for all that is happening to him and which stands a chance of being integrated with the help of another person who himself values the need for satisfying social relationships. This is made even more poignant by knowing that Sullivan is to have said that his own mother's version of him " . . . was so different from me that I felt she had no use for me except as a clotheshorse upon which to hang an elaborate pattern of illusion" (cited in Perry, 1982, p. 13). The young man's loneliness was more threatening than the anxiety he experienced with others and by helping him to manage that anxiety Sullivan was able to help him to learn again.

Making anxiety the principal concept of the clinical and theoretical program allows Sullivan's own work to speak most directly to the therapist because anxiety is an experience we all know something about. Had I been able to grasp that fact as a young therapist and to remember it as a seasoned one I might have learned that the essential task was to try to be with myself while being with my patients so that we both might learn from what was happening between us. Obvious as it may seem, it is this understanding that is made possible by a set of assumptions central to Sullivan's approach as when Sullivan says: "And no one has grave difficulties in living if he has a very good grasp on what is happening to him" (p. 22). Unable to recognize and integrate his hostility towards his mother, this young man was slowly going mad. His anxiety in having to recognize the degree to which his experience with his mother constricted his awareness of himself and others and made social learning difficult, was made possible by a therapist who was less anxious relative to the horror that the patient felt in acknowledging directly his hostility towards that wonderful woman, his mother. The social field of the therapeutic interview made learning from experience once again possible. Sullivan writes: "The instrument is not in the theory but in the person. His principal instrument of observation is the self–his personality, *him* as a person. The processes and the changes in processes that make up the data which can be subjected to scientific study occur, not in the subject person nor in the observer, but in the situation which is created between the observer and his subject" (p. 3). The directness of such a statement places the therapist squarely in the interpersonal field with the data from both patient and therapist as data for the illumination of those patterns of anticipation and expectation that govern experience. Sullivan sees this as a specific version of the more general experience with another person with whom one feels understood and Sullivan argues that this experience is based on respect. He says, "If you will pause to consider the people whom you look upon as 'understanding'–that is, able to handle you expertly–you will notice that they demonstrate a very considerable respect for you" (p. 28). It is then the creation of the therapeutic field, the field of the study of interpersonal relations, that is the principal aim of Sullivan's theory and clinical work.

THE PSYCHOTHERAPEUTIC MINUTE: SULLIVAN AND BRIEF TREATMENT

Sullivan's approach to psychotherapy was an ordered one, moving from what he termed the "reconnaissance," an account of what brings the patient to therapy in the first place and a survey of the patient's history of interpersonal relations to date, followed by the "detailed inquiry" in which aspects of history and current experience are explored in greater detail, to the "termination" phase of the interview itself. What is of particular importance in this time of brief therapy is the degree to which Sullivan made every effort to be clear about what the problem is and then to communicate that understanding directly to the patient. This sense of having a consensual understanding of the problem was the beginning of the inquiry into the specifics of the patient's experience with the problem. For Sullivan, a successful reconnaissance itself could result in a good outcome in that the patient might realize what was happening to him and therefore experience a satisfactory resolution of his immediate concern. Further exploration would depend upon the nature of the problem and the degree to which the patient felt that his or her ability to learn from new interpersonal experience had been satisfactorily enhanced. To the contemporary reader this, of course, sounds much like several approaches to brief treatment. In a footnote to a question concerning the length of the detailed inquiry Sullivan, in his characteristic fashion, comments on what he thinks prolongs psychotherapeutic work: "I have long held that 'brief' psychotherapy was to be achieved by improving the utilization of the psychotherapeutic minute. If one is governed by no principles, but only by some vague beliefs–as in something like 'free association'–I think brief psychotherapy is very likely to be measured in terms of decades" (p. 76). One could find in that concise remark Sullivan's critique of those psychotherapeutic methods that fail to address with sufficient purpose the experience of the person in his relations with others. The freeing of the individual from restrictive and restricting patterns of interactions with others is the purpose of the work and the temptation to sail off with the patient into apparently more interesting waters where islands filled with fascinating artifacts of fantasy and imagined experience can be found is difficult for many of us as therapists to resist. Patients, for their own reasons, often wish to cruise those waters as well. As Gustafson and Dichter (1983) argue, Sullivan was interested in bringing to light the missing data left out of the patient's account of his interactions with others. The operation of "selective inattention" requires a focus on that which remains outside the patient's immediate awareness and therefore limits his ability to know what is happening and to learn from it. The problem with "free association" is its very indirectness as a method of exploration. One might think that we tend to associate in line with our anxieties about our relationships with others, leaving areas in our experience unaccounted for in some direct and observable way. The psychotherapist from this perspective attempts to create a social field where the rise and fall of anxiety leads to collaborative efforts to account for such lost experience. Sullivan's position as observer and participant in noting and questioning the gaps in the patient's story is very much in keeping with contemporary accounts of brief psychotherapy.

CONCLUSION: THE PALE LIGHT OF ILLUSION

It has not been the purpose of this essay to critique Sullivan's theory of interpersonal relations; rather I have hoped to share a sense of the excitement and delight in reading Sullivan again. For me, Sullivan seems less the theoretician who systematically clarified in carefully constructed accounts his view of the person, but a clinician who clearly had something to say about the study and treatment of interpersonal experience and attendant problems in living. In *The Psychiatric Interview*, one finds oneself in the presence of a unique character who saw his task as creating a situation in which the anxieties of interpersonal experience could be explored as an alternative to the terrors of loneliness. His legacy will be enhanced by those of us who rediscover him or find him for the first time as he speaks to us with the directness, wit, and sympathy that characterize his lectures. It is our imaginative engagement with Sullivan, therefore, that must guide us through his work. To varying degrees our relationships with others are illusory. If free to encompass the changing experience of the self and other, such illusions give life its range and richness. Wallace Stevens, in his poem *The Re-statement of Romance* seemed to have such an idea in mind in speaking of the " . . . pale light that each upon the other throws."

REFERENCES

Bloom, H. (1973). *The anxiety of influence: A theory of poetry*. Oxford: Oxford University Press.

Dyrud, J. (1979). Sullivan's concept of the illusory other, *Contemporary Psychoanalysis,* 15: 190-194.

Friedman, L. (1988). *The anatomy of psychotherapy*. Hillsdale, NJ: The Analytic Press.

Fromm-Reichman, F. (1950). *Principles of intensive psychotherapy*. Chicago: University of Chicago Press.

Green, H. (1964). *I never promised you a rose garden*. New York: Holt.

Greenburg, J., and S. Mitchell (1983). *Object relations in psychoanalytic theory*. Cambridge, MA: Harvard University Press.

Gustafson, J. and H. Dichter (1983). Winnicott and Sullivan in the brief psychotherapy clinic, Part I, *Contemporary Psychoanalysis,* 19: 624-637.

Levenson, E. A. (1972). *The fallacy of understanding*. New York: Basic Books.

Levenson, E. A. (1982). Playground or playpen. Comments on *The Psychoanalytic Process* by P. Dewald, *Contemporary Psychoanalysis,* 18: 365-372.

McCaughan, D. L. (1985). Teaching and learning adolescent psychotherapy: Adolescent, therapist, and milieu, *Adolescent Psychiatry,* 12: 414-433.

Perry, H. S. (1982). *Psychiatrist to America*. Cambridge, MA: Harvard University Press.

Schafer, R. (1983). *The analytic attitude*. New York: Basic Books.

Searles, H. (1979). *Countertransference and related subjects*. New York: International Universities Press.

Stanton, A. H., and M. S. Schwartz (1954). *The mental hospital: A study of institutional participation in psychiatric illness and treatment.* New York: Basic Books.

Sullivan, H.S. (1938). Psychiatry: Introduction to the study of interpersonal relations: The data of psychiatry, *Psychiatry,* l: 121-134.

Sullivan, H.S. (1953). *The interpersonal theory of psychiatry.* New York: Norton.

Sullivan, H.S. (1954/1970). *The psychiatric interview.* New York: Norton.

Thompson, C. (1958). Sullivan and psychoanalysis, In: M. Green, ed., *Interpersonal psychoanalysis: The selected papers of Clara M. Thompson.* New York: Basic Books, 1964, pp. 83-94.

Will, O. A. (1970). Introduction, *The Psychiatric Interview.* New York: Norton.

Chapter 9

Clinical Risk
and Brief Psychodynamic Therapy:
A Forensic Mental Health Perspective

James J. Clark

SUMMARY. This article explores the risk environment confronting practitioners of brief psychodynamic treatment, and describes strategies that can help clinicians practice effective risk management. I argue that clinicians can reap only limited benefits from a focus on profiles of high-risk clients and litigation "hot spots." The optimal approach is attention to the contextual dynamics shaping clinical practice. Among the most important are the relational processes driving the clinician-client dyad, the clinician-client-third party payer triangle, and the interface between the mental health and legal systems. I close with a discussion of the ambiguity and uncertainty that characterize clinical decision making and risk management. *[Article copies available for a fee from The Haworth Document Delivery Service: 1-800-342-9678. E-mail address: getinfo@haworthpressinc.com <Website: http://www.haworthpressinc.com>]*

KEYWORDS. Risk management, liability, malpractice, brief treatment, clinical judgment

James J. Clark, PhD, LCSW, is Associate Professor, University of Kentucky College of Social Work, and Faculty, U.K. Center on Drug and Alcohol Research.

Address correspondence to: James J. Clark, Patterson Office Tower 651, College of Social Work, University of Kentucky, Lexington, KY 40506-0027.

The author thanks Professors William Borden and Robert Walker for their helpful reviews.

[Haworth co-indexing entry note]: "Chapter 9. Clinical Risk and Brief Psychodynamic Therapy: A Forensic Mental Health Perspective." Clark, James J. Co-published simultaneously in *Psychoanalytic Social Work* (The Haworth Press, Inc.) Vol. 6, No. 3/4, 1999, pp. 219-235; and: *Comparative Approaches in Brief Dynamic Psychotherapy* (ed: William Borden) The Haworth Press, Inc., 1999, pp. 219-235. Single or multiple copies of this article are available for a fee from The Haworth Document Delivery Service [1-800-342-9678, 9:00 a.m. - 5:00 p.m. (EST). E-mail address: getinfo@haworthpressinc.com].

219

THE CONTEMPORARY SITUATION

The psychodynamic psychotherapist confronts the same areas of legal risk facing other mental health clinicians. These traditional areas include failures to follow statutes and licensing regulations covering informed consent, privileged communications, prevention of foreseeable harm to self and third parties, child and adult abuse, proper assessment and care, and boundary violations including sexual and financial exploitation of clients. This is familiar ground for most practicing clinicians and is covered in detail in most clinical and forensic manuals (for excellent examples of these see Appelbaum & Gutheil, 1991; Bongar, 1991; Dickson, 1998; MacBeth, Wheeler, Sither, & Onneck, 1994; Perlin, 1996; Simon, 1992).

Most clinicians strive to practice responsibly and are committed to their clients' well-being. If the elements of risk were simply in the control of these clinicians, there would be little to worry about. There are, however, a number of internal and external threats to clinical safety that can transform a place of safety into a place of danger for clinician and client (Schafer, 1983). Many clinicians do not understand that the contemporary environment welcomes litigation against even well-meaning and hard-working professionals. Indeed, the most vulnerable clinicians are the ones who believe that they are personally immune to such problems because of special qualities of character or experience. In my role as a forensic consultant for clinician-defendants, and as an investigator and disciplinary clinical supervisor for a state licensing board, I have found that accused clinicians find themselves blindsided by litigation and board complaints, in part, because of this hubris.

This article describes the turbulent environment facing practitioners of brief psychodynamic treatment, and describes strategies that can help clinicians practice effective risk assessment and containment. I argue that although clinicians can benefit from attending to lists and profiles of high-risk clients and practice areas, the optimal approach involves attention to the contextual dynamics shaping contemporary clinical practice. Among the most important are the relational processes driving the clinician-client dyad, the clinician-client-third party payor triangle, and the relationship between the mental health and legal systems. I close with a discussion of the ambiguity and uncertainty characterizing risk management for brief psychodynamic treatment.

THE RELATIONAL CONTEXT
OF BRIEF DYNAMIC PSYCHOTHERAPY

The first requirement for managing risk is to remember the psychoanalytic observation that clients' perceptions of us as therapists and persons are shaped by more than the "real" situation. Persons bring their own needs, desires, fears, and fantasies into the clinical situation. This is the motivation for seeking help and the material for psychotherapy: "Hopes and dreads are transformed, through the analytic process, into rational understanding" (Mitchell, 1993, p. 15). It can be helpful to spend the first encounters becoming attuned to the client's hope and dread and to think carefully about their implications for managing risk. A recent example from my own practice can illustrate this point:

A young woman and her husband arrived at their appointment early, filled out their paperwork and paid in advance. As I escorted them to the consulting room, the young woman remarked, "We have heard that you work miracles for people." While momentarily gratifying, I *suspected* that this encounter might be high-risk; I *guessed* that she had arrived with unrealistic expectations of immense and swift transformation. In response, I spent additional time in an informed consent protocol that laid out what we could realistically expect in an initial, assessment session. I documented this carefully and checked that the couple had signed all of the forms we routinely present to new clients regarding exceptions to confidentiality, fees, etc. As it happened, this young woman was an immature and needy person who expected me to convince her resolute husband to change his mind about filing divorce papers. She became very disorganized and upset as she saw the session unfold without the aforesaid miracle occurring. She angrily told me that she had no desire to pursue therapy if she couldn't save her marriage. In response, I was careful to spend time helping her soothe herself and to turn from her impossible scheme of controlling her husband, to a realistic plan for getting interpersonal support during this period of personal loss and distress.

If I had not worked to correct the client's statement, verbally and behaviorally, I would have implicitly affirmed the statement "I hear you can work miracles." This seems like an obvious approach, but it is surprising how easily I could respond in ways that would exacerbate risk. To avoid becoming a target for the client's negative emotions, it could be tempting to be less vulnerable, perhaps by distancing myself and assuming the stance of a technician. Or I might ignore the remark and unconsciously agree with the client's assessment of my clinical successes–after all, she heard about me from a former patient who was happy with my work. I could combine both stances and assume the grandiose persona of omnipotent technician–an approach of aggressive defensiveness.

Prince (1984) remarks that this "through the looking glass world" of clinical interaction is a place where there is much talk that is unimportant, but that the clinician must look for "seemingly irrelevant, incidental, or sometime bizarre comments [that] have deep meanings which require immediate attention" (p. 50). He brilliantly develops the therapeutic significance for doing this, but here I would like to emphasize the risk management dimensions. Will disappointed, angry clients (such as the about-to-be-divorced young woman) litigate or complain to the licensing board? The definitive answer is: maybe. The empirical evidence shows that when we exclude clients who will never sue for any reason and those who are serial litigators, whether patients do take legal action depends on their satisfaction with the clinical interaction (Bursztjain & Bordsky, 1998; Martin, Wilson, Fiebelman, Gurley, & Miller, 1991; Sloan et al., 1993). If the client believes that a miracle is forthcoming and subsequently invests much of self, time, and income pursuing this fantasy, then the poor outcome might lead her to perceive the clinician as exploitive. If the clinician presents as a "correct," distant arbiter of reality, the client may reason that the poor outcome resulted from incompetence or the absence of compassion. These privations and injuries might be ameliorated by seeking justice against the therapist. Meanwhile, back at the clinic, assuming the case is even recalled, the therapist sees it as routine. Unaware of the standard the client had been using throughout treatment, the therapist is almost certain that he or she has practiced responsibly and experiences any subsequent lawsuit or board complaint as an unforeseeable event grounded in the client's psychopathology.

I employ the above example–a scenario familiar to clinicians treating clients with personality disorders–to introduce a few approaches for identifying and managing risk. One reasonable and popular approach is to follow the forensic experts who profile certain clients as the source of clinical risk (so called borderlines, hypochondriacs, substance abusers, narcissists and others) and profile certain therapists (narcissistic, distant, unempathic, greedy, and exploitive clinicians) as creators of high-risk problems (Bursztajn & Brodsky, 1998). Clients and therapists who have developed such predictable and rigid adaptations are clearly high-risk prospects, especially when the serial litigious client meets the grandiose psychotherapist. We know that such therapists are the central characters in the client narratives of disillusionment and suspicion which have done public damage to psychoanalysis as a treatment and discipline (Hale, 1995, pp. 347-359).

However, the profile approach obscures a more troubling concern: I argue that on any given day, any client and any clinician might embrace distorted appraisals and enact problematic behaviors. The very compliant and nice mother of three might litigate when she finds that she is losing her husband, her home, and her financial security. The typically empathic clinician might be rude to a needy client when under time and financial constraints. If this is true, then it is crucial for all clinicians to attend to the relational contexts of the clinical situation. This observation is consistent with contemporary psychoanalytic theories that emphasize a relational approach to treatment in which client and therapist shape therapeutic process (Mitchell, 1988). Such theories see treatment as a collaborative process rather than as a clinician-driven, manualized form of intervention. We can sometimes overlook that these approaches demand great sophistication and vigilance from the clinician, especially in brief treatment formats. Careful attention to clinical process creates the possibility for positive therapeutic outcome, and that same diligence is required for effective risk management.

Messer and Warren (1995) point to this in their discussion of the difficult client in brief psychodynamic treatment:

> In this view, when we describe a patient as difficult we are saying something about ourselves as much as about the patient. Who the patient is and the kind of therapeutic relationship that can be attained, will inevitably be the function of who the therapist is and how the therapist works. Different therapists find different patients difficult . . . By refusing to anchor assertions about

psychopathology in universal or naturalistic categories, we create the possibility of greater openness to individual patients and their particular psychological configurations, which contain strengths as well as weaknesses. (p. 279)

Openness to the phenomenology of the particular clinical context and the capacity for internal supervision (Casement, 1991) are prerequisites for effectively identifying and managing risk.

THE ECONOMIC CONTEXT
OF BRIEF DYNAMIC PSYCHOTHERAPY

Managed care affects the daily lives of clinicians and clients in obvious and implicit ways. Psychoanalysts have led the field in castigating the loss of freedom for therapists and clients to determine the length and cost of treatment, as well as in decrying the breaches of privacy and privileged communication (Bollas & Sunderson, 1996). Other analytic observers suggest that managed care is the inevitable correction for expensive, needlessly protracted, and sometimes damaging episodes of psychodynamic treatment (Shapiro, 1997). This latter interpretation argues that because therapists prioritized theoretical and clinical attention to the internal realm of the treatment dyad, they failed to develop reasonable attention to the external realms such as the economic, i.e., insurance companies, government, and other payers. These external concerns are now controlled by third-party entities which prioritize cost effectiveness over all other goals. As Shapiro argues:

The outer world has intruded . . . Like our personality-disordered patients, we too, are now facing unanticipated boundaries and limits in the outer world . . . It does not look like we can change this world back into a familiar place. Our difficulty in acknowledging and integrating aspects of the altered external context into our treatment framework may even repeat boundary disturbances characteristic of our patients' families. To maintain our integrity and keep our therapeutic enterprise grounded in reality, we must reexamine the basics of our treatment setting in this new context. (Shapiro, 1997, p. 4)

Risk management also requires an acute awareness of this "new context" because the therapist's relationships with managed care entities substantively transform the clinical configuration from a dyad to a triad–a triangle that is drawn by the contractual relationships among clinician, client, and third-party payers.

While clinicians are well aware of managed care's impact on their business, they may be less aware of managed care's effects on clients' perceptions and emotional responses. Forensic experts have recently noted the growing number of lawsuits and board complaints in which clients perceived the clinician as colluding with managed care companies (see Lifson & Simon, 1998). In such scenarios clients have felt betrayed by clinicians who abandoned them when managed care authorization expired. These clients expected the clinician to advocate vigorously and successfully for extended sessions of care; when this failed to happen, betrayal, and anger led to litigation. The clients' appraisal was that the clinician was more interested in making a profit than providing care–a charge that therapists often level against managed care entities, suggesting the existence of a kind of "parallel process." In some cases, the client perceived the therapist as allied with the managed care company against the client. The practitioner of brief treatment may be unaware of such client appraisals until a complaint is filed. While it is unrealistic to win more hours for every client, this new trend of litigation suggests that the clinician is well advised to act in ways that will help clients individuate the therapist from a managed care company.

We need to discuss the problem of limited resources with our clients and carefully explain how we are advocating for persons who need extended sessions. In those cases where treatment is essential and authorization is denied, we must continue with the client and write off the costs–a foolish business practice but a wise risk management strategy in the contemporary situation. The trend of recent court decisions indicates that the clinician's decision to terminate treatment is quite independent of the managed care company's decision to terminate payment, and that the clinician does not relinquish the duty of care when the managed care company refuses to pay (MacBeth et al., 1994; Lifson & Simon, 1998).

Another approach to managing risk in the triangle is to adapt the primary care model that provides what little conceptual framework managed care entities currently employ. Developing close working alliances with clients' primary care physicians can provide the clinician with the ability to request other kinds of work-ups and referrals–for example, neurological testing, sleep disorder studies, pain management programs, substance misuse treatment programs, and other biopsychosocial rehabilitation services. The primary care physician as gatekeeper can advance the development of a complete assessment database and referral to ancillary services that can supplement and enhance brief treatment. Certainly clinician efforts to develop a multidisciplinary approach to patient care lowers the likelihood that clients and their families will see the clinician as a greedy, uncaring technician. Continuing the geometric metaphor, such actions open up the triangle and potentially create a circle of care which better serves the client's needs and diminishes the problematic intensity of a triad constrained by financial considerations.

THE LEGAL CONTEXT
OF BRIEF PSYCHODYNAMIC TREATMENT

Clinicians may only dimly see how the legal system appraises their professional activities and responsibilities. Persons unfamiliar with the law reasonably assume that if they act in good faith they are insulated from legal trouble. However, as I have argued above, the clinician's intentionality is not the only variable of significance. In fact, the clinician's intentionality may be of peripheral interest to the finders of fact in cases where plaintiffs successfully argue that they have been harmed. Negative outcomes command attention and invite punitive action against defendants. Or as one expert puts it, "These cases don't play well in front of juries" (Bongar, 1991). Clinicians who wish to manage risk effectively need to understand how they will be viewed by finders of fact–licensure boards, judges, and juries–long before they ever face them.

This is a subject of immense complexity, but I would like to present three observations about the legal context that I believe can be helpful to clinicians. The first is that the legal arena is profoundly different from the world of the psychotherapist because it is driven by the adversarial process. Litigation is bureaucratized warfare. "Warfare" is not simply a metaphor to illuminate a high-conflict situation–parties bringing lawsuits and complaints literally target the clinician as the enemy. This is precisely why defendant-clinicians experience such actions as personal attacks. The physician and essayist, Richard Selzer, described his emotions on the afternoon he won the lawsuit filed against him: "I am free. And bruised. One is not taken down from the cross the same as he was when nailed upon it. For one thing, I have learned that civilization . . . is a tiny island in a wild sea. There is always the danger of being engulfed" (Selzer, 1992, p. 123).

Unlike the clinical form of truth seeking that relies on the multidimensional exploration of patient narratives, the legal system is a forum where parties oppose each other with hard-hitting arguments and the most extreme characterization of events. Defendant-clinicians are in an unfamiliar and dangerous zone. If fortune smiles, an experienced and skilled attorney will help the therapist through the battles to come, but even this assistance cannot soften the emotional anguish. Malpractice litigation is a major life trauma (Martin et al., 1991). Further, clinicians must understand that the legal system sees this approach as the optimal form of truth-seeking; the truth emerges from the battle. Those who do not cooperate or who enter the fray reluctantly can be seen as not interested in the truth, or worse, appear to admit culpability by such resistance.

While some forensic experts differ, I believe that the situation is little different with most licensing boards. Although composed of colleagues, professional boards are charged with protecting the public from unscrupulous practitioners. Most boards are represented by their state's office of consumer affairs or attorney general, and proceedings are shaped by legal counsel's approach to fact finding. In addition, licensing boards are more likely to be under public scrutiny than in the past, especially when advocacy groups bring forward a cause celebre (Maltsberger, 1993). For all of these reasons defendant-clinicians usually find "their" board implementing an adversarial process to find the facts and render judgement. This comes as a shock to clinicians who assume that they will receive gentler treatment at the hands of colleagues.

My second observation is that the legal system embraces a different model of the psychotherapy relationship than do many psychodynamic therapists. While clinicians tend to see the limitations of their influence and actions in the life of the client, and consider the therapeutic process as necessarily a collaboration, the law considers the clinician as primarily responsible for the clinical process. Although a plaintiff usually will not claim that the therapist has breached contractual promises made to the client (reversal of psychotic illness, transformation of mood, and reconciliation of marital discord are not commodities deliverable in exchange for monetary consideration), plaintiffs have successfully claimed that their therapist demonstrated serious negligence and committed malpractice. Under this theory, the clinician has specific duties (often defined by statutes and regulations) to the client. If any duty is determined to have existed, the plaintiff must prove that the duty was breached, that harm was done, and that the therapist's breach of duty was significantly connected to this injury (Perlin, 1989).

More recently, courts are allowing juries to hear cases that do not meet contract or malpractice requirements, but do meet the requirements of fiduciary theory. Fiduciary theory establishes an even broader standard of responsibility wherein the therapist is seen in a trustee role in relationship to a dependent, entrustor client. This theory would correlate with the traditional medical-analytic view that patients essentially ". . . . surrender much of their personal inviolacy in the expectation that they will emerge from the encounter more whole and less fragmented than when they entered it" (Erikson, 1964, p. 53). The use of fiduciary theory in mental health law is relatively new and has allowed cases of alleged therapist sexual abuse of patients to be considered even when the traditional malpractice threshold has not been met (Bisbing et al., 1995). I am not lamenting the judicial development that victims of exploitive clinicians will have their day in court. My concern is that therapists must awaken to the fact that their actions can be considered within the standards of a fiduciary theory, even when their therapeutic approach rests on an egalitarian, relational theory.

In addition, I think it is important to understand the broader use of the judiciary in the United States. Cases against mental health professionals that judges might have dismissed in the past are now referred to juries. While judges are undoubtedly influenced by new case law that is animated by fiduciary theory, the more powerful, sociocultural development is that American society is using the courtroom to sort out its response to risk (Hazard, 1990). Third-party injury cases are representative of this development as in the following case:

> A twenty year old male enters treatment in order to comply with his probation agreement. The agency admits persons voluntarily and is not a locked, forensic facility. After attending one group meeting he leaves the residential facility without discussion. A

clinician telephones the probation office, but is unable to locate his probation officer. The clinician drops the matter, moving on to her next treatment session. Several weeks later, the ex-patient shoots and cripples another man during a street fight. The former patient is tried in criminal court, convicted and incarcerated for the assault. The shooting victim files suit against the agency and several clinicians in civil court, claiming that they had duties to foresee future dangerousness and ensure that the AWOL patient was incarcerated for violating his probation agreement. The presiding judge decides to allow the case to move forward since he finds it unclear if the clinicians could and should have prevented the violence. He states that because the jurisdiction's case law is murky, the plaintiff deserves to argue his case before a jury which will determine responsibility.

This judge has found that the plaintiff's claim that it was reasonable to expect clinicians to predict the future as more weighty than the clinicians' claim that such unreasonable expectations deter therapists from even attempting to treat such cases. Recent victories by third-party plaintiffs in "false memory" cases present similar problems for how the clinician is to proceed when faced with an adult patient who claims memories of sexual traumatization (see Applebaum & Zoltek-Jick, 1996). Since most malpractice and fiduciary cases "go away" through insurance settlements, there is growing impetus for plaintiffs' attorneys to represent clients on a contingency basis.

My third observation is that juries, judges, and licensing boards must analyze the procedures and decisions taken by the clinician through a retrospective evaluation of the case. In other words, the decision-makers already have before them a bad outcome as they evaluate what the clinician did or did not do. This heuristic, known as "hindsight bias," always taints the decision-making process because the chain of events takes on a foreseeable and almost inevitable quality (Berlin & Marsh, 1993; Fischoff, 1982). In the above case, the jury might conclude that anyone–especially an expert clinician–could have reasonably foreseen that the probationer would have become violent in the future, despite hearing evidence that he had never been charged with a violent felony in the past. Similarly, although a small percentage of clients who threaten suicide actually kill themselves, fact-finders performing psychological autopsies will be tempted to exaggerate the foreseeability of this rare event (Bonger, 1991).

What can be done? Understanding the legal environment can help clinicians approach risk management more confidently. The prescription for careful documentation and record keeping is especially important here in that the clinician can anticipate what the record might look like under the retrospective analysis of fact-finders in the context of an adversarial procedure. Whatever the true merits of a defense, missing, destroyed, or altered records can automatically lose the case (Macbeth et al., 1994). The clinician should document the rationale for all important clinical determinations and actions, and ensure that these are under the umbrella of accepted theoretical or empirically demonstrated methods. Even highly respected therapists have been successfully sued and have lost their licenses to practice when fact finders determined that they pursued idiosyncratic approaches to treatment–sometimes known as "psychiatric misadventures" (McHugh, 1994). Even if we exclude the proliferation of forensic junk science, there can be significant disagreement among expert witnesses about what clinical approaches are optimal or even acceptable as applied to a specific case; this further clouds the search for truth in the courtroom (Clark, 1996).

Messer and Warren (1995) argue that brief psychodynamic clinicians are called to become more flexible in their methods and more willing to treat clients who would not traditionally be considered for psychodynamic treatment. Clinicians who work in the public and not-for-profit sector, especially in community mental health settings, face the challenge of treating clients with disorders along the entire *DSM-IV* spectrum. Gabbard (1990) claims that psychodynamic approaches are useful for Axis I patients who are nonresponsive to traditional psychopharmacological intervention, as well as paraphilias, selected anxiety disorders, eating disorders, and the Axis II personality disorders. Clinical social work, in particular, has a long tradition of employing psychoanalytically informed treatment in adult and child welfare settings, and tailoring psychodynamic approaches for clients who could never receive traditional analysis (Fraiberg, 1987; Lieberman & Gottesfeld, 1973). And there is an ethical and moral dimension here: "To be sought out, to be asked to attend such a cry, such a call from others, is no small honor and privilege, and ought to be regarded as such by us, even in this day of a medicine increasingly bureaucratized, commercialized" (Coles, 1995, p. xxi).

Messer and Warren (1995) call for the proper adaptation of therapeutic approaches to meet these challenges. If practitioners of brief psychodynamic treatment need to work outside of the traditional analytic setting, they will likely modify traditional techniques to create a feasible match with the client population and the clinical setting. Unfortunately, even ethically animated activities expose clinicians to risks. Trouble often arises when clinicians move into practice domains where they have little experience or when they begin to use practice approaches that have sparse theoretical or empirical support. Faced with difficult cases and adapted or unfamiliar treatment approaches, clinicians need to ask the question, "If legal action was taken against me, would I be able to obtain the testimony of respected experts that I have acted properly and within the parameters of current practice standards?"

Monahan (1993) advises clinicians to educate themselves about risk areas and legal requirements, conduct risk-specific assessments of clients and carefully review relevant records, communicate risk problems to persons who need to know, seek consultation in difficult cases, follow-up with noncompliant clients, and develop feasible policies to guide risk management procedures. Although it is counterintuitive for many psychodynamic therapists to look at actuarial and statistical approaches to risk management, the time has come to consider their utility. Such approaches accept the inevitability of clinical error and apply probability theory to reduce the frequency of recapitulated error (for reviews and applications of this literature see Berlin & Marsh, 1993; Gambrill, 1997; Turk & Salovey, 1988). Quantified risk allows circumscribed prediction and control. Murdach (1994) has described a feasible set of procedures which applies findings from quantitative risk studies to clinical settings. She proposes these under the rubric of "clinical prediction," and argues that understanding the psychological and social contexts can be achieved by determining historical patterns, understanding demographics and base rates, assessing current stressors and significant cues, and using debiasing techniques.

Finally, the best way for clinicians to navigate the turbulent legal environment is to retain an experienced attorney who understands mental health practice. There is no substitute for seeking legal counsel in order to demonstrate a serious commitment to complying with statutes and regulations. Clinicians, whether they know it or not, usually need individualized interpretation of complex case facts and the case-specific application of legal reasoning. Further, existing statutes can be unclear or contradictory, providing little guidance for making risk management decisions. An experienced attorney can help the clinician to understand the meaning of recent court rulings within their jurisdiction, as well as the relevant principles underlying pertinent case law. This kind of consultation–sought before any subpoena arrives–can be of inestimable help to the clinician.

DECISION MAKING UNDER UNCERTAINTY

An article like this runs the risk of demoralizing clinicians or, at worst, encouraging a masochistic approach to their work (see Prince, 1984). It might be fitting to heed the advice given by Lord Salisbury in his 1877 letter to Lord Lytton: "No lesson seems to be so deeply inculcated by the experience of life as that you should never trust experts. . . . If you believe the doctors, nothing is wholesome; if you believe the theologians, nothing is innocent; if you believe the soldiers nothing is safe. They all require to have their strong wine diluted by a very large admixture of insipid common sense." Salisbury's counsel points to the embrace of a wry pragmatism in the face of an uncertainty and ambiguity that has grown more profound since he wrote near the end of the nineteenth century. I have argued that the best way to manage risk is to understand the contexts that shape clinical practice in contemporary society. Calculated, thoughtful risk-taking is *essential* for meaningful work with persons who are in psychological distress.

Despite the troubling developments I describe above, I wish to make it clear that there is still a strong defense for the professional who behaves as a "reasonable person," and approaches clinical work in a thoughtful, informed manner with the good of the client as the primary, ethical stance. It is also important to note that psychodynamic therapists embrace particular principles that serve them well in identifying and managing risk. These include the premium on self-analysis, careful attention to the transference-countertransference matrix, focus on the client's subjective experience, tolerance for the client's ambiguity about personal change, and a willingness to encounter the dark aspects of the client's fantasies and intentions–especially those dominated by rage, revenge, and violence. The clinician who is attentive to these phenomena will be less likely to stumble into high-risk clinical contexts and will be ready to respond effectively when facing risk. The same cannot be said, I believe, for clinicians trained in treatment approaches that focus on and intervene only in the arena of the manifest and the explicit.

Beahrs and Rogers (1993) argue that forensic experts need to support colleagues who are being sued for bad outcomes when these have emerged from reasonable and compassionate treatment approaches. Many courts are still loathe to support frivolous suits, knowing full well that such actions deplete the morale and resources of professionals willing to work with high-risk clients. We live in a time where common sense often does not hold, and the dichotomous roles of victim and perpetrator are readily marketed by attorneys, advocacy groups, and the media. Unfortunately, these perspectives are sometimes advanced even by intelligent persons who refuse the bleak intelligence that modernity's technological and medical processes are error-embedded, high-risk activities (Giddens, 1991; Perow, 1994). Clinical error is inescapable: "The sorrow of this work is not only that mistakes are inevitable but also that they will go on happening in the tomorrows of work" (Paget, 1997, p. 139).

Clinician-defendants like Selzer (1992) relate the experience of being "engulfed" in the cultural "wild seas" that drive malpractice litigation; the courts, too, are swept up in these waters and there is little indication that this will soon change. The contexts of practice demand a good measure of personal courage. Clinicians must come to understand the nature and movement of these currents and take intelligent risks as they practice their important, if often, "impossible" profession.

REFERENCES

Austin, K.M., Moline, M.E., & Williams, M.E. (1990). *Confronting malpractice.* Newbury Park: Sage.

Appelbaum, P.S. & Gutheil, T.G. (1991). *Clinical handbook of psychiatry and the law.* Baltimore: Williams & Wilkins.

Appelbaum, P.S. & Zoltek-Jick, R. (1996). Psychotherapists' duties to third parties: *Ramona* and beyond. *American Journal of Psychiatry,* (153), 457-465.

Beahrs, J.O. & Rogers, J.L. (1993). Appropriate short-term risk in psychiatry and the law. *Bulletin of the American Academy of Psychiatry and the Law, 21* (1), 53-67.

Berlin, S.B. & Marsh, J.C. (1993). *Informing practice decisions.* NY: Macmillan.

Bisbing, S.B., Jorgenson, L.M. & Sutherland, P. (1995). *Sexual abuse by professionals: A legal guide.* Charlottesville: Michie Press.

Bollas, C. & Sundelson, D. (1996). *The new informants: The betrayal of confidentiality in psychoanalysis and psychotherapy.* NY: Jason Aronson.

Bongar, B. (1991). *The suicidal patient: Clinical and legal standards of care*. Washington, D.C.: American Psychological Association.

Bursztjain, H.J. & Brodsky, A. (1998). Patients who sue and clinicians who get sued in the managed care era. In L.E. Lifson & R.I. Simon (Eds.), *The mental health practitioner and the law*. Cambridge: Harvard University Press, 237-249.

Casement, P.J. (1991). *Learning from the patient*. NY: Guilford Press.

Clark, J.J. (1996). Dilemmas at the nexus: Criminal law and the mental health professions. *Journal of Law and Social Work, 6* (2), 43-56.

Coles, R. (1995). *The mind's fate: A psychiatrist looks at his profession*. Boston: Little, Brown.

Dickson, D.T. (1998). *Confidentiality and privacy in social work: A guide to the law for practitioners and students*. NY: Free Press.

Erikson, E.H. (1964). *Insight and responsibility*. NY: Norton Press.

Fischoff, B. (1982). For those condemned to study the past: Heuristics and biases in hindsight. In D. Kahneman, P. Slovic & A. Tversky (Eds.), *Judgement under uncertainty: Heuristics and biases*. NY: Cambridge University Press, 335-354.

Fraiberg, S. (1987). Psychoanalysis and the education of caseworkers. In L Fraiberg (Ed.), *Selected writings of Selma Fraiberg*. Columbus: Ohio State University Press, 412-438.

Gabbard, G.O. (1990). *Psychodynamic psychiatry in clinical practice*. Washington, D.C.: American Psychiatric Press.

Gambrill, E. (1997). *Social work practice: A critical thinker's guide*. NY: Oxford University Press.

Giddens, A. (1991). *Modernity and self-identity*. Stanford: Stanford University Press.

Hale, N. (1995). *The rise and crisis of psychoanalysis in the United States: Freud and the Americans, 1917-1985*. NY: Oxford University Press.

Hazard, G.C. (1990), The role of the legal system in response to public risk. In E. J. Burger (Ed.), *Risk*. Ann Arbor: University of Michigan Press, 229-248.

Liebermann, F. & Gottesfeld, M.L. (1973). The repulsive client. *Clinical Social Work Journal, 1* (1), 22-31.

Lifson, L.E. & Simon, R.I. (1998). *The mental health practitioner and the law*. Cambridge: Harvard University Press.

Macbeth, J.E., Wheeler, A.M.N., Sither, J.W., & Onek, J.N. (1994). *Legal and risk management issues in the practice of psychiatry*. Washington, D.C.: PPG, Inc.

Maltsberger, J.T. (1993). A career plundered. *Suicide and Life Threatening Behavior, 23* (4), 285-291.

Martin C., Wilson, J.F., Fiebelman, N., Gurley, D.A., & Miller, T.W. (1991). Physicians' psychologic reactions to malpractice litigation. *Southern Medical Journal, 84* (11), 1300-1304.

McHugh, P.R. (1992). Psychiatric misadventures. *American Scholar* (Autumn), 497-509.

Messer, S.B. & Warren, C.S. (1995). *Models of brief psychodynamic therapy: A comparative approach*. NY: Guilford Press.

Mitchell, S.A. (1988). *Relational concepts in psychoanalysis*. Cambridge: Harvard University Press.

Mitchell, S.A. (1993). *Hope and dread in psychoanalysis*. NY: Basic Books.

Monahan, J. (1993). Limiting therapist exposure to *Tarasoff* liability: Guidelines for risk containment. *American Psychologist, 48* (3), 242-250.

Murdach, A.D. (1994). Avoiding errors in clinical prediction. *Social Work, 39* (4), 381-386.

Paget, M.A. (1997). *The unity of mistakes: A phenomenological interpretation of medical work.* Philadelphia: Temple University Press.

Perlin, M. (1989). *Mental disability law.* Charlottesville: Michie Press.

Perlin, M. (1996). *Law and mental disability.* Charlottesville: Michie Press.

Perow, C. (1994). Accidents in high-risk systems. *Technology Studies, 1* (1), 1-20.

Prince, R.M. (1984). Courage and masochism in psychotherapy. *The Psychoanalytic Review, 71* (1), 47-62.

Schafer, R. (1983). *The analytic attitude.* NY: Basic Books.

Selzer, R. (1992). *Down from Troy: A doctor comes of age.* Boston: Little, Brown.

Shapiro, E.R. (1997). *The inner world in the outer world: Psychoanalytic perspectives.* New Haven: Yale University Press.

Simon, R. I. (1992). *Clinical psychiatry and the law.* Washington: American Psychiatric Association.

Sloan, F.E., Githens, P.B., Clayton, E.W., Hickson. G.B., Gentile, D.A. & Parlett, D.F. (1993). *Suing for medical malpractice.* Chicago: University of Chicago Press.

Turk, D.C. & Salovey, P. (1988). *Reasoning, inference and judgement in clinical psychology.* NY: Free Press.

Index

Self-righting, 46,65
Self-soothing, 46,92,106
Self-sufficiency, defensive, 60-61
Separation-individuation, 16,26-27,31
Sexual abuse
 of borderline personality disorder
  clients, 88,95,98,99,104
 "false memories" of, 229
Sexual exploitation, of clients, 220
Sexuality, self psychology of, 189-190
Shakespeare, William, 8
Sifneos, P., 18,20-21,89
Single-session consultations, in brief
  therapy, 35
Social work, clinical, 230
Social work clinicians, interpretation
  style of, 126-127
Socratic questioning, 14
Stanton, Alfred, 205
Stern, Daniel, 4
Stevens, Wallace, 216
Stonewall Inn, police raid on, 165
Strengths, of clients, 64-67
 of borderline personality disorder
  clients, 107-108
Stress response syndromes model, of
  brief psychotherapy, 28-29
Structure, psychic, 46
Strupp, Hans, 25-26,29-31
Studies on Hysteria (Freud), 12-13
Substance abuse, by borderline
  personality disorder patients,
  102
Suicidal ideation/behavior
 of borderline personality disorder
  clients, 88,94,96-97,100,
  103-104
 of gay clients, 175,176,182
 legal implications of, 229
Sullivan, Harry Stack, 5,8,24,203-217
 brief therapy and, 214-215
 Interpersonal Theory of Psychiatry,
  208
 The Psychiatric Interview, 209-124,
  216
Super-ego, 93
Supportive-expressive therapy,
  176-177

therapist interpretation content and
  frequency in, 115-129
Supportive techniques, in therapeutic
  interventions, 28
Symptoms, of self psychology clients,
  58-60

Tavistock group, 19
Telephone answering machines, use in
  therapy, 100-101
Termination, of therapy, 79-80
 influence of managed care on, 225
 premature, countertransference-
  related, 175
Therapeutic alliance, 12-13,15,162
Therapist
 homosexual, interaction with
  homosexual clients, 161-201
 internalized homophobia of,
  163-164,166-168,186
 lawsuits against, 225
 as participant-observer, 25,30
 training in brief therapy, 35-36
Thompson, Clara, 16,207,209
Transference, 12-13,204-205
 Alexander's management of, 17-18
 in anxiety-provoking brief
  psychotherapy, 20
 drive models of, 20-21,22
 Ferenczi's management of, 15
 French's management of, 17
 Freud's management of, 12-13
 with gay clients, 177
 idealizing, 54,82n
 in intensive brief psychotherapy, 21
 interpretation and, 115-116,125
  extra-transference, 121,122,123
  genetic transference,
   120-121,122,123,124
  here-and-now transference,
   121,122,125
 intersubjective context of, 52
 positive, 174-175
 of selfobject needs, 64,67-69
 systemic interpretation of, 21

Transitional objects, 100-101
Traumatic events
 narrative interventions for, 33-34
 stress response syndromes model
 of, 28-29,31
Treatment planning, collaborative, 56
Triangle of conflict, 19-20
Triangle of person, 19
Twinship, 45

University of California at San
 Francisco, Center for the
 Study of Neuroses, 25-26
University of Pennsylvania, Center for
 Psychotherapy Research,
 25-26,117
Unsafe sexual practices, of gay clients,
 4-5,169-170,178-193. *See
 also* Bathhouses, gay

Vanderbilt Center for Psychotherapy
 Research, 25-26,29
Violence, by clients, 228-229
Vitality, loss of, 58,59,60
Vulnerable client groups, brief
 psychotherapy for, 32-34

Walter, Bruno, 13
Will, O.A., 205
Will, Rank's concept of, 16
William Alanson White Institute, 208
Winnicott, D.W., 1,4,8,11,23-24,
 133-134,204,208

YAVIS (young, attractive, verbal,
 intelligent, and successful)
 concept, of clients, 123-124

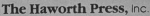

TO ORDER: CALL: 1-800-HAWORTH / FAX: 1-800-895-0582 (outside US/Canada: + 607-771-0012) / E-MAIL: getinfo@haworthpressinc.com

☐ **YES, please send me The Therapist's Notebook**
___ $49.95 ISBN: 0-7890-0400-3. (Outside US/Canada/Mexico: $60.00)

Please complete the information below or tape your business card in this area.

- Individual orders outside US, Canada, and Mexico must be prepaid by check or credit card.
- Discounts are not available on 5+ text prices and not available in conjunction with any other discount.
- Discount not applicable on books priced under $15.00.
- 5+ text prices are not available for jobbers and wholesalers.
- Postage & handling: In US: $4.00 for first book; $1.50 for each additional book.
  Outside US: $5.00 for first book; $2.00 for each additional book.
- NY, MN, and OH residents: please add appropriate sales tax after postage & handling.
- Canadian residents: please add 7% GST after postage & handling.
- Payment in UNESCO coupons welcome.
- Please allow 3-4 weeks for delivery after publication.
- Prices and discounts subject to change without notice.

Signature _____

☐ **BILL ME LATER** ($5 service charge will be added).
(Not available for individuals outside US/Canada/Mexico. Service charge is waived for jobbers/wholesalers/booksellers.)
☐ Check here if billing address is different from shipping address and attach purchase order and billing address information.

Signature _____

☐ **PAYMENT ENCLOSED $** _____
(Payment must be in US or Canadian dollars by check or money order drawn on a US or Canadian bank.)

☐ **PLEASE BILL MY CREDIT CARD:**

☐ AmEx ☐ Diners Club ☐ Eurocard ☐ Discover ☐ Master Card ☐ Visa

Account Number _____

Expiration Date _____

Signature _____

NAME _____

INSTITUTION _____

ADDRESS _____

CITY _____

STATE _____ ZIP _____

COUNTRY _____

COUNTY (NY residents only) _____

E-MAIL _____
May we use your e-mail address for confirmations and other types of information?
( ) Yes ( ) No. We appreciate receiving your e-mail address and fax number. Haworth would like to e-mail or fax special discount offers to you, as a preferred customer. We will never share, rent, or exchange your e-mail address or fax number. We regard such actions as an invasion of your privacy.

☐ YES, please send me **The Therapist's Notebook (ISBN: 0-7890-0400-3** I will receive an invoice payable within 60 days, or that if I **decide to adopt the book, my invoice will be cancelled.** I understand that I will be billed at the lowest price. (Offer good only to teaching faculty in US, Canada, and Mexico.)

Signature _____

Course Title(s) _____

Current Text(s) _____

Enrollment _____

Semester _____ Decision Date _____

Office Tel _____ Hours _____

THE HAWORTH PRESS, INC., 10 Alice Street, Binghamton, NY 13904-1580 USA

(14) 06/98 BIC99